GROUNDHOPPER

GROUNDHOPPER

Tales from Football's Equivalent of Trainspotting

Matt Coughlan

pitch

First published by Pitch Publishing, 2025

1

pitch

Pitch Publishing
9 Donnington Park,
85 Birdham Road,
Chichester, West Sussex,
PO20 7AJ
www.pitchpublishing.co.uk
info@pitchpublishing.co.uk

A CIP catalogue record is available for this book
from the British Library.

ISBN 978 1 80150 937 4

Typesetting and origination by Pitch Publishing

MIX
Paper | Supporting
responsible forestry
FSC
www.fsc.org
FSC® C010615

Printed and bound on FSC® certified paper in line with
our continuing commitment to ethical business practices,
sustainability and the environment.

Printed and bound in India by Thomson Press

Contents

Introduction

Grounds 1–65

IT STARTS innocently enough. Someone asks you how many grounds you've been to and whether you're on the Futbology app. You think to yourself, I don't need an app to count the number of grounds I've been to. Then you wonder how many you have *actually* been to, and how close you are to completing a certain league or region, and before you know it you're watching Sporting Bengal United v Athletic Newham on a bitterly cold Wednesday night in January, but it's all harmless fun, right?

It should be harmless fun but, like many pursuits, there is always the danger of it becoming the source of mockery for being an anorak-wearing trainspotter-type, or it becomes an obsession that alienates friends and family. I confess I have been guilty of such behaviour in the past. In my defence, trainspotting was my dad's idea of a distraction, jotting down train numbers we happened to see, on extensive railway journeys as a child – Railriders Top 100 Super Traveller of the Year 1986, no less – rather than hours spent on a platform at Crewe. I have no such excuses for trying to visit as many pubs in CAMRA's (the Campaign for Real Ale) inventory of historic interiors, racking up as many parkrun courses as possible, or watching all the top-rated films in the *Halliwell's Guide*. I would like to think pursuing such a variety of interests makes me less of an obsessive weirdo. In reality, it means I'm not very good at completing sets of things and have lots of small collections.

It was therefore only a matter of time before my interest in non-league football led me into groundhopping. Once I realised I had been to enough grounds to concern a non-football-mad wife, but not so many to impress dyed-in-the-wool groundhoppers, I was bound to be drawn in. Unlike the big hitters of the groundhopping world – think gold sequin cagoule, diamond-encrusted notepad, flask of weak lemon drink – my total stood at a mere 65 grounds visited. This is my quest to reach 100, which feels like a suitable qualification to consider myself a groundhopper. I expect weak lemon drink has been spat out in disgust by some readers at these figures. This may not be the last time that happens in this book, as I am bound to break many of the unwritten rules of groundhopping.

Groundhoppers tend to be at pains to say there are no rules to groundhopping, and then proceed to explain their own rules for what they will watch and how they will record it. This leads other hoppers to express their own rules, and online arguments ensue. It should be a simple case of watching a football match (to keep a total of games watched) at a new ground (to keep a total of unique grounds visited). The question of what constitutes a match becomes unnecessarily complicated if you don't see the full 90 minutes. What if you arrive late? What if you leave early? What if the match is abandoned? What if the result is annulled at a later date? Was that really a match at all? Does anything below step six really count? Should you count friendlies, schoolboy football or Sunday league games?

Then there's the question of what constitutes a new ground. What if parts of the ground are rebuilt? What if the whole ground is levelled and rebuilt on the same site? What if they rotate the pitch during rebuilding work? After that you get the even more obscure personal rules, where games must feature the ground's usual home team, the match can't finish 0-0 or you need to revisit, or that a printed programme must be available to warrant a visit. Can you say you've been to a game if you don't have a physical memento, like a programme or pin badge?

My own rules are likely to be incredibly loose. I will count most games, so I can tick off a ground. My totals already feature a friendly, youth-team games, a match at step seven and an abandoned game (albeit on a revisit). I have some standards. I won't count stadium tours of the Nou Camp or Bernabéu, running around the track at West Ham's new ground, attending a conference in a windowless room at Stamford Bridge or capturing a few minutes' play while at a children's party in a sports centre adjoining another ground.

All matches need to be recorded, and most serious hoppers will have a notebook, diamond-encrusted or otherwise, and keep extensive records of their 'ticks'. My record keeping until this point has been non-existent. I can't even be certain what the first game I attended was. I vividly recall my first Arsenal game at Highbury, but may have watched Burnham Ramblers in the Essex Senior League before that, and possibly even Charlton Athletic during their groundshare at Upton Park. I can't remember how many times I saw the Ramblers or the Addicks, or even Chelmsford City many years later, so I'll never know the exact number of games I've been to. Most of these games didn't matter to me when all I cared about was Arsenal. I can blame them for my lack of grounds visited, with away tickets scarce, and then a long hiatus from football after I stopped going.

Once I started going to matches again, I spent far too long over one Christmas holiday manually adding all the old games I could recall to my Futbology record, making sure I logged Charlton games with my dad at The Valley, Fratton Park for a friendly, Kenilworth Road and Priestfield among others, albeit without recording the correct season or scoreline.

Most of the new grounds visited were instantly memorable. Arsenal's FA Cup runs took me to Wembley (old and new), the Principality Stadium (originally called the Millennium Stadium) in Cardiff, while Wembley was being redeveloped, and to the classic semi-final venues of Villa Park and Old Trafford. My futile quest to build away match credits led me to Selhurst Park to see tenants Wimbledon, Fulham's Craven Cottage, Portman Road for a League Cup semi-final first leg against Ipswich, and the old White Hart Lane for a couple of League Cup ties.

A visit to the Etihad to watch Manchester City v Arsenal was only possible using a friend's credits and continuing to boost his rating. It had all the makings of a great weekend away. There were plenty of historic pubs the night before with my brother. I saw Australia lose the Rugby League World Cup Final from my hotel bed on the morning of the game, and we added the Marble brewery tap before kick-off. Arsenal then surrendered meekly in a 3-0 defeat, with Nicklas Bendtner's performance even moving my Charlton-supporting brother to lose his rag with him.

My first Arsenal away game was over a decade earlier, when my northern uncle got tickets for a trip to Sheffield Wednesday at Hillsborough. Our tickets were in the home end, right in front of the irritating drummer and I was under strict instructions not to cheer for Arsenal. He needn't have worried as they lost 1-0 without registering a shot on target. Defeats on the road always seemed more likely, which didn't encourage me to go the extra mile to get hold of tickets.

The glamour of a European tie lured me in on a couple of occasions, when I got tickets for Champions League games at the San Siro and the Stade de France final in 2006. I also went to Barnet's Underhill to see Arsenal's reserves play their Spurs counterparts, and lose 3-0, so it was an eclectic mix of games.

Spurs featured unexpectedly when I visited Carrow Road to watch Norwich City v Spurs with my under-15s team, after we played at the Canaries' training ground in the morning. It would be a push to claim this was a trial, although if I had proven to be a big ginger Messi then I'm sure it wouldn't have gone unnoticed, but I didn't cut the mustard for them.

I wasn't League One standard either. In goal for another junior team, we faced Peterborough United's under-16s in a trial match. I kept a clean sheet in the half I played, albeit only showing that I took goal kicks rather poorly. A couple of team-mates were handy and had drawn the attention of scouts, but the nearest they made it to the first team was as ball boys for a game later the same day between Peterborough and Birmingham City. I wasn't minded to expose my dubious ball-handling skills in front of a rowdy away end, where they were positioned.

My mate Phil was behind several trips to see Leyton Orient at Brisbane Road, notable for an insufficient number of urinals at half-time, resulting in one of our group using a sink. We travelled to watch the O's play Bristol Rovers, Brentford at Griffin Park with its corner pubs, and Southend at Roots Hall with its heavy police presence. This included an Alsatian that made Big Sweaty Martyn shriek like a girl, after he peered into the back of a police van, wondering what it contained. There was Leeds at Elland Road, with what seemed like an unnecessary police escort to the ground, until one idiot on the top deck of the bus thought it would be clever to make a Galatasaray jibe at the home fans as we arrived. We got into the ground in one piece and found one of our seats was on the other side of a camera gantry; Orient were later denied a goal when the ball crossed the line in plain view of everyone bar the match officials. Away games further down the pyramid always promised variety if nothing else.

There was Phil's greatest moment as an Orient fan, when they clinched promotion at Oxford in a pulsating 3-2 win at the Kassam Stadium, which also condemned the hosts to relegation. It was easy to get carried away in the emotion of some of these games, which showed there was more to football than just the Premier League. A police officer nearly ruined our celebrations by sending us towards the notorious Blackbird Leys estate when we asked for directions back to the station. Luckily, someone noticed in time, otherwise it would have been bad news for a group of us, who a drunken fan accused of looking like a boy band, apart from me, who he singled out as looking more like Steve McClaren. We made it back to Paddington station and joined the chorus of 'Oh, Paddington is full of bears!

It's full of bears, bears and more bears. Oh, Paddington is full of bears.'

Bear-free, but certainly not beer-free, awaydays with other friends included Meadow Lane for Notts County v Shrewsbury, Layer Road for Colchester v Luton, and a game at St Neots Town, which took me a while on Futbology to work out must have been a 1-0 defeat to Kettering. Further afield were trips to KV Mechelen in Belgium and the Olympic Stadium in Munich for Bayern v Freiburg during Oktoberfest, which was either the coldest stadium I've ever visited or a testament to my all-round bad sense to only pack a small denim jacket. My poor judgement was eclipsed in Berlin when, for reasons lost in among the steins and schnapps, we visited the Stasi Museum rather than a Union Berlin game. We saw a couple of other cult clubs on trips to Germany, which took in games at St. Pauli's Millerntor-Stadion and Dortmund's Westfalenstadion.

My first book, *Turncoat*, covers most of the grounds I visited until now, except for Sporting Bengal United, Billericay Town, Stansted and Hornchurch. It was at Sporting Bengal's Mile End Stadium that I realised I was getting drawn into groundhopping, so let's revisit that experience.

It was after work, and a chance to both add to my ground tally and let rush hour die down. Most of all, going to games is enjoyable no matter what the level. There's the excitement of travelling somewhere new and the tiny sense of adventure that comes with that. Made tinier still in this instance, since I've done Mile End parkrun in the park adjoining the ground, so I'm familiar with the stadium. Looking into the history of the ground and the teams is always of fascination to me, expanding my wider knowledge of the game and getting the sense of another community.

Sporting Bengal were set up in 1996 to promote football among the Asian community in London, which is a laudable aim given the paucity of Asian players making it at the higher levels. A few Bengal players have gone on to represent the Bangladesh national team, but the current side was languishing at the bottom of the table with one win all season.

Opponents Athletic Newham were formed more recently in 2015 and were doing much better in the league. They went into the game sat in sixth place with games in hand and the league's top scorer, Richard Kone, in their ranks. Newham started out as a youth team, then called Lopes Tavares London after their founder, and were playing their first season at this level. The Kings were also the last remaining side from the Essex Senior League in the FA Vase.

It promises to be a one-sided encounter. Part of me hopes that any game I go to will end 5-4, with screamers into the top corner, missed penalties, sendings off, a late twist and maybe something for the 'What happened next?' round of *Question of Sport*. In short: drama. The prospect of goals and avoiding a dreaded 0-0 was a more realistic expectation, but even that didn't matter. The joy is in the unscripted. I could just as easily have spent the evening in a warm cinema watching the latest half-baked interpretation of the same storyline, but here I didn't know exactly what would be in store.

I walk from the office, which revealed another part of London I would normally bypass on the tube. I approach the sports centre in front of the pitch. There is nothing to indicate a competitive fixture is about to take place, and I make my way around the perimeter fence in search of the entrance. I pass several five-a-side pitches. On the first, most of the opposition team surround a player in possession, a Karel Poborsky scoop takes them all out and sets up a team-mate to blast it in. On the second, a more straightforward ball down the line tees up a presentable chance, but the shot is straight at the legs of a keeper who seems to be trying to get out of the way of the ball. If nothing else, I have now at least seen one goal on my night out.

When I reach the entrance, it appears to be another way into the leisure centre, with a large reception desk and not-at-all clicky-clacky turnstile. I pay £7.50 for entry and a programme. I do like a programme, even if it's a few disappointing pages like this one, as there's usually something of interest about the club but, unlike many others, I'm not too worried if it's online only. I like a 50-50 draw even more than a programme, but there isn't one here. Neither is there any catering. The club can't have expected enough of a turnout to make it worthwhile. I do like to buy something at the ground and put a bit extra into club coffers, even if it's a soggy burger.

There's no danger of getting soggy myself at this ground, with its large 1950s cantilevered grandstand, offering a splendid view of the pitch. I take one of the bench seats, towards the back of the stand, as close to the halfway line as I can manage. I look for the team sheets online, having not seen one on the way in. There's nothing on Twitter and no tannoy announcement. I complete my rituals of checking into the Futbology app and taking some cliched photos, making sure I get some of Canary Wharf in the background. I can't do a lap of the pitch as it's fenced off, so the groundhopper who reputedly likes to touch both crossbars at each ground he visits would have difficulty doing so here. It denies me my standard photo of a corner flag.

The teams come out with little fanfare, as most of the crowd seems to consist of groundhoppers taking in a conveniently timed game. Newham start by keeping the ball on the ground and building with neat passing triangles up the wing. Mistakes creep in, and robust challenges are made. Newham create a half-chance as Joel Appiah hits the post with an attempted bicycle kick. Bengal keeper Kevin Rrushi clears into the night sky above the floodlights, causing the full-back trouble picking the ball out when it drops back to earth.

The game stops for an injury, and Newham rather unsportingly contest for the ball after kicking it back to their hosts. This might have provoked outrage in a packed stadium. Instead, it just edges Newham further upfield. A few throw-ins later and Newham play the ball inside to Benjamin Bodipo. He looks like he's about to hit one far on to the running track, but checks inside, composes himself and drives it low into the corner. Rrushi gets down, but it squirms past him for 1-0. Folders are opened around me and records are updated.

No sooner have folders been stowed away and a deep cross finds three Newham attackers against a lone defender at the back post. The ball falls to Rasheed Salau, and he pokes it home for 2-0. Half-time arrives before the score increases further. I could leave satisfied now I've seen goals and ticked off another ground, but am keen to see if Richard Kone can pad out his stats at the top of the scorers list. I let the game wash over me. Newham hit the woodwork from a corner and quickly revert into defensive positions to stop any threat on the counter. It's a relaxing experience just sitting back watching the game ebb and flow. Kone is getting more and more irritable as he tries to get on the scoresheet. He wins the ball in midfield and races clear of the Bengal back line. He rounds the keeper but, with the goal at his mercy, he skews it well over.

I sense his growing frustration, as he continues to be foiled like a five-a-side player thwarted by a cowering rush goalie in a high-scoring kickabout. He looks to shoot more and more often. He cuts in from the right and can only send a tame shot from distance straight at Rrushi. It's not his night. The folders don't need to be opened again before full time, as it ends 2-0. It hasn't been a classic, but there's been absorbing moments watching Newham's neat approach play, and Kone's travails.

For the assorted groundhoppers it's another game done, and more goals witnessed and logged. 'That's six I've seen this week!' I overhear an old boy say on the way out. The stats are a shorthand for the experience of seeing a game. There's no confirmed number of those in attendance, but it can be no more than 100 people. It's a shame there aren't more home fans, as something akin to the atmosphere generated at Test cricket with touring sides from the Indian subcontinent would be incredible and the catering would surpass the supermarket I find myself using. Then again, the five-a-side games still going on are testament to the various local communities being more interested in playing than watching, which is no bad thing either.

I've had my entertainment from seeing a game and getting a feel for a new ground. The experience added some variety to my week and helped me learn a bit more about a couple of clubs. It's that search for variety, novelty and entertainment which is behind me wanting to go to more grounds, rather than just logging grounds for the sake of it – although the numbers are nice to know and it's easy to find ways to give those numbers importance. I've half an eye on visiting all the grounds in the Essex Senior League and all the other senior grounds in Essex.

The main aim is to reach 100 grounds, which is easily doable. The challenge will come from selecting games that fit around family life. It will be a pyrrhic victory if I end up divorced by the end of this book. Trying to get to a mix of old, new, loved and loathed grounds, mostly on odd weekday evenings when the kids are tucked up in bed, will add some degree of difficulty and hopefully give you a sense of the appeal of groundhopping. I'm also aware that some level of gatekeeping can apply to hobbies, so I will need to make sure I don't fall foul of any of the unwritten rules and fail on those grounds over the next couple of seasons.

Ground 66

White Hart Lane

THE 2021/22 season has only just concluded and while serious hoppers are hunting around for any grassroots fixture or obscure summer league, I've got a trick up my sleeve. I'm ticking off a big one and, by my own rules, it counts as a new ground. Spurs' rebuilt stadium fits most hoppers definition of a new ground and would warrant a revisit. It's a giant spaceship of a stadium that bears little resemblance to its predecessor and the pitch has been moved, as far as I can work out.

The controversy is the type of football I'm going to watch. I'm not going to see association football. I'm going to see rugby football league, or rugby league as it's more commonly known. It is undoubtedly a different sport and I'm not going to argue about the shared heritage of both games, nor am I going to manually add it to the Futbology app. I am going to include it here, because I've no time for Spurs, and there's a lot about rugby league that should appeal to groundhoppers, although maybe only the northern ones.

Southerners don't seem to appreciate or understand rugby league. They have an inexplicable attraction towards the ball hiding and end-to-end kicking of the 15-man version of the game. My mate Phil calls league 'basketball for northerners' and pretends there's some sort of nuance to all the rucks and mauls of union. I grew up in Yorkshire in the 80s and have fond memories of going to see local rugby league side Bramley play. I recall standing on what felt like a vast terrace (which old photos reveal was only about six steps) with my dad and his friend. We would all be in cagoules, as it was still a winter game, although, latterly, as a summer sport, I remember snow at a Leeds Rhinos match in June. There would always be a bag of sweets and a distinct feeling of wanting to get on the field and burst forward with the ball. I was there when Bramley held the mighty Wigan to a draw in the Challenge Cup, or so I'm told.

It was gritty. The urinals were four walls with no roof and a trough in the floor on three sides. This sort of basic facility perhaps explains why I'm drawn to non-league football, which has a similar charm, albeit with slightly better toilet facilities. Like a lot of non-league football teams, Bramley's McLaren field was sold to developers, and the club folded before being reformed.

After moving down south, I tried to get along to the odd game. I watched London Broncos host the likes of Wigan, St Helens and Leeds, until the Broncos became less competitive. I also went to a couple of Challenge Cup finals at Wembley (which, along with seeing American football there, I don't count in my total for that ground). Like football's showpiece FA Cup Final, it's played in May, they sing 'Abide With Me' and the national anthem before the game, and fans of most teams tune in to watch. The big difference is that as a neutral you can buy tickets before the competition starts and the game tends not to sell out, even with tickets costing as little as £25, which is how I ended up at this year's final at the Tottenham Hotspur Stadium to see Huddersfield v Wigan.

Huddersfield Giants are looking for their first win in the competition since 1953. They are up against record 19-time winners Wigan Warriors, who haven't lifted the trophy in nine years, but that won't stop most neutrals backing the Yorkshire side. The Challenge Cup Final is an excuse for a day out in London by fans of all clubs and plenty of other teams' colours are on display as I catch the train to the general vicinity of the ground.

Quite a few of them find their way to the industrial estate containing the Beavertown and Pressure Drop breweries (two more trading estate breweries I can tick off that list), where I catch up with northern mate and Giants fan Adam. Talk turns to player wages and how a lot of talented academy players are leaving the game, as they can get better money in the army for fewer injuries.

After being told about a few players to watch, we head off to separate parts of the ground. The one part of the ground I'm glad not to be going to is the roof walk, which is where the poor girl singing the national anthem is stationed. I could probably hit a few high notes myself if I was up there. Instead, I take my seat in the second tier of the steep-sided bowl for an excellent view. I'm loath to admit, but it is very impressive. I may love a ramshackle non-league ground, but seeing the pristine turf from upon high in a new stadium is always a thrill. It is better still in the absence of 60,000 Spurs fans. The walk up Tottenham High Road could even be described as pleasant. The glorious sunshine and carnival atmosphere was in stark contrast to my previous visits, skulking into the away end on a cold winter's evening.

There wasn't my usual nostalgia for the old ground. I didn't miss a place I considered a dump, with its police control room looming over the away end. I did miss the old prices for refreshments, as I pay £6.75 for a pint of Beavertown's Neck Oil, which is brewed on site and filled from the bottom of the cup upwards, in order to fleece thirsty fans at the fastest possible rate. I can take my alcoholic beverage to my seat, as I'm not at a professional football match, although not before I double-check with a steward that it's OK. He doesn't seem to care either way. I'm soon walking back past the steward since the block number on my ticket doesn't lead me to my seat, as there's a camera gantry position blocking the way. It's another black mark against the ground. I'm willing to find any sort of fault I can, even if the RFL did the ticketing.

Before I upset Spurs fans finding more faults with their shiny new ground, the game gets under way and the Giants start stronger, looking to cause their own upset. They gain an early territorial advantage, but their probing finds no chink in the Warriors' defence. The underdogs can't find an opening and when Wigan concede a penalty Huddersfield settle for the two-point kick. Wigan fans taking up the large single-tier stand behind the goal boo as Tuimoala Lolohea opts to go for goal. It's an obvious choice, to convert territory into scoreboard pressure and he duly converts to make it 2-0.

Huddersfield continue to make the early running and keep Wigan on the back foot which, as someone from the white rose county, is pleasing to see, especially as Wigan are the game's equivalent of Manchester United. Their wingers do no better than the likes of Beckham and Giggs would manage against Ricky Leutele, as he jinks his way over the line for 6-0. Lolohea misses the conversion, unable to hit the target from out wide. Perhaps a garish advert for Dragon Soop on the electronic hoardings distracted him. The equally garish-sounding 7.5 per cent vodka and caffeine drink is clearly targeted at northerners for whom some London-based marketing exec deems Stella to be too soft. An advert for mushy peas then follows.

Wigan don't play up to northern stereotypes of grittiness to get back into the game and show real guile to create their first chances. First is an offload out of the back of the hand to create a pocket of space out of nowhere. Then they quickly shuttle the ball, with a sharp pass and an offload to Harry Smith, who goes over for the try. He converts to level the score at 6-6. If there's a sense Wigan will have it their own way from now on, the Giants are having none of it. They continue to get forward. Wigan's defence seem to have them covered and Huddersfield lack a certain inventiveness to their play until a dummy run leaves Chris McQueen with an overload. He skips past a defender and is in for a try, restoring the Giants' advantage. The conversion is missed, leaving the score 10-6 at the interval.

The feeling is tense with the underdogs holding a narrow lead, or that may just be the fact there's a large queue for the toilets. I've reason to be glad rugby is five minutes a half shorter than football. I decide against another pint, having already taken advantage of legally being able to drink within view of the pitch in a Premier League ground. If I expected more tension in the second half, then Jai Field suggests order will be restored. He goes over three minutes after the restart, with the conversion putting the Warriors up 12-10. Giants keep their heads up and soon have a chance to draw level. Lolohea misses a kick that appears more straightforward than his earlier missed conversions.

It doesn't appear to be Huddersfield's day when a high tackle goes unpunished. Most of the not-entirely-neutral section appeals for a sin bin against Morgan Smithies. On the next play, Giants work the ball to the opposite flank. It reaches winger Jermaine McGillvary. He holds off three defenders to force his way over the line to give Giants a 14-12 lead, which Lolohea can't extend.

It's late in the game. An attendance of around 51,000 is read out, which is as exaggerated as Spurs' claim to be a big club. Huddersfield's McQueen receives the prestigious Lance Todd Trophy as the man of the match. There are only a couple more sets of six tackles to see out until McQueen's side will lift the Challenge Cup itself. Wigan appear to be contained on the last tackle of one of those sets. Suddenly, Tommy Leuluai throws a long pass that opens up the field. Smith has time and space to put a grubber kick in between the defensive line, and Liam Marshall is in for a try out of nothing. It's 16-14 to Wigan after the conversion is missed. I'm hoping for one last twist, but Giants can't get close to the try line on their possession. A hopeful up-and-under kick on the last tackle doesn't put the Wigan defence under any pressure and they claim the ball and with it their 20th title.

On the way out, there is fatalism, disappointment and confusion that Giants didn't win. One fan is so bemused that he bought a hot dog he didn't want and offers it to those who pass him on the stairs. Another tells his kids not to be disappointed and that Huddersfield don't do winning. He expects the football team will lose the play-off final the following day. Adam planned to watch this as well, but noted few fans followed both teams, despite sharing the John Smith's Stadium. The Giants' support is largely restricted to the Far Town area.

Far from White Hart Lane are the nearest train stations, so I stop at the ORA brewery on another trading estate. A few other fans make their way here for craft beer and pizza. ORA was originally set up in Modena, Italy, before being transported to north London. It's another successful import to the capital and makes for a perfect end to the day in the same way a rugby match is perfect for my groundhopping needs. I visited Spurs' new ground without having to watch them, or put money in their coffers. The game was also a back-and-forth spectacle, full of sporting drama.

There's little drama to be had in pre-season fixtures, so I resist the lure of Hendon v an Arsenal XI. It represents a chance to see a historic non-league team, albeit one who left their historic ground, against the mighty Arsenal. Their might appears diminished when anyone vaguely close to the first team is away on a summer training camp, so it's a team made up of youngsters I struggle to identify. I don't want to go to a game for the sake of it. There has to be something riding on it, so I bide my time until the 2022/23 season starts in earnest.

Ground 67

The Hawthorns, Stanway Rovers (not West Bromwich Albion)

THE ESSEX Senior League is one of the first leagues to start back up, on the last weekend in July. I'm torn between going to a ground I like the look of or to a game I expect to be more competitive. The ground that is tempting me is Sawbridgeworth's Crofters Road, although much of that is because I fancy cycling there on a warm summer's afternoon. The more intriguing fixture is Ilford's visit to the outskirts of Colchester to face Stanway. I've a bit of a soft spot for Ilford, as a one-time giant of the non-league game fallen on hard times and revived by a small group of volunteers.

After being in a crowd of only 12 people to see a listless defeat last season, I feared for their future, even though they finished well clear of relegation. In pre-season, chairman Adam Peek made some bold changes and brought in Richard Ponsford to take over the manager's role Peek had been fulfilling. Ponsford came from Ongar Town, fresh off the back of winning the Essex Olympian Football League, after successive promotions. This league was two steps below Ilford, so something of a gamble, but a new approach and a new pool of players that comes with any manager at this level made it one worth taking and I was keen to see them, so I headed to Stanway.

Stanway Rovers finished in mid-table last season, after playing with little distinction since forming in 1956. They didn't appear to be the most interesting team playing in Stanway today either. Stanway Pegasus were making their bow in senior football, at the step below and under a rare female manager, Rosie Webb. Pegasus were playing less than a mile away and fewer than five years since they formed. They were also playing on an artificial pitch on school grounds, which for me has all the appeal of the league equivalent, the modern identikit stadium surrounded by a car park.

It's a brief but sweltering walk to the turnstiles from where I park. I go to pay by card, but am told I need to go back to the clubhouse and pay there. To avoid any further delay and intruding on a wedding reception, I use £7 of the £8 in change I have on me. That means no programme. With my remaining pound coin, I have the choice of entering the raffle and hoping I win a bottle of wine to quench my thirst or the guarantee of doing so with a can from the kiosk.

I head for the kiosk, but not until after the person reading out the team sheet has moved out of the way. He has at least alerted me to where the team sheet is posted, so I can photograph it, although neither of us are any the wiser to how certain names of the visiting team are pronounced.

There's a pronounced lack of shade from the sun beating down on the 100-seater main stand, and I realise I've not applied sun cream, which isn't a typical part of my pre-match routine. I find shade under the cover running along the touchline behind the dugouts. As I lean on the hoardings, I notice there are wooden pallets filling previously open railings to meet ground grading requirements. The pitch is yellow from weeks without rain, and it's not level either. The only green is a strip of astroturf for the linesman to run up and down. There's a splash of yellow paint on the stands and railings to match the club colours.

It's the visitors, in their change strip of red and white hoops, that I'm more interested in, but I also have a side mission. During pre-season, I exchanged messages with the manager of another club in this division. He was after someone to scout on opposition teams when he wasn't able to. I assumed this would be a simple job at this level, as teams had plenty of faults to highlight. I then saw reports someone had put together online 'for fun' and they had enough detail for Marcelo Bielsa. They captured positions at offensive and defensive set pieces, where corners and free kicks are directed and generally more detail than I had noted at games. All with handy diagrams. I only expected to make a few notes along the lines of the keeper struggles with crosses under pressure, the centre-halves lack pace, and the left-back can't use his right foot.

This match is an opportunity to see if I can observe a bit more about the team's strengths and weaknesses, if only I'm able to tune out what is going on off the pitch. My task is more difficult with the sizzle of burgers being cooked on the griddle coming from the kiosk behind me. The smell wafts over, but it might as well be coming from someone's back garden, as I don't have time to get some more cash before kick-off. I make sure I am watching as Ilford get the new season under way, although I don't sketch out how the teams are lined up. I need to ease myself back into the new season as I haven't had a pre-season to get my eye in, and get used to the rhythms of the game. I'm playing catch-up, but luckily the gaffer isn't expecting a report on this one, so I set myself the challenge of jotting down my observations on general styles of play and any individual traits.

Almost immediately the Stanway keeper Bradley Davison, who isn't the tallest, spills a free kick. His defence smuggles it away before an attacker can pounce. I just had to see him kick the ball a few times and have a look at his starting position and that would be one of the 22 players covered. Rovers predominantly look to get the ball out wide to the right, with pacy full-back Olumide Akinode the primary outlet. Stanway send several crosses into the box, but nowhere near the forwards. This seems like a useful observation about their general attacking play, but is it better to let them get on with an ineffective tactic or try to stop it?

While I ponder this, I overhear a discussion about the stadium and remember I am also here to write about the ground. Some younger fans are keen to see the club move into a new facility. The lure of prefabricated stands and synthetic playing surface outweighs the quirky, slightly ramshackle appeal of The Hawthorns for them. I'm surprised, as most fans typically want to hold on to old grounds. The ground isn't especially old, being built in 1982, but it is looking frayed around the edges. It wouldn't take too much to smarten the place up but, at this level, finding the money to install a sprinkler system for the pitch and finding someone to go up a big ladder to fix the nets to stop balls sailing out of the ground isn't easy. The alternative is selling up for more housing to add to those which already surround the ground on three sides, and hope the contractor builds a suitable facility as part of the deal. That would risk another ground being lost and potentially not being replaced.

Davison is also taking a risk in Rovers' goal. With a high starting position, he offers himself as an option for his defenders to pass their way out of trouble. He's nearly charged down on a couple of occasions, before cutting inside the onrushing attacker and clearing less convincingly than when he's under pressure. I'm taking far more notes about the goalkeeper and defenders than anywhere else. I've even written where goal kicks are directed. It's either my familiarity with those positions or I'm getting drawn too far into a daydream that I'll be the next Mourinho off the back of my astute defensive observations. In fairness, there hasn't been an awful lot of attacking play to draw any conclusions from. Ilford keep looking for balls into the channel between centre-half and full-back, but it hasn't yet paid off. Joe Lilly plays in right-back Delphin Noorat on the overlap, but his cut-back catches out Freddy Matlock, who stumbles and can't keep his effort down.

Lilly drifts out wide from the number ten position again when Ilford clear a corner high into the clear blue sky. With a surprising touch of quality, he brings the ball under control and turns a defender in one movement. Noorat has burst from right-back over to the left wing. Lilly plays him in with a defence-splitting pass. Noorat has time to bring the ball under control and slot past Davison to make it 1-0. Ilford punish Rovers for playing a high line and failing to push up for offside as a unit. I'm scribbling this down as the visitors celebrate. I'm also glad that I've spotted something a bit more nuanced than the centre-halves' lack of pace, which is also in evidence.

I expect both sides are glad when the half-time whistle blows on a boiling afternoon. They retreat to the shade of the dressing rooms and I take that as my cue to go for a saunter around the ground. Upon reaching the goal Rovers have been attacking, or rather not really been attacking, I get a better look at the topography of the pitch and note where the uphill areas are. Stanway will shoot slightly downhill in the second half, certainly from one of the corner flags. Maybe this is a preference and one to flag to the gaffer in case he wants to upset them and make them swap ends and shoot to their least preferred end in the second half.

I'm not sure how much detail the gaffer would want, so I make a note anyway. I also note there's a gap between the fence panels into an adjoining builders' merchant's yard, which a supporter is taking advantage of to retrieve a ball. This will be of little interest to the gaffer or any groundhoppers, and I can't tell if this is from a lack of maintenance or if it's just convenient. I pay little attention to the main stand, which I usually like to get a good look at, but it's the warmest part of the ground, so I up the pace to reach the covered terrace behind the other goal. Scattered along the terrace are a random assortment of chairs which, while tempting, are clearly for the old regulars.

I return to the covered touchline and can't quite find the exact spot I was in, so I stand nearer to the Ilford bench, as a small sign of my loyalties on the day. There are a few others loyal to Ilford, or at least their players and manager, as shown by their anguished cries when Jake Chadwick can't direct a glancing header on target soon after the restart. There's nearly more anguish when Rovers have a goal ruled out for offside, after sub Ernest Okoh played the ball in. I realise I've seen Okoh and fellow sub Joel Older play before, which is always a simple delight, as I expect teams to be full of anonymous players and this makes them seem more important. It also makes scouting them easier, knowing what to expect.

Ponsford looks to give Stanway's ponderous defence something unexpected to deal with when he introduces Calib Kofi-Admako Mensah and Jack Zielinski from the bench. Ilford are being penned back, although I'm still not sure what the midfield are doing to assert this dominance. I can tick off another cliche of the left-back being one-footed, though, as Stanway's Harry Savage comes under pressure trying to use his favoured foot, which leads to the concession of a throw-in. This might not seem like much, but when a lot of teams have a long-throw specialist, or at the very least can box opponents in from a throw, this is useful intel.

The through ball also looks like being a useful weapon, and Ilford continue to deploy it. Mensah is caught offside to the fury of friends and family, who blame the linesman. I pass up the opportunity to blame their man for failing to time his run better. I do sympathise, however, when they appeal for several shoves in the back that go unpunished, as Rovers' centre-halves make up for their lack of finesse with brute force.

Stanway try to force the game along by throwing new balls on to the field when the old one hasn't left the ground. Ilford's defence are nearly caught out of position on a couple of occasions, before the referee has a word with those in the home dugout. Capturing the sort of shithousery that goes on at this level feels like a useful observation.

Zielinski makes a more useful intervention when he gets on the end of a through ball. It takes a while for him to get it under control on the bouncy surface, and he can only scuff a bobbling shot. Davison saves with his knee. His opposite number doesn't have to use any body parts to deny Rovers, as Older can only drag his effort across the box. It isn't the weather for the hosts to mount a spirited fightback and it ends 1-0 to Ilford.

Neither the game nor the ground captured my imagination, but the possibility of a revival in fortunes for a historic club like Ilford made the trip worthwhile. When I saw that Stanway Pegasus won 7-0 just down the road, it made me question my choice of game. Pegasus drew the larger crowd as well. Rovers didn't announce theirs, but the league website gave the suspiciously round attendance figure of 70.

The size of a crowd isn't always a measure of the experience. Not long ago women's football would have been lucky to attract that figure. The day after the Stanway game, England women's team contest the European Championship Final at a packed Wembley. I'm unable to watch more than 20 minutes. Not because of the football, or some form of misogyny on my part. I have a fever and retire to bed. In my delirious state, I follow the game, imagining I'm the coach from *Chariots of Fire* waiting to hear the equivalent of the winning anthem, in this case cheers from nearby pubs. This blends into a thought that I can be the next Mourinho, so I compose a report on Stanway for the gaffer, once I notice his team plays them in a week or so.

My ravings must have been more paranoid late-era Mourinho than anything else, as the gaffer's team lost.

I don't think either of us recommended leaving players unmarked from a corner, which led to the opening goal. One of Davison's attempts to dribble past a striker was almost charged down for a leveller, but the gaffer's team lost the midfield battle and things became a little fractious towards the end as they were beaten and with it went any hope of my eventual rise to becoming a grumpy manager who occasionally gets to sprint down the touchline and shush opposition fans.

Ground 68

The Brentwood Centre Arena, Brentwood Town

IT'S NOT until the end of August before I get to my second game of the 2022/23 season. Experienced hoppers will be well into double figures by now. I even turn down a couple of opportunities to go to games while Mrs C is away with the kids at her parents'. The fact I decide to try and cycle twice round a six-mile loop of local roads slightly faster than I did the previous month, instead of going to watch Sawbridgeworth, would be understandable if I wrote more poetically about time trialling. Not fancying Athletic Newham at the Terence McMillan Stadium, complete with running track and much-lamented playing surface, is likely to be more understandable for those who have been.

Instead, I wait until the bank holiday Monday to watch Brentwood Town v Hashtag United. There's both interest in the fixture, as I like to follow Hashtag in the Isthmian North (at step four), and in the ground, since it's the nearest one to home I've yet to visit. The stadium itself is fairly unremarkable, built in 1993 on the playing fields surrounding the Brentwood Centre, a sports centre boasting an 'International Hall' although I'm not entirely sure what international events have taken place inside it, and the lettering has either fallen off or been taken off. I do know that I played five-a-side in there, albeit far from international level, and suffered the sort of bizarre injury goalkeepers sometimes manage. I was swinging on the crossbar of the goal, which fell on me and broke a finger, which is up there with dropping a jar of salad cream on your foot or being hit with a puck watching ice hockey.

I have no such calamities on the short drive to Brentwood and there's plenty of room to park in the sizeable car park. I join a queue that's forming at the one open turnstile. The card machine isn't working. Someone in shorts and a training top with their initials printed on it turns up and opens a large gate for anyone wanting to pay in cash. It feels like he's collecting player fines for turning up late. I reluctantly hand over the last of my cash rather than wait for the card machine to work.

There's no team sheet on display, but I locate the team dressing rooms from the pungent smell of Lynx coming from one of the huts. I continue to the plywood main stand, passing a block of seating, the tunnel, press area containing Hashtag's usual media team, and another block of seating. I pick a seat that has extra legroom, only to find several roof supports and floodlight pillars obstructing the view. Given how many there are, I decide it will be easier to peer round them rather than try out the remaining seats.

The old boys sat nearby seem to have found the best views and one even found a programme on sale somewhere. I spent all my cash on the entrance price, so I miss out again and listen intently to the team line-ups, mainly to try and hear them over the R&B music that's also being played over the speakers. I pick out danger man Tom Richardson up front for Brentwood. In among familiar Hashtag names there's new signing Greg Halford, the former Colchester, Reading, Sunderland, Charlton, Sheffield United, Wolves, Portsmouth, Forest, Brighton, Rotherham, Birmingham, Cardiff, Aberdeen, Southend, Waterford and Billericay man. I saw him play for Colchester as a highly rated youngster, who I didn't rate, but had to concede was high, standing at 6ft 4in. He looked incongruous playing at full-back and was linked with Premier League clubs because of his versatility. He made 28 Premier League appearances and plenty more in the Championship and League One. I am keen to see whether that experience shows at this level.

The announcer asks the fans to make some noise as the teams enter the field. There are a couple of ironic woos. The teams make their way through a makeshift tunnel, which looks like a screen that forensics might use to protect a murder scene. 'Firestarter' by the Prodigy is blaring from the speakers to generate some atmosphere. No signs of the recent scorching sun looking like it's torched the playing surface, which is verdant. The teams shake hands, Brentwood in sky blue and Hashtag in their pink away strip, and for a moment I wonder if I might be at an elaborate baby-gender reveal.

Nothing too elaborate from Halford. He calmly brings the ball under control and sends it long, forcing a Brentwood defence into conceding a corner, which comes to nothing. Soon after, Halford turns past a striker and sends another long ball forward for Toby Aromolaran to chase. Aromolaran is fouled, but the free kick again comes to nothing. There's little in the way of attacking play to distract me from today's side quest to look closely at how a former Premier League player fares at this level. He tells a linesman to 'fucking switch on'. Otherwise, he's coaching his team-mates and shows composure to cushion a header sideways rather than send it straight back into the midfield melee.

Halford is soon on the end of the sort of kick on the knee that must put off a lot of former pros continuing at this level. He's quick to react as a Brentwood forward cuts into the box and blocks, as the Town man goes to shoot. The follow-through catches Halford and he stays down. He's not quick to get back to his feet and comes in for some abuse from the dozen or so Brentwood fans on the uncovered terrace behind the goal. They have him down as a 'Premier League actor'. The physio helps him to his feet and the Brentwood player is booked.

Hashtag seem a better match for their opponents physically this season, with the likes of Max Cornhill and Alex Teniola bringing experience from higher levels, although not quite the Premier League. It's another summer signing from the league above, Pedro Carvalho, who gets on the ball. The pacy winger runs at the Town defence but allows a centre-back to get a foot in and he's lucky to win a free kick when he collides with the defender. Halford lines it up. I'm not expecting him to win the game single-handedly from centre-back, but he nearly opens the scoring when his strike curls round the wall and just past the upright.

Halford gets another rude awakening when he is shoved over in midfield, and nothing is given. The hosts break forward with Halford's centre-back partner, Tom Anderson, isolated. Anderson has a couple of attempts to get at the forward, who goes down for a penalty. Richardson dispatches the kick with a firm drive low to the keeper's right to give Brentwood the lead. The fans behind the goal start a chant of 'Premier League, you're having a laugh' aimed at Halford. He only has a few minutes before the break to respond and sends a long throw into the Brentwood box. The hosts clear and see off another ball into the box before the half-time whistle blows.

I've avoided seeing a 0-0, but the game deserves to be goalless given the lack of action. There's a lack of music playing over the tannoy, which is pumping out white noise. It's only fixed in time for another blast of 'Firestarter' to greet the start of the second half. The track doesn't get either side pumped up for the second 45. Several minutes pass before Carvalho controls a long free kick by Anderson. He skips past his man, only to be tripped. The referee awards a penalty. Carvalho steps up to take it, but Harry Girling gets down well to his left and makes the save.

Neither side can fashion chances from open play, but Brentwood do allow right-back Billy Willis the full length of the pitch to burst into. He exchanges passes with Eman Okunja and sends in a low cross. Teniola challenges for the ball with Girling and it breaks to Lewis Watson. He shoots and levels the score with the aid of a deflection. It's a deserved piece of luck and on his birthday as well, with some Hashtag fans greeting the equaliser with a rendition of 'Happy birthday to you'.

Brentwood aim to be party poopers with a long ball to Matt Price. He beats Anderson and fires in a shot towards Anthony Page's near post. Page sticks out a leg to stop the hosts from retaking the lead. The game becomes more end to end, with several appeals for penalties and Brentwood missing another presentable chance after Halford is caught out. Okunja looks more like Premier League material, having been billed as the non-league Kante. He's all action

39

and bursts through the Brentwood lines. His low pull-back is turned in by Carvalho to atone for his penalty miss and give Hashtag the lead.

The match ambles along. Hashtag are afforded half-chances that they fail to hit the target with, while Brentwood struggle to build a platform. Home fans, now mostly stood on the covered stand behind the goal, grow restless and look for the referee to help them out. The attendance of 281 is read out, which shows we must be approaching full time. The visitors are engaged in a passing move that appears to have the sole purpose of running down the clock until it's laid back to left-back Matt Wooldridge on the edge of the box. He fires a low drive that finds its way through Girling for 3-1. The Tags even have time to work a presentable chance for one of their subs before the final whistle, but he lashes wide.

At full time, I'm buoyed by the result, if not the ground I've been to. I text my brother a picture of the stadium to see if he can guess where I've been. He goes for Billericay based on an advert he can see and asks if there were any former league players in the teams. It's one of those universal thrills at this level. I mention Halford and he gives me his verdict on his Charlton days, 'Dogshit, had a long throw on him, no idea how he made a career for himself in the Premier League.' Wikipedia tells me he did only play 17 games in the Premier League after his spell at Charlton. Wikipedia also seems to have influenced my dad's verdict when I ask him about Halford, as his recollection is uncannily similar to the entry.

The next Saturday it's other family commitments that stop me from taking in one of the many tempting local fixtures. Mrs C is away and I've got the kids. I try to explain to them the magic of the FA Cup in the hope it might tempt them along to a qualifying-round tie and a new ground. In the end, it's the promise of a souvenir from the club shop that tempts them to Melbourne Stadium for Chelmsford City v Havant and Waterlooville. It's a repeat for me, but stadium number two for each of them. The medallions they choose in the club shop do little to placate them besides being briefly used as a mirror. Having the foresight to bring sticker books meant I kept my son fully occupied, so I'm not sure he can really tick this one off after missing all seven goals in a 4-3 defeat for City. My daughter fared slightly better and caught about half of the goals, aided by a couple of penalties. She disagreed with Cloughie's famous saying, 'It only takes a second to score a goal', and felt it took far too long. I saw all the goals, but got no real feel for the game, so it wasn't a roaring success and family outings won't be a way to complete my mission.

Ground 69

Oakside, Redbridge

MIDWEEK AFTER work presents a much better groundhopping opportunity. I'm in London and have the chance to either tick off another senior ground in Essex, a ground in the Essex Senior League, or both. In the end I opt for Redbridge who, unlike Frenford and Buckhurst Hill, don't quite play in Essex but, like Buckhurst Hill, are members of the Essex Senior League.

Redbridge play at Oakside, which backs on to Barkingside tube station. Barkingside FC were the original incumbents when the ground opened in 1957, once Second World War tank traps had been cleared. Financial difficulties led to Redbridge taking over the lease and keeping Barkingside on as tenants. This lasted until a rent increase forced Barkingside into a groundshare at Cricklefield with Ilford.

The journey along the Central line to Barkingside is littered with reminders of grounds past. Leyton is typically associated with Orient, but Leyton FC played at the Hare and Hounds until 2011, when they folded due to financial difficulties. This was a sad end for a club with a fine history dating back to 1868 and encompassing two FA Amateur Cup wins and countless regional trophies. The ground just about survives, although the stands are in poor condition and the pitch is partly used as a car park and not one of the Mourinho bus-parking variety. At the time of writing, there's an ongoing campaign to save the ground.

While Walthamstow is not on the Central line, Walthamstow Avenue's latter years became intertwined with clubs in these parts, through various mergers. Their Green Pond Lane stadium is another lost ground I didn't have the chance to visit and exists in my mind as only a black-and-white photograph of a large grandstand reminiscent of the single stand I had with my Subbuteo set. Avenue were unable to build on their two FA Amateur Cup wins and taking Manchester United to a replay in the fourth round of the FA Cup.

Leytonstone is next and used to boast a club who played at Granleigh Road and were three-time FA Amateur Cup winners. Their ground backed on to another nearby railway line, with arches cutting across part of the terrace along one touchline, which had a small whitewashed stand perched at the top. Photos of this are pretty much all that's left and there's a sense of regret that I didn't get to see a venue that existed within my lifetime, although it would be harsh on my six-year-old self to have had the foresight to get along there.

The tube continues to rattle along on an overcast autumnal evening: Stratford, where West Ham now play, their reserve and youth teams having taken over Redbridge's old Rush Green stadium; Redbridge station, where tonight's Redbridge team don't play near, as the club are named after the wider borough. I pass Newbury Park, which is close to the site of Ilford's old Lynn Road ground that hosted games in the 1948 Olympics and was another grand old non-league venue lost to developers. Newbury Park is also where I've had to take many a replacement rail service home from, which can even take the joy out of a north London derby win.

I reach Barkingside station and it's a short walk to Oakside, although not as short as it would be if there was an exit from Platform 1 into the main stand. The turnstiles are cash only, so I'm directed inside to the clubhouse to pay by card. While I'm there I order a burger, bottle of lager and a chocolate bar. It comes to £13.50 for a two-course meal, drink and entertainment. I'm already entertained when I see on the television that Chelsea are losing their Champions League tie with Dinamo Zagreb. Once again, I don't buy a programme. This time because it's a digital programme, only available online. I've already read it before leaving the office, which helps build the anticipation for the game. It's slightly odd that it's laid out like it's supposed to be printed, but there's a nice bit about the history of the clubs and I check to see if there are any names I recognise. There's no one with Premier League experience, but I've seen Redbridge's Samraj Gill play for Hashtag. Opponents West Essex have Callum Bloss in their squad, a player with one of the most lucrative sponsorship deals in non-league. YouTuber Smiv paid £700 to sponsor him for the season, an amount that goes a long way at this level.

It's nearly time for kick-off, so I leave the bar and head to the stand. I'm blocked by the tunnel to the dressing room where the players are lining up, ready to enter the field. It starts to rain and once the players amble on to the pitch, I dash under cover. The roof is made of scaffolding, but is watertight. A lone fan with a brolly braves the terrace behind the goal. Those around me bemoan the fact that kick-offs are always late in this league. One of them notes that in Scotland they take less than a minute from exiting the tunnel to kick off. I can only presume there's a need to keep moving in those cold, midge-infested lands. It also reveals I'm in the company of far more seasoned groundhoppers.

I don't see any notebooks poised when West Essex win a corner. Bloss delivers it into the six-yard box and Cameron Gray gets a head on it and flicks it into the bottom corner to give the visitors an early lead. 'You need to think about taking fucking responsibility!' comes a shout from the Redbridge bench. I take that as a sign to stop sending my brother pictures of the ground to guess where I am and concentrate on the game. I finally notice something resembling a pattern in midfield. Redbridge are pressing in a concerted manner and it takes some neat passing from West to escape.

When Redbridge get on the ball, they look to get it forward quickly, either through the pace of Solomon Ogunwomoju or an early ball. There's a slick pass from Milesy, which I can tell by someone on the bench saying, 'good ball, Milesy,' but I can't tell who Milesy is from his hastily scrawled name on the team sheet. He finds Jake Brocklebank, who brings the ball under control and turns his marker in one movement, before slotting home from close range to equalise.

The hosts build momentum. Someone obscured by the opaque dugout drags a shot on to the post. Milesy goes for a chip. Ogunwomoju-ey is found in space at the back post, but blasts over. West remain a threat on the break but have lost their grip in the middle. 'We can't start lumping it. We're not them' comes an instruction from a diminutive member of the visitors' dugout. 'Lump it like us boys. Don't play it short like he is' comes the sarcastic reply from a Redbridge player not in the side. Both sides try to gain the upper hand, but it's honours even as the half-time whistle blows.

Silence descends on the ground. The rain has stopped. A tube rumbles into the station. My brother finally guesses where I am. I decide to move seat, figuring I want to be near the exit and not waiting to get past the players' tunnel when there's a distant rumble of a southbound tube train after the match. This part of the stand is concrete with plastic seats, including a row that has been knocked over. There is a canvas poster tied to the perimeter fence facing me, which describes the work being done to improve the ground. They have replaced the fence and dugouts and now want to replace the stand opposite. I notice where it's fenced off and find a picture of it online along with Barkingside fans reminiscing about times spent on there. Redbridge are after 100 people to pay £5 a month towards the rebuild. The sad truth is there aren't 100 people in the ground. It's always a shame to see clubs struggling, but more so in a vast metropolis known for its wealth.

The media team are doing their bit to promote the club. They take a seat in the press box and discuss the game and updates to the Twitter feed. There's a substitution early in the second half and they need to agree the minute it took place. Having relied on club Twitter feeds to check points of detail in my writing, I'm alarmed by the haphazard way they conclude it was after 52 minutes.

I would make a dreadful media team member, as I can't fire out updates on crucial passages of play like the best ones do. My notes from what felt like a significant passage of play read, 'No foul west. Appeal. Break to fed [I think I mean Red as in shorthand for Redbridge and not a player resembling Roger Federer]. Two slides [tackles]. Work ball. Lose it up in air bad west header. Red sting palms then head of def[ender].' It was inconsequential to the game, but to me signalled the point where I had become invested in it, that point where I'm fully immersed in the contest and I am acutely aware of the little details that could sway it either way, like the towel.

The drama started in the first half when the ball needed to be dried for a long throw-in. A training bib was good enough for one throw. A player not in the squad went to fetch a golf towel he had in the changing rooms. It then had to be ferried to the player with a long throw and safely stowed should the opposition dugout pilfer it. In between times, the squad player is chatting to someone in the crowd who used to scout for a league club about the general standard of officiating. The referee then has a job to do in response to an off-the-ball incident. A Redbridge player is down and the ref calls over West's Pascal Thornton, a burly white man. He then sends off Salid Lo-Seye, a sinewy black man. The stark difference between the two players deemed to be involved calls into question what the officials saw. West have the last quarter of an hour to hold out with ten men.

As soon as a Redbridge player slides into a tackle, the visiting bench are on their feet demanding the referee evens things up. The fact he was nowhere near a West player means the ref waves their appeals away. Lo-Seye is less animated, stood forlornly near the bench. A couple of supporters go over to commiserate with him and no one is any the wiser about why it was a red card.

The clock is running down, Tony Martin fires over for the hosts. Another ball ends up going over the site of the former covered terrace, prompting one fan to remark, 'They will need a two-week all-inclusive to go and fetch that.' Redbridge have one last chance in stoppage time. Ogunwomoju lines up a free kick left-footed from fully 30 yards. It could be much nearer, but that's the only way free kicks from a reasonable distance seem to be referred to. His strike brushes the crossbar and finds its way into the net. It's a world-class finish and would comfortably grace one of the night's Champions League ties. Seeing the Redbridge team run the length of the field to celebrate, as Lo-Seye slumps further over the perimeter fence, is far better than watching a game on television as I've become fully invested in the drama.

There's even time for one of those observations of little things that go into the match at this level. The social media team are trying to work out who has come on as a substitute. 'Who has come on?' 'Fifteen.' 'We don't have a 15.' 'Yeah, we do, look he's over there.' 'Well, he's not on the team sheet.' I edge my way towards the exit, so I'm past the tunnel before it's blocked off. I get a closer look at the fenced-off terrace and the final whistle blows.

I head back to the tube station, glad that I've explored another part of London and seen a decent game of football. The ground didn't have any distinguishing features and could easily be dismissed from looking at the photos. That this unassuming venue has been overlooked for development, unlike some of the grander, lost stadiums, is a good thing. It's a charming spot, within easy reach of central London and well worth the visit.

Ground 70

Hertingfordbury Park, Hertford Town (and St Panteleimon)

AWARE THAT I don't want to focus entirely on grounds in London and Essex, I make my next stop the Midlands; well, the Spartan South Midlands League. That I'm only just over the Essex border in Hertfordshire suggests a rather loose interpretation of the Midlands, which is often the way with regional leagues. I'm in the county town of Hertford, which is only about 20 miles north of London, but not without good, solid, groundhopping reasons.

Pictures of Hertingfordbury Park, and more specifically the main stand, lured me in. All it takes is an old stand. It doesn't have to be an Archibald Leitch, but anything that looks like it's seen its fair share of laced-up balls hoofed around by clodhopper boots on a heavy pitch is good enough for me. This stand dates back to 1959 so just about qualifies. Hertford Town have played on the site since 1908 and are now in the Southern League Division One Central, at step four, which means I'm watching their tenants St Panteleimon in step five. This probably counts as cheating in some groundhoppers' books.

Saint Panteleimon is the patron saint of lottery wins and crying children, among other things, so I'm on the lookout for a 50-50 draw and hope the kids behave for Mrs C while I'm out. St Panteleimon FC are a Greek heritage side, formed in 2015, and previously groundshared with several north London clubs.

Quite how they ended up out here is a mystery. Google tells me there isn't so much as a Greek restaurant in town. Walking up to the turnstile, there isn't anyone there either. I walk through an open gate and realise that I'm unlikely to find a programme to tell me any more about the team or find a 50-50 draw.

I find out a bit about Leighton Town, today's opponents, who hail from Leighton Buzzard. They were formed in 1885 and are disappointingly nicknamed the Reds and not the Buzzards. This is the highest level they have played at and they have won nine trophies in their history, which makes me wonder which team has won the fewest trophies in the longest time, as there's usually a smattering of lower-division titles and county cups on most clubs' honours boards.

What Leighton do have is their team line-up posted on Twitter. In the absence of a team sheet in the ground or anything on the hosts' feed, I'll have to refer to all the home players using a stereotypical Greek name. I'll go for Uncle Lou, after my Greek uncle, which is also easier to write than most Greek surnames.

I survey the ground. There's a newly laid 3G pitch, which is always helpful when teams are groundsharing. Several sets of goals stored around the place suggest it's getting plenty of other use as well. The wendy house grandstand isn't as old as it first looks, being concrete. I make my way up to the back of the stand in front of a press box that's just being used for storage. The seats are a hotchpotch of different plastic and wooden ones and have an elevated view of the pitch.

I see the teams limber up ahead of this clash between second and fourth. The Leighton warm-up descends into players belting the ball as hard as they can at each other, which doesn't seem appropriate ahead of a top-of-the-table clash. The referee and club officials discuss an appropriate mark of respect following the recent death of the Queen, with a period of silence agreed. This is already being observed by a small crowd. I count 39 people in attendance, which includes two babies. I'm not sure any count at the turnstile would include them anyway, as they won't have paid, but since no one has paid, I might as well include them.

Uncle Lou gets us under way. Although, now the teams have changed out of training tops, which were yellow with white numbers, to yellow shirts with blue numbers, I can at least distinguish the players that way. They are looking to play the ball out from the back, which always feels risky at this level. The visitors have a less-cultured approach and send a hopeful punt forward. Leon Lobjoit takes a touch and finishes low past the keeper to open the scoring.

Despite the contrasting styles, both sides are getting stuck in. Things are already feisty when a ball is booted into a Leighton player who is on the ground, which raises temperatures up a notch. The Saints' manager, who you might imagine being a Demis Roussos lookalike with José Camacho-style sweat patches, liberally using the word 'malaka' in every other sentence, is nothing of the sort. He's very much a London geezer who is audible from across the pitch, telling his team, 'Fucking work, that's fucking pathetic,' as if he's berating waiting staff at a Toby Carvery.

His team serve up a through ball that's a different gravy. Uncle Lou #20 gobbles up the chance, drilling it low past Xavi Comas to level the scores.

Before I fall into too many stereotypes about Greek football, it's worth noting that, yes, most of their play goes through a playmaker in a number ten shirt, but the keeper does look to catch everything. It's Leighton who need to beware of bearing gifts just before half-time as a back pass finds Uncle Lou #18, to give Saints the lead.

I do a lap of the ground at the interval. There's the Stables End, a covered terrace that's all rusted metalwork, but more than anything looks like it could do with a raucous crowd on it. Instead, there's just a stone Buddha, the sort you might find in a garden centre. Someone has also put into the ground a few plants on the far touchline, where there are the remains of some old turnstiles and another previously covered terrace. The cover has been pulled down and the concrete steps appear to be going the same way. This all adds to the charm of the place. There are recent additions too. Something is being built to prevent me from doing a full lap. I return past a small clubhouse and think I've spotted a team sheet, but it's one for Hertford's last under-18 game.

It's an under-18 who causes the main talking point early in the second half, not long after Saints go 3-1 up. A child wanders on to the field and doesn't seem inclined to leave. Everyone stands around perplexed. He's too young for anyone to manhandle him off, but there aren't enough fans around to make their displeasure known. Eventually he wanders off, back out of the open gate. A couple of Saints officials sat nearby wonder why the gate is open and why people keep walking in for free. They can't understand why people aren't using the other gate, which I've yet to see.

I wrestle with the moral dilemma about whether I should offer some of my loose change to the club officials, who are the first I've seen. I've no idea how much entry is supposed to be and it would look slightly weird. Another customer is making his views known, repeatedly saying how boring it is that Saints are slowing play down at every opportunity. The on-pitch game management is certainly better than the off-pitch, but even then Leighton's Ethan Flanagan heads a corner on to the crossbar. The visitors sense they could get back into this. 'How are we fucking losing to these?' enquires a defender, before his team-mates almost concede an own goal and he slices his own clearance out for a throw-in.

Leighton earn a set piece late on. They direct the free kick towards the penalty spot and Lewis Toomey nips in front of Uncle Lou #1 to head home to close the gap to 3-2. There's enough time for Leighton to get forward again. Uncle Lou #1 is booked for time-wasting. The visitors have one last chance. A red-shirted head connects with the ball. It flashes wide and Saints hold on for the win.

Despite seeing five goals, some decent play and experiencing the old ground, I'm left with a feeling of disappointment. Or more accurately, it's a feeling of *saudade*, that melancholic nostalgia for something lost. Supporters should pack the old terrace. It suggests I should have seen the landlords rather than the tenants, but even then numbers aren't what they should be at certain non-league grounds. For my next stop, I decide it needs to be more of an occasion.

Ground 71

SCEFL Groundhop Weekend (Friday)

SIX GAMES over one weekend. The chance to tick off six new grounds and watch 540 minutes of football (plus stoppage time). I dip my toes into the SCEFL groundhopping weekend. Groundhop UK run several groundhop events during the season. In conjunction with various leagues, they put on games over a weekend to allow hoppers a chance to meet up, experience new grounds and bump up their stats. Groundhop UK arrange a coach, accommodation, and tickets with a guaranteed programme. Since this was just over the river for me, I made my own plans and accepted the risk of missing out on a programme again.

The SCEFL is the Southern Counties East Football League, with a Premier Division at step five and Division One at step six. It was formed in 1966 as the Kent Premier League, but unlike its Essex counterpart, it changed its name to reflect the number of teams from outside the county taking part. Previous winners include relatively well-known sides such as Cray Wanderers, Sittingbourne and Maidstone United.

Friday night's SCEFL Premier Division game between Punjab United and Stansfeld in Gravesend is first up.

Members of the local Sikh community formed Punjab in 2003 but are keen to show they are open to all. They worked their way up to step five and play at the Steve Cook Stadium, named after their former groundsman, who was a popular figure, and passed away in 2020. The pitch is in good condition and the ground has been built up piecemeal as the team progressed. Momentum had stalled at this level and Punjab found themselves second from bottom.

Visitors Stansfeld, or Stansfeld Bermondsey & Oxford Club to give them their full name, hail from further up the league table after starting strongly following promotion last season. They were formed in 1897 by doctor, priest and philanthropist John Stansfeld and were one of two teams named after a 'John' featuring this weekend. I could have studied to become a doctor myself in the time it took to get over the Dartford Crossing, but I arrive in enough time to bag a programme and to join a sizeable queue for food.

The food hut and decking area outside is a popular spot, as everyone's keen to sample some traditional Punjabi fayre. Confusion reigns about how to get hold of a mixed platter. That is on offer elsewhere and a ticket needs to be bought to get one. No one seems to know where to get a ticket or collect the food. All they know is that it isn't the queue we are in. There's no use getting frustrated about queuing, as it's always going to be busier than the club are used to. In the meantime, it is good to see the club let their junior teams use the main pitch in front of a crowd, and other youngsters enterprisingly trying to flog some merch to those in the queue. A steady parade of hoppers get their photo of the team sheet pinned next to the service window, while others diligently write it out for themselves. I get my photo as I edge closer before eventually ordering lamb in a naan-like wrap, and a samosa. It is well worth the wait and preferable to a standard burger.

The teams come out with dhol drummers accompanying them, which adds to the occasion. Rain drums on the corrugated iron-covered area I find myself under, with the two small seated areas already full. The match gets under way and the wet conditions look like they might cause some problems. A high ball into the Stansfeld box skids off the head of a defender. It could go anywhere, but lands safely in Charlie Cottrell's hands. At the other end, Dan Parkinson hits a skidding free kick from distance, it rears up in front of Sam Mott, who does well to parry, before smothering the rebound.

There are few other chances in the first half. The visitors are marginally on top and judging by their defenders' shouts of 'fuck this game' and 'we ain't even got started yet', they're evidently frustrated at events and the officials in particular, who come in for some abuse. The half ends goalless. Chatter on the terraces continues unabated, covering how the Isthmian League and Southern Leagues have sat in relation to each other over the years, groundhopping in Scotland where Gala Fairydean are inevitably mentioned, and how much money Real Bedford are spending, although it's not clear if that is genuine money or the magic beans they are using.

Once the rain stops, I move to the end Stansfeld are attacking, expecting that's where the action will be. The slight slope on the pitch keeps the ball down the other end. At least I get to hear a Punjab defender politely thank the linesman for a decision, which makes me warm to the hosts, if the catering hasn't already done so. Punjab are no shrinking violets and captain Lea Dawson slides in, taking man and ball. He takes the ball cleanly, but the follow-through catches the player and sparks a melee. I had seen a player post a video of his own sending off in similar circumstances and ask for opinions. They were split into referees saying it was out of control and a red, and the 'game's gone, you've never played the game' types. There appear to be a few of those types in the visitors' ranks, but as it was their man fouled, they are unhappy to see only a yellow. Stansfeld aren't best pleased when someone charges down the resulting free kick from closer than ten yards.

The game is gradually coming to life. Punjab's Elliot Sartorius swivels and shoots straight at Cottrell, who reacts smartly. A long ball upfield from Stansfeld finds Ollie Milton. He shrugs off his man and fires at Mott, who narrows the angle and blocks. It isn't frantic end-to-end stuff, but both sides take turns to present each other with chances to score. After a Stansfeld chance, Punjab break down the right. Substitute Lee Friend cuts inside and drills a low finish past Mott to break the deadlock. The groundhop weekend won't start with a dreaded 0-0 and notebooks can be updated. I'm glad people are taking note as I can report it was scored in the 68th minute. In the 70th, Paul Vines meets a Punjab cross from the left with a spectacular scissor kick to level the score.

The goal is met with cheers for its execution and from those pleased to see our welcoming hosts back on terms. We move into 'how long?' territory, when the visitors ask the ref how long he is going to allow Mott to take his kick, and Mott asks the linesman how long is left. There are chances for both teams. Right at the death, it opens up for Punjab. A long ball forward is squared to Emiliano Hysi. He shoots straight at Cottrell, who can only parry back to him. Hysi can't get another shot away, so goes back to Arun Suman on the edge of the box. He shoots, and it's deflected wide. The final whistle goes before Punjab can take the corner.

The 347 in attendance leave happy as the game came to life in the end. We are off to a good start with some goals, and a friendly club earned a deserved point. I retire to my luxurious lodgings for a good night's sleep guaranteed. I will need it as the Saturday is jam-packed with sporting endeavour.

Grounds 72–74

SCEFL Groundhop Weekend (Saturday)

NOT ONLY is this weekend a chance to add to my tally of grounds visited, it is also a chance to add to my tally of different parkruns. I chose my hotel based on its location next to the start of Maidstone parkrun. I can knock out a quick 5k then cycle to the opening game at 11am, or at least that is the plan.

The run starts in the Museum of Kent Life, which I nose around and see those classic Kentish sights: hops and an oasthouse. It is an out-and-back run along a narrow towpath beside the River Medway, with the early morning mist evaporating off the water. It's a lovely run, but it isn't quick, for which I will blame the course and not my lack of fitness. The more important statistics are that I log parkrun number 201, on my 70th different course. I then have to dash to Staplehurst for ground number 72 and match number two of the weekend, Staplehurst Monarchs v Rochester United at the Jubilee Sports Ground.

I thought it would be nice to cycle between grounds, see a bit of the Kent countryside and add to my mileage total for the year. I imagine myself cutting a similar figure to Owen Wilson's bicycle-propelled reporter from *The*

French Dispatch, not realising I'm about to turn up to a match in ill-fitting Lycra. I figure I have enough time to make kick-off, but don't bank on the traffic in Maidstone or on stopping to check directions at every junction outside of Maidstone. The ride takes in some lovely country lanes in bright autumn sunshine. It also takes me until five minutes after kick-off, as I arrive sweating and not at all resembling Herbsaint Sazerac. I miss another five minutes of play getting a much-needed sausage bap and coffee for breakfast. I don't think I missed much, as the game is slow to get going. I work out it is still 0-0 without having to ask a serious hopper, who wouldn't entertain such tardiness.

I looked up some information about the clubs beforehand, which is just as well since I forgot to ask for a programme, assuming they had sold out. Monarchs were formed in 1893 and play in red, United in 1982 and are in their white change strip. Neither had won anything beyond county level and perhaps justified my mate Phil's assertion that Kent isn't exactly a footballing hotbed when he questioned why I would do this trip.

The ground itself is on the outskirts of town. There's a large clubhouse next to the entrance. I go past this and find myself behind one of the goals, which always surprises me when the main entrance doesn't lead on to a touchline. A burger van and beer tent have been added for the occasion, but otherwise there is a lot of empty green space surrounded by trees.

The first chance, or the first I see, falls to United's Luke Mercer after 25 minutes. He hits a half-volley across Steve Lawrence who is down well to save. Rochester are on top judging by the amount of play down my end, although some of that is Monarchs playing it around the back before looking to crown the move, with a through ball to a forward.

Monarchs' Brad Large has a chance that needs a much larger goal for it to threaten the score. A quick free kick finds him in space, as everyone waits, expecting the referee to brandish a card. Large drills one across the box to oohs from another sizeable crowd, with 331 in attendance for this step six fixture. The club officials seem delighted with the size of the crowd and home supporters are unfazed by the early start. With clubs now being allowed to agree earlier kick-offs to reduce electricity costs associated with turning on floodlights in the current energy crisis, it makes sense to move them about. Some well-timed kick-offs might lure in fans going to other games later in the day and ought to be something we see more of.

Whether it is the early start or the bumper crowd, the game doesn't really come to life. There is a soporific quality, like a day at the cricket, which is splendid in the sunshine, but would have been grim if it were wet as there was only one small covered stand. The crowd is so large that people are standing on the grass on one side of the ground, where regulations stipulate only the sides with concrete paths should be used. A nonsense rule on a day like this, but one that makes some sense during most of the season.

An incident straight from the pages of 'You are the ref' livens things up. Large chases a through ball and appears to be shoved over as he challenges United's keeper, Jamie Kelly. Large collides with Kelly, who carries the ball out of his area. The Staplehurst players have the ball on the spot thinking a penalty has been given, but after a chat with the linesman, the officials go with the classic decision of free kick for the goalkeeper. 'Well done, keeper, you screamed just loud enough for the ref to give you that one' comes the response from one of the handful of home supporters in among the hoppers. The number of hoppers near the exit grows as the game wears on, worried about getting to the next game on time. There are worries it might end 0-0 as well.

Fired up by the penalty incident, Monarchs' sub John Osagie cuts in from the right wing, gets across the defender, who is wary of tripping him, and pokes an early finish past Kelly for 1-0. Fears of the day getting off to an inauspicious start with a dreaded 0-0 evaporate. Any hope that this will spark the game to life never materialise, though, and the last quarter of an hour plays out without incident. Hoppers start to leave, another one chides them, saying, 'it doesn't count,' which is easier to tell is a joke than when it's a conversation on an internet forum.

I can't understand why everyone is so worried about getting to the next game. I worked out that even on a bike, I would make it in plenty of time. I question my decision to cycle as there is only one realistic route, down a busy road. I find some nice lanes near the ground and views across the valley from Otham. The only problem is that I've cycled past the ground. Coming back the other way, I pass the Groundhop UK coach and realise I've overshot the entrance. Despite that, I make it to Bearsted v Fisher in plenty of time.

I also drop a shoe out of my bag on Honey Lane, the aptly named road leading to Bearsted's ground, Otham Sports Club. Retrieving this and queuing at the tea bar means I don't quite see kick-off in this Premier Division fixture, featuring the other team named after a 'John'.

Fisher Athletic were named after the saint John Fisher. They folded and were reformed in 2009 as a fan-owned club. In a break from rooting for the host club, I was keen to see the Fish get some points to move off the bottom of the table, as I have something of a soft spot for them.

Fisher are in their away strip of Melchester Rovers red and yellow. I recognise a couple of names from previous visits to their Surrey Docks ground. Imposing defender Sam Fitzgerald scored on both occasions I saw them last season, so maybe he would be inspired to perform some Fitz of the Fish heroics. Their hosts, Bearsted, are hoping to bounce back from a couple of poor results, leaving them in ninth. They are in a white shirt with blue sash, adding a classy touch to a kit and something that's not seen often enough this side of Peru.

The ground is situated inside fenced-off playing fields and has been the Bears' home since 1998, after a move was required for ground grading reasons. They have the requisite concrete path round the perimeter, fencing, dugouts, small stand and small covered terrace. I visit the portacabins housing the tea bar and changing rooms, then find a spot to stand and watch. Views over the valley I had seen on my detour are obscured by trees and there is a stables and paddock behind one of the goals. It's a lovely rural spot.

There is also a game going on. The hosts make the early running but concede a corner. Fitzgerald rises for the header but James Savage claims. Soon after, the Bears win a free kick. Samuel Stace sends it in and Ollie Freeman leaps highest to head home. I then spend far too long trying to summon up words to convey the imagery of a bear catching a fish, as some sort of metaphor. It's clear that concentrating on back-to-back games is something that requires practice. I even struggle to come up with good fish puns.

Fisher set about turning the tide, and some trickery from Jacob Katonia, flipping from side to side, leaves his marker floundering. He sends in a cross and the shot is plaice-d wide. More pressure from the Fish results in a series of corners, halibut they are defended with ease by the home team, who clear it trout of danger. An absorbing half of football ends and the interval gives me 15 minutes to flick through the programme, write up some notes on the game, check in on Futbology, and look at the map for directions to the next port of call. It doesn't take the Fish long after the break to find their way towards the hosts' net. Katonia cuts inside and shoots. Savage claws it away and saves the follow-up. Moments later, Katonia cuts inside again, leaving his marker on the floor and putting a low shot through Savage's legs to level.

This pokes the Bears into action. They win the ball back on halfway and work the ball wide right. A teasing pass low across the box invites Freeman to slide in and restore their lead. The club officials stood behind me are delighted. They are equally pleased after adding up the ticket sales. A crowd of 229, when they would usually expect around 70, has made it worthwhile.

The Fisher bench are less pleased with the official's answer to another 'You are the ref' conundrum. The referee waves play on for a foul outside the box, before another foul inside the box. He goes back for the initial foul. My admittedly biased opinion is to give Fisher a penalty as a reward for their attacking play, mainly because I didn't know the actual laws on this one.

It feels like there will be another goal soon anyway. Fisher keep attacking but can't find a way through a resolute Bearsted defence. The hosts have chances on the break but can't find a final ball to fillet the visitors open. Fisher's chances appear to be over when a player is sin-binned late on. Down to ten men, a hopeful punt finds sub Darnell Bailey-King. He nods it past a defender and flicks it past Savage. The ball bounces back off the post. Off balance, Bailey-King prods it back towards the goal and it's cleared from the line. The visitors just can't unlock the Bearsted defence, in much the same way I can't unlock my bike lock. Everyone files out and I'm still fiddling with it. A tight turnaround before the next game becomes tighter until I give up and snap the thing apart with worrying ease.

The ride back into Maidstone is through the splendid Mote Park, then the not-so-splendid one-way systems and massive roundabouts of the town centre, before finding my way on to the towpath of the River Medway. I pass the Gallagher Stadium and hear the Maidstone United fans in good voice at their National League game against Halifax. I collect the car from the hotel and make my way to the day's final match in Division One, Larkfield & New Hythe v Greenways at the Taray Group Community Stadium.

Larkfield were formed in 1961 and moved into this site in 1967. It's been redeveloped in recent years, as the team progressed from the Maidstone and District League. There's a smart new clubhouse, perimeter fencing, floodlights and the ubiquitous 100-seater stand similar to others I had seen this weekend. Visitors Greenways were formed not long after their hosts in 1965 and play only a couple of miles away in a groundshare with K Sports, although they started out in the Gravesend league before moving up to county level.

I am late for kick-off again, but from the queue for the burger van I have a good view as Luke Burdon slots past a wrong-footed keeper to give the Larks an early lead and put to bed any concerns about it being 0-0. There are some things you don't want to see in football, by which I don't mean the scuffle breaking out on the far touchline, but the burger van running out of food. The downside of cycling to the games is that I feel the need to eat at every one of them. I manage to get one of the last remaining sausage baguettes and turn around in time to see Stuart West double the hosts' lead and put the Larks firmly in the ascendancy.

I find a spot on the touchline. The ground is overlooked by leafy hills in the distance and looks delightful in the early evening sun. I'm struggling to concentrate on the football by this point, but appreciate both sides battling for possession and looking to get forward. The half ends with the hosts 2-0 up. I visit the clubhouse, where Bayern are playing Dortmund, on TV. Dortmund, in the same colours as Larkfield, don't have much appeal for the 243 in attendance here, with only one person watching it. I head out for the second half, where there might not be the beer, chanting and general quality of *Der Klassiker*, but there will be a full-blooded contest.

Greenways start on the front foot. A cut-back finds midfielder Oscar Saxton on the edge of the box. He takes a touch to flick it in the air and hits a volley that's too good for Scott Andrews in the Larkfield goal, to pull it back to 2-1. If anything, this prompts Larkfield to look for a third. Dogged defending keeps the game in the balance, along with several fouls. A long free kick from Greenways is headed towards his own goal by a Larks defender, which Andrews tips over, but the visitors can't create any openings of their own. When they gift one to Burdon, he takes a touch too many and can't settle it. It finishes 2-1.

The sun sets on a great day of groundhopping. My weekend ends there for reasons which are best described in football terms as similar to David Unsworth's failed Villa move and a parsimonious approach to hotels that Mike Ashley would approve of. I only see four of the six games; nonetheless, it's a great weekend full of moments that make watching football in non-league worthwhile. From eating the lamb wrap huddled under a tin shed at Punjab, to an early morning festival feel at Staplehurst, via a competitive game in leafy Bearsted, culminating in a fiercely contested match in the setting sun at Larkfield. There were moments of skill with well-taken goals, aggression on the pitch and friendliness off it.

It was a packed itinerary, fitting in running, cycling and football. I'm tired, but elated, glad to have got along to this event, which really made something of games that wouldn't have otherwise interested me. It's great to see events like this bolster the crowds at non-league, as it doesn't take that many people to create a sense of vibrancy. I was disappointed at missing Sunday's matches and exploring new grounds at Rusthall and Tunbridge Wells, so make a note to look into future Groundhop UK events. Watching random games seemed worthwhile again.

Ground 75

Lower Road, Hullbridge Sports

BEFORE MY next match, I play for my works five-a-side team a couple of times. Unfortunately we're not using part of a 3G pitch a senior club play on, so I can't make a spurious claim for that to be ground number 75. It prompts me to think whether I played on any senior pitches over the years and I recall a couple, albeit ones I've watched games at as well. I also remember the first game I ever watched was between Calverley Cut and a Leeds United XI. It was sometime in the 1980s at the village's Victoria Park, which isn't a senior ground, so I can perhaps bump up my total number of games, if not grounds. The village team were named after the local hairdresser's and were snipped apart 7-0 by several members of the famous Leeds side from the 1970s, with Peter Lorimer quite possibly bagging a few of them.

There is something about the sport that makes you want to go back for more. It may have been seven years or so since my last foray into five-a-side, but when an email came round trying to get a team together to face another department, something stirred inside me. Perhaps it was the amount of step six football I've watched that made me think I could still do a job in goal. Luckily, my work appraisal didn't depend on the job I did in my second outing when I let in a couple of howlers. I had fun, though, being immersed in a game again, willing a team-mate to score, and having the familiar sensation of flinging myself towards a ball and turning it around the post, which made the carpet burns and aching joints worth it. It wouldn't have been much fun for even the hardiest of hopper to watch. There wasn't a programme or a tea bar after all.

Three days after that match and the aches and pains are only just subsiding as I make my way to Lower Road for Hullbridge Sports v Hashtag United. The ground is nearby and gives me the perennial dilemma as to whether I leave it until the last minute to head there or go ridiculously early and bag a car parking space. I arrive at 7.08pm for a 7.45pm kick-off and hear a steward say, 'No more in after this one,' which delights me far more than it ought to.

I pay £10 entry, plus another £1 for a programme and enter the ground. Lower Road started out as a grassroots facility and is surrounded by other pitches. Hullbridge are celebrating their 75th anniversary and wearing a special kit to commemorate the occasion. I pass a strip-lit main stand and its smaller, darker 100-seater sibling, both using the familiar modern prefab construction I'd seen a lot of on the groundhop weekend. I aim to do a lap of the ground, but am thwarted by the far touchline being fenced off where the concrete path runs out. I take some photos of the corner flag and pretended that's what I meant to do all along. I return and take a seat in the small stand in front of where the visitors are warming up.

The teams are soon out. The hosts in their special green-and-yellow-quartered shirts and Hashtag in their change strip of pink. They look like the traditional colours of two grand old Victorian teams rather than the oldest team being one set up just after the war. I wasn't in the mood for conflict myself and rather than ask a couple of dozen people to move, so I could see from the stand, I move to the covered terrace end Hashtag will be attacking. The clubhouse is doing a brisk trade and I get a look at the team sheet before I find a spot near the corner flag.

The Hashtag fans set up their flags and drum and create a bit of atmosphere with 'Is this a library?' Answer – no, they're much warmer. And 'Is this the Emirates?' Answer – behave yourselves. No reply comes from the Hullbridge fans, whose average age suggests their voices aren't deep enough to carry from the other end. Hashtag soon have the play down this end, as Pedro Carvalho uses his pace to try to get in round the back. He's thwarted by a defender sliding in to cut out the cross. Had he been on our five-a-side court, the lack of space between fence and out-of-bounds penalty area would stop him instead.

Hullbridge keeper Lewis Greene cuts out several through balls, sweeping up outside of his area. This was an option denied to me and I'd like to think is the main difference between scorelines in our respective games. I start to worry it might be 0-0 here or, worse, see Hullbridge nick a goal. Their hopeful attempt is well wide of James Philp's goal, though. The home support scream like they're at a fireworks display as he takes the goal kick. In a way, we are at a display, with fireworks going off every so often in the distance just ahead of Bonfire Night. A Hullbridge defender tumbles over like a Catherine wheel at the slightest brush from Hashtag's PK Humble, as he tries to burst through.

No shots could be described as rockets and I hope the game will spark into life when Hashtag win a corner. Carvalho's kick is met by the head of Greg Halford. It's blocked, but new signing Olly Miles turns in the rebound to make it 1-0 not long before the interval. Hashtag break forward soon after the restart. Toby Aromolaran cuts it back to Miles, who is denied by Greene. The Tags keep the ball alive and a PK Humble shot is deflected into the path of Aromolaran on the stretch, but he can't connect.

There's another Greene-Miles reprieve, when the Tags forward is played in one on one, but blasts it straight at the keeper. Miles is denied again by what the bloke next to me describes as a 'good save'. After hearing this shouted as if by reflex whenever I got in the way of a shot, I'd have to say it would have been harder not to save it, but Greene's positioning made it possible. He's kept his side in it, as the half draws to a close after a late flurry of activity.

The tea bar is another hive of activity. I decide to queue up for something to warm me up. There's plenty on offer judging by the array of fluorescent handwritten cards pinned up behind the counter. I spot one for Bovril and decide that it's finally time to sample this traditional football staple.

I make my way to the end Hashtag will be attacking and find a bit of fencing that most resembles a cup holder. The temperature is noticeably colder without the cover of a corrugated iron roof. Younger Hullbridge fans don't seem to notice as they are running around fuelled by sugary drinks. It's all innocent fun until one of them calls another Jimmy Savile for being a bit too hands-on. They can be no more than nine years old. And now old man Coughlan is about to have a sip of his Bovril. Salty gravy is my verdict.

It's not terrible, but I could do with some chips to pour it over. In the end I pour it over the churned-up grass next to the perimeter path.

Hashtag continue where they left off. A deep cross from Miles (the player, not distance from goal) travels over Greene, who isn't impeded by netting over the pitch like I was. It finds Aromolaran, who heads, or more accurately shoulders, it into the net to double the Tags' lead. They look to further extend their advantage. A shot fizzes wide after good link-up play, the ball bouncing back off the fence. Greene doesn't have to worry about this going back into play like I did, but he is becoming just as busy. Aromolaran cuts inside and forces a diving save from Greene, who doesn't have the luxury of having the penalty area to himself to gather it, and his defence smuggle it away under pressure.

The Hashtag fans are in good spirits and start singing the jingle bells song, which is earlier than the supermarkets have Christmas goods in. I'm not joining in the singing anyway. The FA deemed this weekend one for silent support, with clapping only. Clearly, shouting, 'Nice one, well played' is a gateway to 'Fucking hell, ref, are you fucking blind? That was our throw-in you ...' This appeared to be the sort of nonsense to make me question the FA's priorities until I realised it's an initiative for junior games.

A ball over the top to Hashtag sub Kojo Apenteng is then slipped into the path of PK Humble. He has players lining up at the back post, but blasts it straight at Greene. It's the sort of greed you might find in a junior game. Next time in the box, PK squares it to Aromolaran. As I'm turning to move towards the exit, he turns his defender and goes down. I'm most of the way towards the exit by the time the referee points to the spot. I'm passed by dozens of kids supporting Hullbridge running the other way to put off the penalty taker. They don't make it in time. It's unlikely they would have fazed Halford. He sends Greene the wrong way to make it 3-0. With that, the full-time whistle blows.

A crowd of 457 disperse into the night. For most, it wasn't the anniversary celebration they had hoped for, but for me, it was a pleasing result and great to see so many turn out on a Friday night. Some clubs find a niche midweek slot due to a combination of pitch-sharing and avoiding clashes with bigger rivals and it would be good if more sides could do so, not least as the groundhopper will always be on the lookout for unusually timed games to watch.

Ground 76
Terence McMillan Stadium, Athletic Newham

THE ODDLY timed winter World Cup has started in Qatar, but rather than watch Belgium v Canada on TV, I decide to see some live non-league action at the Terry Mac after work. This ground is widely derided as one of the worst in the Essex Senior League, with both Athletic Newham and Clapton tenants. Complaints mainly focus on the lack of facilities and poor standard of the playing surface. The latter has been recently addressed, but just like Qatar, there is no beer available to purchase. At least it wasn't built at the cost of the lives of thousands of migrant workers.

I may have low expectations of the ground, but I'm expecting a decent game. Saffron Walden's matches this season have been high-scoring and both sides are towards the top of the table. Walden lost their long-serving manager, Jason Maher, to Coggeshall Town only a few weeks ago and were in danger of losing their way after last season's promotion push fell at the final hurdle.

This ground is a hurdle I need to overcome to complete my side quest of visiting all the stadiums in the Essex Senior League. Being a fan-owner of Clapton Community, I don't want to put any money into the coffers of the other tenants at this ground, Clapton FC, so a Newham game suits me. That said, they don't seem all that keen to take anyone's money. There's no sign advertising the game on the main road. It's only because I know a match is on that I find my way through the sports-centre complex and head towards the floodlights. A bloke loitering by the gate, a small wooden shed, appears to wonder why I'm there, giving me a quizzical look. 'One adult. To see the football,' I ask, feeling thrown by having to offer a justification. 'Seven pounds,' he responds, confirming he is actually manning the turnstile. I pay and ask if there's a programme. 'No, I will put it online later,' he offers vaguely.

There's a more welcoming feeling emanating from the portacabin clubhouse as I see two supporters emerge with cups of tea. This catering offer is beyond what I had been led to believe was available. I overhear the supporters lauding the setup at Enfield Town, where they too have a running track, but have added stands behind the goal for more atmosphere. Here, there is just a single stand, with three rows of seats, tacked on to the side of a sports hall. There's no access to the rest of the ground so I look for a seat on halfway. I pass a booth for an announcer and hope there will be someone to read out the teams, as there's no sign of a team sheet. I find a seat in the back row, barely much higher than ground level, and look for team news online and find nothing.

Walden are warming up in front of me, with passing drills made harder by a bobbly, but no longer lethal, surface, as the giant cracks have been filled. This is my first time seeing the Bloods in a while, and I usually try to visit their Catons Lane ground a couple of times a season. It's my favourite ground in the division and perhaps the county. It has the charm of the cow shed-style main stand and sloping pitch, but a gradual upgrade of facilities keeps catering for fans' needs. Here a Walden official climbs the perimeter fence to hand over the subs boards, on actual boards rather than an electronic one.

A Newham official approaches a group sat near me, who appear to be part of the club, and there's a conversation about them needing to sign in for safety reasons. It sounds spurious, as a headcount of the entire crowd wouldn't take long. There's more precision on the pitch as Newham practise set pieces with attack versus defence, while Walden just rehearse hoofing it in the channels. The teams leave the pitch and I have to admit the ground isn't as bad as it's often made out to be. It's even better for some Walden fans. One boasts that he and his wife got in for a fiver each. Another says he paid a nice round figure, zero. The bloke on the gate had wandered off, and they noted it was a similar story last season. I glean some team news from them as well, which is just as well, since there is no announcement.

The teams return from their shipping container changing rooms which, if they are good enough building material for the 974 stadium in Qatar, are fine at this level. They spare the teams from having to share with those using the badminton courts. Walden are in their change strip of blue and white stripes, giving the game a feel of a Covid-era Sheffield derby. The Walden supporters next to me, including family members, cheer on their team and wonder why their change strip didn't include any large shorts for forward Stan Leech, who appears to be wearing hotpants.

We kick off and Walden look to get the ball forward early. I recognise a few players, including right-back Deon, who I recall playing for another team, possibly Ilford. In a slow opening quarter of an hour, I eventually find him on a photo of an Ilford team sheet on my phone. He's Deon Lewis-Kirwan and I'm equal parts pleased and alarmed that I'm developing this sort of knowledge. I question my knowledge of the Newham team, as goalkeeper Wilkinson Boateng impressed last time I saw him, but this time he unconvincingly pats a Walden cross out for a corner. It's drilled in and Palvy Manduaklia flashes a header wide. It takes a while to retrieve the ball from the running track and I hope the recent FIFA edict to add on more stoppage time isn't in force here, otherwise I might be here all night.

Boateng scuffs a goal kick. Leech pressures the defender and wins a throw high up the field. Lewis-Kirwan is able to throw long, but it comes to nothing. It's good to know Walden have replaced long-throw specialist Gavin Cockman, who moved to early pacesetters Enfield along with striker Solomon Ofori. There's no one to convert and Newham clear. The ball finds its way to Anderson Baro on Newham's right and his pace causes the Walden left-back problems. 'Go on, Monkey' comes a shout. This could be misinterpreted, but it's aimed at Walden's Louie Monk, who recovers. I work this out once the Walden contingent agree among themselves to post the team on social media, but only after one of them offers a rave review of the Turkish restaurant near the entrance to the car park.

The description of succulent lamb is more appetising than the football on display. Lewis-Kirwan almost serves up an inadvertent goal. He crosses around the outside of his marker and it loops all the way round to the far corner and Boateng does well to tip it over. We are left waiting for our starters here and one critic complains, 'This is not football.' Newham have a shot blocked.

Boateng clears long to the right. It bounces through to Richard Kone. He crosses low for Joel Appiah to sweep home first time. A single cheer comes from the stand. The lack of enthusiasm perhaps explains the lack of yellow cross-hatch markings in front of the seated area, which Walden officials complain about, assuming it was a requirement. They discuss whether the fence should be filled in as well, before remembering they ought to add the score to their social media feeds.

Then comes the main flashpoint of the half. Leech goes for a loose ball in midfield. His foot is raised. He's late. There's the sound of studs on shin pad. Newham's Abdul Shobowale goes down, clutching his leg. Team-mates pile in. The Walden fans think it's another instance of play-acting. The referee brandishes a red card to a shocked Leech. The bloke next to me asks for my verdict, as I'm clearly neutral. 'Definite red,' I say with the conviction of Roy Keane doing punditry and perhaps the same scowl, which I may still have following my walk to the ground through a less salubrious part of town. There was no malice from Leech, but it was late and over the top. Leech trudges off. Shobowale is helped off, unable to continue. A Walden club official openly discusses how they will mark down the match official on their report. Others want the cameraman to show the video to the ref, by way of makeshift VAR. Not long after Leech and Shobowale leave the pitch, so does everyone else as it's soon half-time.

I go to check out the tea bar, which is the clubhouse for the East End Runners athletics club. The only items on the menu are tea, coffee, hot chocolate and Penguin bars. I order a hot chocolate and scan the noticeboards for a team sheet, but there's nothing relating to football. One hopper asks a Walden official to AirDrop their team sheet, which I've tracked down online. No sign of Newham's, though, until I find it on the league's Twitter feed. I have an easier time finding out Belgium are leading Canada and could even watch it on my phone if I wanted to use up all my data allowance.

Walden make no allowances for being a man down and start the second half brightly, before Newham find their feet and look to create chances. Daniel Izekor threatens to get in round the back. He cuts it back, but the ball is well behind the forward. 'Oh, my days!' comes a cry from the pitch. 'Fucking hell, how much space!' is the response from a Walden fan. One reason for that extra space joins us in the stand. Leech has changed, he's out of his short shorts and still can't believe his luck. He's commiserated by family and friends. One jokes, 'You couldn't have got him with a high boot, those shorts were too tight.' On the field, the referee dishes out another card, which is yellow and a £12 fine for the recipient. There are complaints when Boateng goes down under a challenge looking for a foul that wasn't there. 'You don't get that in women's football,' the bloke next to me opines. It's an opinion I wasn't expecting.

Walden have a spell of pressure before Craig Carver is brought down on the edge of the box. He expects a card to be forthcoming. 'It's him again!' he claims, but there's no card and nothing from the set piece. Newham threaten on the break and soon find themselves with a four on two. Kone goes it alone and curls home from the edge of the box for 2-0. It's game over and I long for the sort of contest I saw at the Emirates in the Rugby League World Cup semi-final between England and Samoa a few days beforehand and I do question why I'm watching a poor game in a near-empty stadium.

The game peters out. Even the patients watching from the lit-up windows of the adjacent hospital have long since given up on it. The ground wasn't actually as bad as I had expected, and the club couldn't be blamed for their rented facilities. They were a new team trying to grow and were OK on the pitch, but the experience left me feeling cold both emotionally and meteorologically. I couldn't even sit through the highlights video afterwards, which proved Leech's tackle was a definite red.

I take an equally red bus back to Stratford station through the endless sprawl of east London. I find out the official attendance was just 32 but, unlike Qatar where reported attendance figures exceeded stadium capacity, this was surely an underestimate with the amount of people allowed to wander in unaccounted for. Yet somehow in the world of groundhopping I've done something far more significant than watching a Rugby League World Cup semi-final.

Ground 77

King George's Fields, Corinthian-Casuals

THE FIFA World Cup has reached its round of 16 stage and Portugal v Switzerland clashes with my next game. It's no contest who I'm going to see, as I'm off to that most Brazilian of non-league sides, Corinthian-Casuals. I expect a carnival atmosphere, street food and football that might be more Roque Júnior than Rivellino. Formed via a merger in 1939, the Corinthian side popularised the sport abroad, inspiring the Brazilian club of the same name, among others. Their sense of sportsmanship and fair play was well renowned, epitomised by their refusal to score any penalty they were awarded or, defend any they conceded.

Corinthian were a fine team, who supplied many full England internationals and gave the top sides of the day a run for their money in prestigious friendlies, inflicting Manchester United's record defeat of 11-3 on them. Public school old boys started the Casuals, and they were former FA Amateur Cup winners. The merged team retains Casuals' distinctive chocolate and pink colours. They also retain a following among Corinthian fans in Brazil, playing a friendly against their illustrious Brazilian namesake in 1988, with Sócrates featuring for both teams.

Tonight's visitors, Bishop's Stortford, appear far less exotic at first glance, but boast an FA Amateur Cup and FA Trophy themselves. The Hertfordshire side lost in the Isthmian Premier play-offs last season having finished second. They are in the play-off mix again this season, albeit with a mixed away record. Casuals' position is more precarious. A come-from-behind win at the weekend helped them move off the bottom, but there was still much to do. They hadn't been helped by a long sequence of games away from King George's Fields after a tree fell through the clubhouse roof. The ground itself isn't as storied as the club, with the side moving to the site in 1988, after an itinerant history, taking in the Oval, Dulwich and various other London grounds.

I had a fair bit of London to cover myself to get from my office to the game. I let several packed tube trains pass before eventually squeezing on one to Waterloo and just about making the train to Tolworth, which is an infrequent service on the Chessington branch. From there it was a walk along the A3, which makes the walk from Seven Sisters to White Hart Lane seem delightful in comparison. I wonder whether I should include the Oval in my total, based on all the cricket I've watched there, using the exception I created for Spurs' new ground. Somehow that feels wrong, given how long ago football was played there and the exception was very much created to avoid having to watch a team I dislike. Before I can reconsider, I turn down a dimly lit lane and reach the entrance. I pay the £12 entry and another £2.50 for a programme and pass through a turnstile that's much older than the ground itself and must have been taken from somewhere else.

The clubhouse is covered in scaffolding. Part of that is a temporary-looking cover, part results from the tree that fell on it from the adjacent railway embankment. I ask the chap running the souvenir hut if there's somewhere selling food. He explains that an accident on the A3 has delayed the burger van and it's running late. He's apologetic and suggests there might be some extra food put on as they do the players' meals or the chairman will order in pizza. 'It's so non-league,' he laments. Not holding out much hope for a club chairman to shell out on something, I read the information boards about the club's history to distract myself.

I take a seat in the main stand, where there are several pink and brown banners adorning the back wall. The covered terrace behind the goal has a large 'Brothers in Football' banner and a smaller one with the Sócrates quote, 'Beauty comes first, victory is secondary. What matters is joy.' I'm not holding out hopes for any of these things in a mismatched Isthmian League game on a freezing-cold December night. The locals have stayed away as well. It's a sparse crowd gathered moments before kick-off.

A bloke behind notes that it's not just the World Cup, but there's a charity quiz at the Swan that's likely to have had an effect on numbers. It turns out he is part of the club's media team and he's joined by a couple of other volunteers and a man with a distinctively Brazilian accent. There's interest in the club even if the crowd doesn't reflect that. The media man is quietly pleased that his match report will at least get more hits than usual, although he's disappointed the usual cameramen are sitting with him and not braving the elements pitchside.

Another volunteer reads out the team sheets from a nearby booth. She has the smoothest voice of any stadium announcer I've ever heard. Admittedly, the competition is generally rather poor, with most announcers sounding like they're reading from a list written in hieroglyphics, with a mouth full of cereal, while being millimetres away from the mic. Her soothing, well-spoken tones reveal the names of 22 players I've never heard of before, and one Bishop's Stortford sub who may have played for Chelmsford City.

The first entry into the match report is when Stortford's right-winger cuts inside and sends a left-footed cross into the box. It's met by Donnell Thomas. He crashes a header on to the crossbar. There's a buzz around the ground, although that's only because the announcer's microphone has been left switched on and is giving feedback. Someone asks the media man to tell Lisa to turn it off. Another home fan implores Casuals to switch on. They tentatively pass the ball around. It's not like watching Brazil. The closest to samba football is alliterative, when a defender called Simba gets involved. He wins a slide tackle and slams the ball into the hoarding in front of me, which may not be Sócrates's idea of beautiful, but always brings me some joy.

The media man is glad it's not a night he's brought someone along for the first time, as the game is slow to get going. One debutant, likely to be glad of the quiet start, is 16-year-old Casuals keeper Benas Libikas. The media team debate whether he's their fifth or sixth goalkeeper this season. Their regular number one or, more accurately, goalkeeper number four or five, was recalled by Eastbourne earlier this afternoon, thrusting Libikas into the side.

Visiting Stortford fans have yet to find cause to goad the young stopper and start a chant of 'Where's your burger van?' The media team lament the fact the club will probably be fined for not having catering. It's out of their control but also something they ought to have a contingency for. A burger van would have seen more action than either goalmouth, as Casuals only manage a single shot deflected wide and Stortford only have one further attempt that's fired over the bar before half-time.

After being turned off, the tannoy won't turn back on again and, when it does, I wish it hadn't as the Proclaimers come on. I walk far less than 500 miles to the clubhouse. Portugal are 5-1 up on the big screen and I join the queue for the bar. I admire various pieces of Casuals memorabilia, including from their 1956 FA Amateur Cup Final defeat to Bishop Auckland. I order a pint of a pale ale that appears to have been brewed for the club, and the most substantial and nutritious meal I can, some salted peanuts. I hoover up the peanuts and drink the unsubstantial pint before the second half gets under way.

Lisa announces the attendance of 112. She could announce that there are no more trains back to Waterloo and I'd be fine with that. Things are less calm and soothing for the Casuals defence when pinball ensues in their box. 'How did that stay out?' asks the media man. 'No idea,' someone replies. My hurried notes can only reveal the ball looped over someone, Libikas flapped (harsh on the lad, but it's an easy word to scribble down). A defender went down and the ball looked to go over the line. I can't rely on the official match report to elaborate on that and there are no cameramen for me to study the footage from. The upshot is that the game remains 0-0.

I'm starting to think it might stay that way and need a revisit. Under my own rules, I don't deem that necessary, but I don't feel I have caught Casuals at their best. A few blokes try to create a bit of atmosphere, but it's more banging on the walls to keep warm than carnival rhythms. The Stortford fans aim a few jeers at Libikas on the odd occasion he's put under pressure, with his defence protecting him well. It's last-ditch stuff and the media team are impressed by their resolve. They note how many of the players have come to Casuals following serious injuries and have taken a chance on them, comparing them to the children's TV programme *The Raggy Dolls*. Some imperfect goalkeeping is nearly punished when a cross is knocked out of Libikas's hands. No free kick is given and the ball rolls across the goal. Stortford shoot, but Casuals block.

The media man highlights a lack of physical confidence in the young keeper, which is better goalkeeping punditry than I imagine is on the televised game, with the standard 'he should've done better there' (when clearly unsighted and it's only the slo-mo that makes it look like the keeper had ages to take several steps and leap across goal) or 'great save' (when it would be harder not to save it). He's talking to the dad of another youth keeper in the club, who is surprised at how close his son must be to a first-team call-up. I realise how much worse I would do at that age, given I couldn't cope with the physical threat of players who hadn't all gone through puberty, let alone the grizzled veterans at step three.

Casuals clear the stuff of my teenage nightmares, an innocuous free kick sent hopefully into the box. There's pushing and shoving over by the far touchline but play continues and Stortford send in another cross. Libikas doesn't come. This time, his defence can't clear. Stortford's captain Ryan Henshaw backpedals towards goal and flicks a header over the stranded Libikas to give the visitors the lead. 'One-nil to the blue Brazil' sing the handful of away fans. As a comparison with Cowdenbeath, it might stand up.

Lisa announces a 'goal in the 73rd minute for Bishop's Stortford, and I'll let you know the scorer as soon as I find out'. The media team can't tell whether it was number six, number eight or number 18. There's almost a second goal to worry about. Libikas passes to his full-back, who is in space, but takes a poor touch and his back pass presents Stortford with a chance. Libikas does well to smother and keep Casuals in the game. Despite being camped in their own half the media team hope that one potshot could go out for a corner and give them a late chance.

Into stoppage time, a potshot is deflected out for a Casuals corner. A few fans call for Libikas to go forward. He doesn't. There's another melee, shots are blocked. Casuals recycle the ball and put a couple of neat passes together. They can't work a clear opening and eventually a shot is blazed over. I can't be certain it happened in that order, but at least the club's match report won't contradict me as the media team turn back into fans. It's a frantic end, but Casuals can't snatch the point their spirited performance deserves.

I'd grown to like Casuals. There wasn't a carnival atmosphere, street food or samba football. There was very little atmosphere, no food and it was one of the poorer games I had seen in a nondescript ground. The club had something special about it that made me glad I had made the journey. It may have been the friendliness of the volunteers, or something about discovering for myself another one of those marvellous stories in the sport's history. It was impressive that the club remained amateur, and are the highest-ranked amateur team in the English pyramid, albeit with a fair few players on loan from other clubs. I was pleased to contribute in a small way to keeping that going.

Ground 78
Hartsdown Park, Margate

I DIDN'T keep my run of games going into the festive period as the weather hit several potential fixtures. Although it's not entirely clear if I would have been excused from Christmas shopping to go anyway, I could at least look forward to a rearranged game at some point. The next match I went to was with my dad on Boxing Day. I nearly took him to Bishop's Stortford as the nearest ground not yet visited with a game on. Instead, I opted for a revisit to Hashtag United, which bumped his new ground total up, if not mine.

I fail to bump up my total on a visit to the in-laws in Yorkshire. It took us longer than a Stoke City clearance to get everyone packed and into the car, so I didn't so much as miss kick-off as still be 150 miles away in a windswept service station when Emley came from 4-0 down to draw 4-4 in front of a bumper crowd. These sorts of games make you realise anything is possible and prompt you to go more.

Mrs C suggested I could go to watch Huddersfield while we were up there, but the sight of the John Smith's Stadium in the middle of a trading estate didn't fill me with excitement. The old stand at Barnsley nearly tempted me on the same night, but paying £30 for League One football soon put me off. I am not inclined to complete the '92' league grounds, given how soulless and pricey many had become, which is why come the end of the year I had only been to 25 games while serious hoppers were posting annual stats boasting of 150-plus games. I didn't want to rack up numbers with trips to identikit concrete bowls or 3G cages, even if I miss the odd high-scoring thriller as a result. Would my fussiness somehow mean I didn't reach 100 grounds before I was due to submit this to the publishers? For now, I wanted to keep things special and exciting, which is why my next stop was Margate in the Isthmian Premier.

I love an out-of-season seaside resort, devoid of day-tripping hordes and full of evocative seascapes. When I suggested a few games I could see close to my birthday, my mates Phil (15 to 30 grounds visited) and Mark (about 20) leapt on the suggestion of Margate. Phil was taken by them being sponsored by one of his favourite bands, the Libertines. And Mark is always keen to recreate the Jolly Boys' Outing from *Only Fools and Horses*.

A train strike nearly scuppers our plans until Mark suggests to his wife Katie that they have a romantic weekend away. Only when she goes to book the hotel does he ask her to add a second room for me and Phil, and that we would need a lift. The door-to-door service was far better than a train, but if I'm nitpicking, some homemade pastries could have been provided, like the box Katie made for us to take to a morning's play at the cricket.

We hit the micropubs of Margate straight off the bat. I open with a pint of something with a name like Twatwaffle. A fruity pale ale that would be the best pint of the day, either because of the taste or being the only one

I could distinctly recall. We run a quick single to the Two Halves, since the name suits the occasion. A few home fans thought the same and they lament their team's chances while we all stare out at a sullen sea.

We wash up in Fez, where various fairground items, old signs, trumpets and a hair salon hairdryer have made their home among the eclectic decor. We leave Katie (zero grounds visited and not keen on changing that) in the capable hands of Phil the owner. He will keep her supplied with pink Manhattans while we head off to the football. Mark insists on a detour to check in to the hotel, despite a queue of people needing every aspect of staying in a hotel explaining to them in great detail. Google Maps helps us find a shortcut to the ground, but the alleyway is blocked.

A dash across Hartsdown Park, within which the ground sits, means we at least have a view through the fence as the players hold a minute's silence for Pelé. Our only philosophical reflection is whether it's worse to attend a 0-0, or a 1-0 and not see the goal. A payment of £12 at the turnstiles gets us in by the corner flag, or slightly beneath it, as the terrace behind the goal is on a slope, while the 3G pitch is level. We haven't missed a goal.

We check out the outside bar next to the far stand, a basic modern affair, but the bar has only a basic offering of cider or cooking lager. We return via the hotchpotch terracing to the clubhouse behind the goal, to see if there's any ale on in there. There is, but it's very nondescript. The ground rises above that, despite the main stand having been knocked down and yet to be replaced. It's got that mix and match feel I like.

We are still faffing about getting drinks when Matty MacArthur opens the scoring for Margate. Visitors

Brightlingsea Regent struggle to kick into the wind. One clearance is sent near a hovering seagull. 'Go on, take out that fucking gull' is an outburst I surprise myself with, clearly still traumatised by previous chip thefts. My eyes alight on the sign telling me to mind my language, it's a family club. The nearby families are too busy singing 'C'mon the Gate' to notice the wild-haired man swearing at seagulls, which might not be uncommon in these parts. Goals direct from a corner are pretty rare, so when former Inter Milan player Ben Greenhalgh whips in a corner kick and the wind helps it find the top corner, we are taken aback; 2-0 to Margate. Phil insists he scored these all the time.

Brightlingsea eventually make it down our end, so Mark, who is partially sighted, gets to see something rather than just listen to me and Phil debating the effect of the conditions. Our audio description is somewhat lacking, though. 'Erm, there's been a cross. Someone's got a shot in. Corner.' The next thing he knows, there's a small cheer from the visiting fans. The corner has been stabbed in from close range by Littlejohn. You couldn't make it up! At least I can inform Mark there are three fans celebrating.

Our commentary goes back to the wind. Phil is of the traditional view that it's a distinct advantage being at your back. Margate look to prove him right with a series of potshots from distance. While I concede I wouldn't want to be facing them, it appears to restrict their play and, when kicking the other way, a through ball can hold up nicely. Regent fail to prove my theory when a free kick, taken as the ball was still rolling backwards, somehow ends up being over-hit.

Regent battle upfield and once again I'll leave my audio description to evoke the scene. 'Oh, someone's jinking into the box. Tackle. Still going. Erm. Oh. Chance. [Long pause while the three fans celebrate.] Yeah, he's swept that in left-footed. Two-two Jeff.' Suleyman Zuhdu the scorer.

As Margate are left stunned, it seems like an appropriate time to show Mark the way to the portacabin toilets. I pause as Greenhalgh lines up a free kick on the edge of the centre circle. This shouldn't be worth a second glance, but in these conditions it's a chance to restore the Gate's lead. He drills the ball, and it flies towards Charlie Turner in the Regent goal like a carrier bag in a force ten. It is straight at him and he saves at the second attempt.

That's the last meaningful chance Margate have to take advantage of the wind. We retire to the bar at half-time. I make a particularly bad attempt to explain that while I don't think Pelé is overrated, we can't fully appreciate him from the available footage. Grainy black-and-white clips don't do his early career justice and a highlights reel from the 1970 World Cup bears a little more scrutiny. He's clearly good in the air, but so is Peter Crouch. There's skill, but one dummy ends with him missing an open goal, and an attempt from halfway goes wide. Mark's conclusion is that I'm saying 'Pelé is shite, he's worse than Jason Lee', as the *Fantasy Football* ditty went.

Mark and Phil linger in the bar as the second half begins, presumably as much to disassociate themselves with my inebriated ramblings as to stay warm. I'm keen to see whether Regent have any imaginative use of their newfound blustery advantage. They too opt for potshots and the first one is bound for the sky. A Turner sky. With Mark and Phil still absent, it's perhaps inevitable they miss a key moment. Regent's Dominic Locke curls one into the top corner to make it 3-2. Of more interest to them would have been Turner, the goalkeeper, gesticulating to the crowd after they had given him some stick about his weight.

A fan nearby is imploring the Gate to 'hold it' every time they make it up our end. Now Phil is with me, he joins in and shouts this advice as well, before asking who are we supporting. I feel I should be loyal to the team from Essex, while the two actual Essex boys decide to back our hosts. The nerves over Regent hanging on, or several pints, get the better of me and I go to make use of the facilities. I'm sure I see the referee wave play on for an advantage in the penalty area. I think that can't be right as there's no possible advantage. Regent manager Brett Munyard will say as much post-match.

A more sensible decision is me remembering to eat some food while out drinking. I get a burger and chips from the catering van. It's a six-minute wait on the burger, so I enjoy a decent portion of chips and continue to watch the game. I expect to see a Margate player requisition the van's sink as they're pretty much throwing everything else at Regent. The linesman flags for another free kick taken with a moving ball, which the referee ignores as there's no way it's going to remain stationary.

When I return to our spot behind the goal, Phil has very much become a Margate supporter. He's vehemently demanding they 'hold it', throwing barbs at Turner and appealing for a penalty. We enter stoppage time and the Gate win a corner. It goes to the far post. Emmanuel Oke plants a downward header on target. Turner comes across and it squeezes between him and the post to equalise, with the keeper clattering the goal frame out of position.

The pleasing nature of a 3-3 scoreline and crowd of 333 is nearly upended when Regent have a chance at the death. Gate breathe a sigh of relief, especially the old boy next to Phil, who he asks what he thinks of the result. 'Could've been worse' is the resigned response to a draw that should've been a win, but could've been a defeat.

We're feeling triumphant as we embark on a journey round several micropubs. We visit Ales of the Unexpected, where the most unexpected ale is brewed down the road from us, and there are several dogs to continue the non-league feel. From there we venture on to the harbour wall for the Harbour Arms, which is a cosy port in what us landlubbers might consider a storm. A fair bit of water is getting in through the roof as we get through a fair bit of liquid ourselves, encouraging Mark to head clear the plastic football in the fishing nets strung across the roof. Reunited with Katie and her friends, we finish off in Fez. Whatever I may have learned from owner Phil about the micropub and local brewing scene is lost in a haze of pink cider and northern soul.

It's been a great day out, with the football adding to a sense that we did somehow accomplish something. Unlike the Jolly Boys' Outing, we aren't booked into a horrific B&B, although Mark does leave his room with regurgitated pea fritter all over the bathroom floor for Katie to walk in the next morning. Watching football at Margate may not be the most obvious attraction, set back from the seafront, but it beats slowly losing all your twopence pieces on the arcades.

Ground 79

Rookery Hill, East Thurrock United

IT'S ANOTHER birthday celebration that prompts my next choice of game. I need to ferry my kids to several birthday parties taking place over the weekend, so I'm pleased to see East Thurrock United v Hashtag United moved to the Friday night. I'm at a ground that is due to turn 40 next year, but may not see much football beyond that. East Thurrock owner Alfie Best has plans to build a new ground in the next year or so. It may become another lost ground. Rookery Hill may not share some of the history or architectural delights of others, but it will be a shame, nonetheless. It's reason enough to make the trip to Corringham, if views over the London Gateway Port aren't enough for you. I park on an unlit lane overlooking the port and follow a couple of other blokes to the ground. It's not entirely clear where the turnstiles are in among the huts and I follow them into the clubhouse, comfortable in sticking to the 'tops on' rule, on a chilly night. I realise there isn't an entrance from the clubhouse into the ground and am forced into asking directions.

I find the turnstiles next to St Mary the Virgin Church. There's a tantalising glimpse of the pitch, lit by floodlight. I pay £10 entry and another £2 for a programme before embarking on a lap of the ground. I pass the two covered terraces split apart either side of the goal, which is filling up with pre-teens wearing bumblebee-coloured scarves. There's seating on the far touchline, in line with the penalty box, then the dugouts before I reach the Tyler Security Stand. In what is possibly a great advert for their services, they have kept everyone out as it's fenced off. Unable to complete my lap, I return past the turnstiles and a busy kiosk to find a seat in the main stand.

There's a certain amount of character to the ground, with various improvements as the Rocks made it as far as step two. They were relegated from step three last season and find themselves mid-table in the Isthmian North, with visitors Hashtag on a nine-game winning streak. Both teams are warming up, with a youth team also getting to train on the pitch under the lights as a large crowd gathers. The young Rocks fans are warming up their voices, and next to me a couple of old committee members are forced to ask people to vacate the seats allocated for home officials. They can't believe people didn't read the signs. I'm surprised to see officials using their allocated seats for once.

The hosts get off to a solid start, but an appeal for a penalty is waved away early on. Both sides hurl the ball forward early. Hashtag find Pedro Carvalho, who brings it under control, but is undermined by the surface and scuffs it wide. The Tags' Max Cornhill is composed in the middle of the park. He gets hold of the ball in a melee and plays it wide to Toby Aromolaran. His pass to Matt Wooldridge is under-hit, but the full-back gets a toe on it and finds an opening before dragging his shot wide. The match has started with the same staccato rhythm as a drummer behind the goal, who sounds like he is trying to replicate machine-gun fire rather than any recognisable tune.

The Rocks look to bombard Hashtag's penalty area. A long free kick breaks to someone in a yellow shirt but his shot flashes wide. Soon after, a yellow-shirted forearm connects with Hashtag's Jermaine Francis's face as he latches on to another direct through ball. Nothing given.

A free kick to Hashtag deep in their own half gives goalkeeper James Philp the chance to send one long. He finds the head of Greg Halford, who flicks it into the box. The ball bounces once and Aromolaran latches on to it and hits a Van Persie-like half-volley into the far corner from an acute angle. A section of supporters behind the goal are evidently cheering on the visitors as they celebrate Hashtag taking the lead. A corner soon after gives the Tags a chance to double their advantage. They swing the ball into the near post, and defender Tom Anderson connects to make it 2-0.

The hosts look to fight back, but can't find a clear-cut opportunity. A ball breaks for 6ft 7in striker Brian Moses, who manages to send an overhead kick looping over the stranded Philp, only for Anderson to clear off the line. Thurrock are out of luck and, as the half-time whistle blows, their kiosk is all out of hot food. The bloke behind the counter is taken aback by the size of the crowd and remarks there might have to be a few more Friday night games. I go for the classic hot chocolate and chocolate bar combination to see me through the second half.

I retake my seat, and the home officials retake theirs, having to turf out another group who haven't read the signs. On the pitch, it's the visitors dispossessing the Rocks, as Francis wins the ball in midfield and releases Aromolaran, who blasts wide. Both sides battle for the ball, but again the Tags create the more presentable openings. Harry Haysom heads wide from a free kick, before Francis returns the goal kick with a diving header on halfway. Aromolaran is in again. He squares to Halford, but his tame shot is smothered.

The Rocks bench think a foul on Halford is just as tame. They leap up to appeal the decision. PK Humble lines up the free kick and angers them further by pacing out the distance to the defender not quite ten yards in front of him. His kick finds its way to Halford. He lays off to Francis. His bobbling shot is spilled by the keeper and Cornhill wheels away with a celebration fancier than the finish for 3-0.

East Thurrock keep going, their young supporters remain in good voice and they don't look like a side being well beaten. Cornhill practically has to wrestle an opponent to stop the Rocks from rolling up the touchline from a throw-in. Hashtag soon send the ball clear into the left channel. Francis chases gamely, with the full-back favourite to shepherd it out or feel the merest hint of a touch to earn a free kick. He doesn't and Francis is in round the back. He's tripped and wins a penalty. A defender, looking for some afters, trips him again. The referee takes his time to settle things down, before Halford casually sends the keeper the wrong way for a flattering 4-0.

The hosts continue to look for a consolation, but the nearest they manage is an effort skied into the next field, which prompts 20 young fans to rush through the back of the terrace and play ball boy. They return in time to goad Philp as he takes the goal kick, and seem to have had fun despite the result soon confirmed by the ref. The home officials seem pleased with the evening, even if the result didn't go their way. The attendance of 607 will have helped swell the coffers, and it's great to see those sorts of numbers at this level.

I plan to see if Hashtag can extend their club record number of wins in a row with a midweek trip to Coggeshall, but I'm thwarted by the eternal nemesis of the groundhopper, a postponement. It comes as no surprise, after a cold snap renders pitches unplayable. Serious groundhoppers tend to have backup plans involving artificial pitches, but even some of these fall foul of the conditions. I did find an alternative, with Ebbsfleet United hosting my hometown team, Chelmsford City, but popping to the shops at lunchtime put me off standing on an open terrace. I regretted my decision when I saw pictures of Stonebridge Road and some of its historic features, which may not be around for much longer if their redevelopment plans come to fruition. City's 2-0 loss barely registered.

Soon after, another decision means that Chelmsford wouldn't be my hometown club for much longer, as we decide to move up north. Excellent news for ticking off some new grounds in a different part of the country, but not so good for completing all the senior grounds in Essex. It brings into focus which grounds I really want to visit. I book a return to Lewes and one of their beach huts, but this also succumbs to the elements, which in this case is a small frozen patch that can be no harder than pitches baked solid in summer. It's impossible to keep everyone happy with postponements; call it too early and everyone complains if it ends up being playable, too late and it's a wasted trip.

I'm determined not to waste our trip, but backup options at Whitehawk and Hastings both fall. The pubs of Lewes are some consolation, and the next day we go on an excursion, so the kids can lob rocks in the sea. We pass through Bexhill and I propose a detour past the Polegrove's mock-Tudor grandstand. There's no game on, but I get to wander across the pitch and admire the stand. It's not the same as having 90 minutes to take in the surroundings and I need more than a dog fetching a ball to watch in that time. I add another stop at Hasting's Pilot Field ground and get a glimpse through the railings. It's a less-satisfying look at the main stand, but gives me more of a feel for the place than looking at photos. I end up adding more grounds to my bucket list, although postponements and any delays due to moving might hamper me reaching 100 grounds before my deadline.

Ground 80

The Old Spotted Dog,
Clapton Community

ONE MUST-VISIT ground on my list is the oldest senior ground in London, the Old Spotted Dog. Dating back to 1888, it's the home to Clapton Community. Original tenants Clapton FC squeezed in a record attendance of 12,000 into a ground hemmed in by terraced housing without any major grandstand. That was some time ago and in recent years attendances dwindled, before they developed a following of continental-style ultras. Disputes between the owner and several public bodies, and between the owner and the fans, led to the formation of Clapton Community in 2018. After some further legal wrangling, Community were awarded the leasehold of the ground.

Not wanting to get embroiled in any legal matters myself, I'll withhold my opinions on this situation. I became a fan-owner of Clapton Community, so it's pretty clear where my loyalties lie and it's not with the team I heard referred to as 'zombie Clapton'. The owner's newsletter set out the scale of work needed to revitalise the ground and make it suitable for the men's first team. The 100-seater stand was reduced to 20 seats because of rotten floorboards at the back, the perimeter fence needed to be replaced in places, turnstiles were required and, most importantly, a recently acquired warehouse on adjacent land needed refurbishing to be used as changing rooms.

I was unlikely to resolve any of these issues, but when I announced on social media I had bought into Clapton Community last summer, I received a hero's welcome. My tweet had 62 likes, which is much the same thing. I'm sure most of those were looking at what culturally inappropriate attire they could wear to the next game to mark this momentous occasion. Only they wouldn't, as this is one fanbase that is highly unlikely to accept an oligarch or ruler of a dubious regime taking charge. It was these principles that drew me to the club, along with the atmosphere on the terrace. Everyone was welcome, even if they did lack the most basic handyman skills, or live miles away and not be able to help with so much as a clear-out.

Instead my first act, as with any vain, self-obsessed owner, was to propose a radical redesign to the kit. In fairness, the club was asking for entries in a competition. I didn't make the shortlist, as other owners evidently have design skills. My polka-dot effort was both a nod to the Spotted Dog ground and the limit of my ability on Microsoft Paint. I had an inordinate amount of fun reliving something I often did as a child. Perhaps my mistake was not getting the felt tips out and going for a garish 90s design. The winning design based on a supporter's flag would have been hard to beat, though.

The team wearing the kit today are the women's first team, as regulations deem it fine for them to get changed in a nearby school. They were the first Clapton Community side back in the Old Spotted Dog and this isn't the only factor putting their attendances on a par with the men's team, with fans backing both sides equally. The women's team are in the sixth tier and are today facing fifth-tier AFC Acorns, from Lingfield. The competition is the London and South East Regional League Trophy, for those teams knocked out of the first round of the South East Regional League Cup.

Potentially the most meaningless-sounding fixture imaginable, but this Clapton side enjoys a cup run and the crowd invariably enjoys themselves no matter what the occasion. I'm just glad to fit in a game before I move. It's taken a great deal of work from volunteers to get the ground even up to this level of readiness. So, there was no swanning into the directors' box for me and Mark, who has joined me for the trip, as we would be well down the pecking order behind the many other owners and fans who had made the return possible. We did swan in just before kick-off, as we felt it appropriate to support a small local brewery beforehand, with a visit to the Pretty Decent Beer Co. The IPA and sour lived up to the brewery's name and there was a somewhat illicit thrill of having a few beers on a Sunday. I've never enjoyed going to games on a Sabbath, mainly for transportation matters over ecumenical ones. Sitting under the silenced railway arches, looking at a high metal fence, there was a strange calm. No one is around and locals are oblivious to a great sporting occasion on their doorstep.

Nearer the ground, the pub, from which the football ground takes its name, is boarded up. We pass along the alleyway I recognise from supporter protests, when they watched games from outside the ground. I hoped to be a more popular owner and put some money in the coffers with a donation at the gate, in a moment of Dave Whelan largesse. I also donate to the food bank, although like many football club owners my motivations weren't entirely pure, as it helps me get rid of a few tins ahead of the house move. To regain some sort of man-of-the-people appeal, I get us a couple of cans of 'I could get better at Tesco for a quid' from the Pretty Decent Beer Co being sold at the bar for a very reasonable £4, which would allow me to do a Mike Ashley impression in the crowd.

We join the crowd in the scaffold (both name and description of the main stand), making a note to get something from the fusion food stall at half-time. We find a spot on halfway and before long the stereo cuts out and the game kicks off. I'm confronted by football at a level of the women's game I've not seen before and my instinct is to find a standard to compare it with. In men's non-league, the worry is that a match will be Sunday league, pub football. The opening passages of play suggest this may have something in common with those on the pitches adjoining West Ham's training ground we saw on the train journey in. The Spotted Dog pitch isn't helping, with the ball bouncing all over the place. This is no criticism of the ground staff, as grass pitches are notoriously difficult to maintain and given my own back garden resembles Derby's old Baseball Ground I'm in no position to comment.

The Tons' defence looks like being cracked apart by an Acorns team who have started brightly. Clearances aren't convincing and the midfield are taking tentative touches with back to goal. Everything needs an extra touch that time doesn't allow. Before I'm moved to comment on the standard of play to Mark, the hosts work the ball down the near touchline. Full-back Chelsie Osborne gets forward to cries of 'C'mon Chelsea', which is one chant I can't bring myself to join in. Before I make myself so unpopular with a group of East End fans and face the sort of protests David Sullivan did, I should note that the atmosphere is great and we're enjoying ourselves. Mark is filming, so he can watch back through adaptive software.

Pretty soon we need to replenish our beers, so we pass behind the goal Clapton are attacking and get another round from the clubhouse. We take up a position behind the goal on the rusting barriers. The Tons have grown into the game and are sending the play our way, with some interplay on the flanks. The pitch stops several crosses from reaching their target until Larissa Vieira lashes a venomous strike over the bar. Another shot from range briefly has me concerned for my beer, and another smashes into a bicycle chained to the fence.

Clapton are on top and support from the scaffold continues, so I won't be forced to do a Delia and ask where they are at half-time. There's no breakthrough in the scoreline, nor in the conversation Mark and I are having about how sport can be inclusive towards trans competitors and remain fair to cis women. We are mainly relieved that the old gender stereotype for shorter queues at the men's toilets holds true for a half-time comfort break, which is notable for some customised CCFC tiling.

Back in the bar, it's my round and I notice a 'no dickheads' sign on the bar back. I try to think of a humorous way of saying to Mark, 'I'm sorry I can't get one for you,' without sounding like a dickhead. As with many situations, the best thing is to say nothing and just order more cans of Tescos. Mark is keen to take them to the far end of the ground, where a separate group of ultras are gathered. There's a queue at the food stall, so we have what seems like the bright idea of deciding to go during the second half when it has died down.

We sidle up to the ultras, who are stood on crumbling terracing. The trees behind have been felled, which reveals enough elevation to explain how record crowds could have fit in here, but for now it is a small uncovered enclave. The lead ultra beckons us over so we join a group of around 15 fans, surprised by their friendliness. The lead ultra instructs the drummer to start a tune, which sounds familiar. We guess the tune in two and are adding our own oohs and lahs more or less in time. I notice one of two enormous flags unattended, waiting for someone to waft it around. While weighing up scenarios in which I manage to sour our warm welcome or get the game abandoned, another new joiner cannot resist and becomes the flag man. At some stage the second half gets under way.

The song continues for a good ten minutes and I'm entranced. We're at the end Clapton are attacking, so we should see any crucial action. The singing doesn't abate for a corner. The lead ultra then starts another song. We are soon chanting 'Clapton is my passion/I just sing along/ We don't need no Premiership/We just sing the same old song' for another ten minutes or so. Mark can't resist some pedantry between repeats. 'Surely Premier League, not Premiership.' We can't disagree with the sentiment, though. Mark then veers between some Schteve McClaren-style matching of the continental accents and then intoning the slower run-throughs like an old luvvie enunciating his lines, as he enjoys the singsong.

The constant singing doesn't seem to be appreciated by the visiting goalkeeper, and when Marta Casanovas is played in with a through pass and shoots across her, the ball slips through in a manner reminiscent of my five-a-side howler. The Acorns' stopper will want to forget this moment in a hurry, but my experience suggests she won't. It's an easy-to-excuse mistake. Mark and I are both keen to take credit for our group providing some sort of assist, surely forcing the lapse.

We need to return to the clubhouse for another beer to celebrate with, and to use the toilet facilities. We don't want to leave, as it looks like we are abandoning our comrades soon after an amusing pro-immigrant song. Eventually Mark's bladder forces the issue, and we set off to complete our lap of the ground. The lead ultra shakes our hand and we promise to return. We pass the small seated stand, which has a few people in the usable seats, and find another set of toilets. The urinals are taped off and I can't in all good conscience send Mark into one of the traps, so we continue to the clubhouse.

On the way back from the bar, we forget about food, keen to rejoin the band of ultras. The teams continue to battle it out with only the odd opening. It doesn't matter. Clapton look like they will hold on to their lead and progress to the quarter-final. Before we know it, the full-time whistle goes and they do just that. The team come over to high-five the ultras before the traditional 'lo lo lo lo' back and forth with the scaffold.

We make our way out of the ground and the match officials are getting changed near the clubhouse. 'That was a real midfield battle,' remarks one of them, meaning I had caught the gist of the game in my trance-like state. It's tempting to stay for music in the bar, but with it being a Sunday, we decide to embark on the journey home.

If churchgoing is in terminal decline, and with football often compared to a religion, this offers a proper sense of community in a crowd of 265. There is a real purpose in how the club has come together, fought for a historic old ground and are looking to bring it back to life. Being part of the choir invigorated us, and I can't help but be evangelical about the club and the work they do. A long pilgrimage south for a revisit will certainly be in order. It's closer than Italy, which must be the next nearest equivalent experience.

Ground 81

Meridian Sports and Social Club, Meridian VP

ANOTHER TEAM I felt I should visit was Meridian VP, for the tenuous reason of the official club account following me on Twitter. I felt I should repay their perceptiveness in identifying that I was the sort of egocentric writer who would visit if they followed me. Their ground was also close enough to my office to warrant a midweek trip.

A quick hop on the Elizabeth line took me to Woolwich. The images of cannons on pubs and road names with military connotations showed I was in the area of Arsenal's birthplace. A push over the top of Barrack Field would have revealed views of Woolwich Common and Charlton Park were it not pitch black. The lights of Canary Wharf come into view as I reach the ground, but I am more pleased to see the floodlights of the various pitches at the sports and social club.

I enter the main building to check out the facilities, since I'm not sure what there is beyond the turnstile. A friendly barmaid asks if I want a drink, while I am still getting my bearings. I immediately give myself away as a socially awkward groundhopper. 'I'm here for the football,' I say, when clearly that's what everyone is here for, whether that's playing or watching whatever was being shown on various big screens. I check that this is where the food, drink and toilets are and am directed to the conveniences. On my way back, I find myself in the players' tunnel and could get into the ground for free. Instead, I retrace my steps, go through the turnstile and pay the £7.50 entry, which comes with a free programme.

For once I remember to ask the turnstile operator where the team sheet is posted and for once it is in a place I can't miss, directly in front of me, as I pass through the turnstile. I find a spot in the main stand, well, the only stand, a modern prefabricated 100-seater familiar to me from the SCEFL groundhop.

I feel a fondness for this league after the hop and am watching Division One at step six tonight. I take a seat on halfway and can almost make out the twinkling lights of Canary Wharf through the trees on the opposite touchline.

The ground is basic, but doesn't feel as grim as the picture on Futbology makes out, which reminds me to check in. A flick through the programme tells me Meridian were formed in 1995 as a five-a-side team by Dawinder Tamna and his brothers. Their rise might not seem meteoric, but anyone who's tried to get four other people to turn up every week will know that going from that, via a merger with Valley Park, to being five points off the play-off places is impressive stuff.

Visitors Sporting Club Thamesmead aren't doing so well on the pitch, being a place above the relegation zone. Although off the pitch they have a decent modern facility, by which I don't mean some sort of 1960s brutalist construction that you would normally associate with the area. The club, in its current guise, was formed in 2011, with predecessors dating back much further.

The programme is a double-header covering Meridian's next match against Lewisham Borough, who are yet another club formed this century, in 2003. Among the usual information and a couple of original articles, I also notice that Bridon Ropes share this venue. This leads me to look them up. Formed in 1935 as a works team for the British Rope factory in Charlton, it suggests they are the senior partner in this groundshare and I should have seen them in one of their Wednesday midweek games, but crucially they hadn't followed me on Twitter.

The followers of Meridian and Thamesmead fill up the ground, although 'fill' is doing a lot of heavy lifting there. One supporter is pleased to have avoided some heavy lifting, as she only had three sets of kit to wash at the weekend and usually it would be four. She asks her companion, 'Are you Thamesmead then?' 'Yeah, my grandson is over there,' he replies. 'Oh, mine's in goal,' she says, beaming with pride. It turns out he was hard done by at his former club, who brought in another keeper. The new stopper was apparently on more money, and Larkfield & New Hythe, far from being the friendly, progressive club I had come across on the groundhop, were the Manchester City of the SCEFL Division One. There's always one team in every league people suspect of distorting the market and talk turns to how they must be being bankrolled, as the ball is rolled back for a hoof into the channel at kick-off.

Some early chances come about because of good wing play. Charlie Martin, in the Thamesmead goal, denies Meridian's Julius Roy-Macaulay, before the ball is worked back down the line and a cross is deflected towards the goal and headed off the line. Meridian hold a tight defensive line to play Ryan Solan offside and the referee firmly instructs the grandson goalie to move the ball to the correct position, but not so firmly it attracts the ire of his gran. Or maybe I just expect female relatives to cause such a scene, based on bitter experience.

Comparing the game to the women's match I saw prior to this would be a futile experience. It's frantic stuff. Thamesmead break with pace but someone treads on the ball. The move slows and I wince in anticipation of a crunching tackle. The couple nearby are seamlessly moving from talking about male relatives playing to female relatives and even their plumber's mate's niece playing. It's just yet more football to those of us who like to consume as much of it as possible. Although it's debatable that instructions emanating from the pitch are ones the purists would approve of. 'I don't care whether I shank it or not, I want you to run,' a visiting defender implores.

The Thamesmead defence has more concerns when Douane West gets a shot away. It's deflected into the path of Romayle Wade lurking at the far post. he turns it in, to calls for offside, which are ignored by the officials; 1-0 to Meridian, which prompts Thamesmead to argue among themselves and with the playing surface, which is branded 'shit', albeit looking better than the Spotted Dog.

There's plenty of industry and chasing the ball down from both sides. Meridian have a second chalked off for an offside and I decide to do a headcount of the crowd. I make it 42, but it's hard to tell how many are lurking in the shadows of the overhanging trees on the far touchline. I once again find myself in a group of ultras, as more members of the Meridian keeper's family turn up, proclaiming themselves to be the Meridian ultras. There's no chanting, only more complaints about Larkfield, before the half-time whistle blows.

At the start of the second half, I do a recount of the crowd and we've lost an entire football team with only 31 in attendance now. We've also lost the Thamesmead keeper, who has been replaced at half-time. The new stopper looks to make his mark by shouting at his defence. His first act is to pick the ball out of the net. Fortunately for him, it's the net protecting the car park behind the goal and he wrestles with it like it's part of the *Krypton Factor* assault course, and retrieves the ball.

His opposite number, Frankie Leonard, is soon called into action. Sacha Gibson shoots. Frank (as he's known to the ultras) can only parry into the path of Fred Agyemang to tuck it away from close range to level the scores. Soon after, Agyemang looks to return the favour to Gibson, laying the ball off to him, before the Thamesmead number 11 fires a shot bound for the far corner. Frank gets a big hand on it to turn it round the post and make up for any fault in the equaliser.

The game picks up as a contest and I'm drawn into proceedings in a way that belies the level of football. At Clapton, it had been the crowd. Here, it's a back-and-forth tussle. Play is broken and sporadic. Both sides battle for possession and look to use their pace down the flanks. Meridian play in West (the player, not the compass point), down the wing (which I'm guessing is south). West centres, with a teasing ball between onrushing forward and keeper. It breaks to the Meridian man and rolls towards the line but is cleared by a covering defender.

The other 30 people gathered are also getting drawn into events. Three people over on the far side boo a decision to award a goal kick rather than a corner to the visitors. There are more appeals when Gibson takes it past Frank. He's running out of play, but goes down under the challenge. No penalty. Thamesmead are in the ascendancy now and I can't help but have a big grin on my face, enjoying the back-and-forth contest. I expect the almost primal satisfaction of bulging net at any moment. The ball breaks to Howard Newton on the edge of the box. He connects sweetly and a rising drive looks for all the world that it will nestle in the corner of the net. Frank is well beaten, but in the end has to fetch the ball from the undergrowth behind the goal for a goal kick.

The game swings back in Meridian's favour. A set piece is volleyed over. Bursts of frenetic action are interspersed with lulls in play. Out of nowhere, Agyemang exchanges passes to give Thamesmead a chance, which is saved. Either side could win it. Meridian have a chance from a corner which flashes wide. Another lull. A long free kick from the visitors causes panic. Frank spills the cross, and it falls to Agyemang, but Frank recovers to save. That's the last chance, and the match finishes all square.

I head back to Woolwich station and only when I set off do I realise how cold I am. I'm shivering as I make my way to a bus stop, although I'm not as cold as the residents I pass on Cemetery Road. Before I'm in danger of joining them, a bus pulls up almost immediately and I can warm up. I look online and notice the official attendance is given as 31. The contest deserved a bigger crowd than that and, who knows, an extra hundred on the gate and Meridian may challenge the likes of Larkfield & New Hythe.

Ground 82
Royal Oak, Harwich & Parkeston

AFTER MY cold midweek game in London, the perfect tonic is served up at the Royal Oak. Serious hoppers will be familiar with this ground as it boasts arguably the finest grandstand in Essex. It's one I've been meaning to tick off for a while. Those hoppers can rest assured that I don't decide to stay warm in the pub from which the ground takes its name and claim a glimpsed view of the pitch counts. I am keen to fit in a proper visit before the move up north.

The drive takes just over an hour, which gives it something of a day trip to the seaside feel, even on a grey February afternoon. Football tourism can take you to some obscure and far-flung places. Photos of grounds in the Faroes have the allure of a desert island in a brochure. I wouldn't have gone to the industrial city of Dortmund were it not for Borussia. Now I've got 45 minutes until kick-off to kill in a place mostly famous for its ferry route out. I decide not to just stare at the rear of the grandstand, which has been patched up, and go for a stroll.

I make my way to the seafront to get a bit of sea air. It takes a moment to tell where the grey of the North Sea ends and the overcast sky starts. I turn towards the old town, with the container port of near-neighbour Felixstowe on the opposite bank of the estuary looming large in the distance. My short loop gives me a brief taste of the faded grandeur of an old seaside town and a look at a branch of R. Gwinnell & Sons funeral directors, who sponsor the ground, making it the R. Gwinnell & Sons Royal Oak to give it its full name.

I reach the perimeter wall, which I had sped past on a previous visit, catching just a fleeting glimpse of the stand. It captured my imagination. The more I looked into the club, the more I realised it was a well-regarded non-league venue dating back to 1898, with the classic pitch-roofed grandstand added in 1948. The team were formed in 1877 and reached the FA Amateur Cup Final in 1953. They faced Pegasus, a team formed of students from Oxford and Cambridge, who did the footballing equivalent of hurling thunder from the air to run out 6-0 winners. Despite losing, the visit to Wembley was still a matter of great pride for Harwich. Today's fixture against Leiston Reserves in the Thurlow Nuun Eastern Counties League Division 1 North at step six is a more austere occasion.

Once inside the ground, with a programme safely buried in my pocket, I get my first proper look at the grandstand. There's a fresh lick of black and white paint from when the club renovated it in 2020. The seats bear the names of those who donated towards the fundraising. Tarpaulin covers all bar the front two rows of seats on the steeply sloped stand. I edge my way to one of the few vacant seats near a pillar. I choose a seat where it only obscures the view of the centre circle rather than a penalty box. More modern cantilevered stands don't have this problem, but I'm happy to crane my neck in return for the traditional charm of a stand that appears to have retained several regulars.

The teams come out from the modern changing rooms behind the goal, which sports an electronic scoreboard. Harwich, known as the Shrimpers, are in a sharp black-and-white-striped kit, which looks freshly bought. Leiston Reserves, known as the Blues, are in blue. Harwich make the brighter start but the only action worthy of note is when Alfie Smith screws a shot well wide.

I struggle to concentrate on the game. If I was being generous, I would say I'm still taking in my surroundings. It is a lovely spot, but neither side seems to be capable of spotting a pass. The only notable action is a long ball into the Shrimpers' box that's headed towards his own goal by a defender and saved by Brad Cook, and a bloke coming around with a clicker to count the crowd.

'You don't have to blow for every one,' remonstrates a Harwich defender after yet another stoppage. A long hopeful ball is cleared. I realise in my reverie for an old stand that I've forgotten to look for the team sheets, so I search online. As I'm looking at my phone, the ball rolls down the slope and the net ripples. Since the pitch slopes from one touchline to another, it's a misplaced pass rolling into an unused goal. I've missed nothing in the way of action.

The Shrimpers' number seven (I'll look him up later) gets on the ball and breaks forward. He twists past a defender and puts goalkeeper Harrison Podd on the floor. Podd is able to stick out a foot and prod clear. The ball naturally finds its way down the slope. Harwich send in a cross and Smith attacks with a diving header. Podd pads it away. This passage of play isn't enough to get the crowd going. Only when the Leiston full-back tries to take a throw-in from the wrong position do they become more animated. This boils over into a few people jeering a free kick and one bloke calling the fouled player a shithouse.

There's the potential for shithousery in a more literal sense, as the pigeons who have made their home in the rafters above are making a commotion. Feathers fall into someone's pint in front. I notice the tarpaulin is covered in bird poo and I take this as my cue (or should I say, coo) to leave for half-time refreshments. I make my way to the kiosk in the corner next to the changing rooms. There's no queuing or cooing and I get a burger, hot chocolate and chocolate bar for under a fiver.

I see out the first half by the corner flag at the end Leiston are attacking. They have barely gotten past the halfway line all match and at the moment my hands are full; they play the ball into the channel in front of me. For a moment, I'm concerned that I might need to deal with a stray ball. I needn't have worried, as there is more action in the game a group of kids are playing on a patch of grass between the kiosk and changing rooms. Those are the only cheers for a goal I hear before the half ends.

The kids continue to be more prolific in their game than the subs are in their half-time shooting practice. The subs aren't even facing a goalkeeper. I walk round to the covered end to face the direction Leiston are shooting second half, mainly for a quick getaway afterwards. Home fans are gathered on picnic benches outside the social club in the corner and eye me suspiciously, like I've just walked into their local and ordered a white wine spritzer, or as if I'm an away fan. To my surprise, there are a few fans from Leiston despite the first team being at home, but they remain near the kiosk.

The covered end looks smart from a distance, with its black and white painted roof. On closer inspection, the concrete steps are too high for a terrace, but have no seats on them. I perch with my legs dangling, as netting strung up behind the goal protects me from wayward shooting practice. It also makes it harder to see the game when it kicks off, but I'm not missing much. 'I've seen ten-year-olds play better than this,' complains one old boy nearby. The sound of the ball being thumped long and headed back and forth echoes around the ground.

The netting can't prevent the best effort of the half ending up near me in the stand. I fetch it for Cook to get the game going again and notice the ball isn't as rock-hard as expected. The game may not have come to life, but maybe I've uncovered something big. Like the groundhopper who noticed a set of goals were the wrong height as part of his routine touching both crossbars, maybe I've come across an attempt for the home side to gain an advantage. I then realise that given how fastidious the ref has been, he's unlikely to miss a flat ball. I deduce it was more a case of it being an old worn ball, which explains the reverberating sound it has been making.

At the point I'm about to look up the rules on match balls, I notice the Shrimpers' number nine, Joe Knight, who has been putting himself about a bit, sent from the field. He trudges off, but despite being down to ten men Harwich are galvanised. They keep the play down the other end but can't find an opening. The Leiston defence are switched on, like the newly installed floodlights, but there are few bright moments. It crosses my mind that this has 0-0 written all over it. I've been to other games where I've felt the same, but they've been entertaining, where I could wax lyrical about the contest, only for a late winner to add to the occasion.

This is looking much less promising. There's a comical passage when Harwich are under pressure. They can't clear. The defender recovers and slices a clearance. It's blocked. Leiston cross, which is met with another sliced clearance that is skied back to Cook. After another long lull, in which an attendance of 223 is announced, a Leiston sub goes on a jinking run, evading tackles in the box, until Cook pounces on the ball at his feet and snuffs out the chance.

The scoreboard is showing ten minutes remaining. I wonder whether I would revisit if it ends 0-0. It's a nice enough ground, and I'd happily explore the town a bit more, but it would be a trek from Yorkshire and I'd want to see a better standard of football. Maybe I'll just have to go to another game and not count this for the 100 in this book. Harwich win a corner. They send it deep to the far post. Dan Keeble, up from the back, heads it into the ground. It bounces awkwardly past Podd and into the net for 1-0. I'm only marginally less relieved than the home fans who could see two points slipping away.

Slipping back on to the field is Joe Knight, who was only sin-binned when I wasn't paying attention. I do see a red card brandished following an incident at the other end of the field. A Leiston player is down, but then another Leiston player is sent off for something I've not seen as I edge towards the exit. I slip away when the final whistle blows. The match was a disappointment. I don't regret it, though. I appreciated the fine venue. If I could blend the best bits of the last three games – the ground at Harwich, the match at Meridian and the crowd at Clapton – I would have the perfect football outing. As it is, those individual trips still beat watching the same team in the same concrete stadium.

I read a match report afterwards and it's clear I didn't miss some sort of nuanced tactics on display, but I notice the attendance is reported as 170. I dismiss the notion of a scandal of gate receipts being fiddled, as I know from experience a counting error within a margin of 25 per cent is entirely plausible.

Ground 83
West Street, Coggeshall Town

HASHTAG UNITED are on an implausible 16-match winning streak and I'm off to see them next in their re-arranged fixture away to Coggeshall Town. I'm going with my friend Lewis, who is watching his first-ever live game of football. He is a rare beast in my circle of friends, having never been to a match. I am keen to right that wrong, especially as he bears a passing resemblance to Statto from *Fantasy Football League* and it always seemed wrong that he couldn't come up with a single stat. I want to see what he makes of the groundhopping experience as an outsider. Lewis is more interested in Formula 1 and photography, so I tell him to bring his camera and he drives us there, albeit more in the style of a rally driver than an F1 driver.

We arrive at West Street, on the edge of Coggeshall, in good time for kick-off. The small town is famous for its timber-framed buildings, most notably Paycocke's House. We pay our £10 entry and pass through a historic Ellison's turnstile. I don't clock the serial number and Lewis is left wondering how old it is too. The ground itself dates back to the 1960s, but the last decade has seen several improvements, as the team reached the highest level in their 144-year history, which is currently under threat.

After being formed by the JK King seed company and having played at a couple of other sites in town, the Seed Growers were well established here. They grew with the help of pop star Olly Murs, whose influence was evident in the smart new clubhouse bar, with red neon strip lights and large club crests that was more in keeping with an episode of *The Only Way is Essex* than a spit and sawdust non-league bar. A Coggeshall coach is drilling the team in a pre-match warm-up, which sounds like a one-sided argument from *TOWIE*.

We pass behind a small stand nestled at the bottom of a slope, with the path around the top offering a good vantage point. Lewis remarks that it looks like an asbestos roof. We head for the covered terrace and realise the route for a full lap past the dugouts and gantry is blocked, so we hang around behind the goal, watching Hashtag warm up. I explain to Lewis the current league positions, players to watch, and players who used to play for the opposition. This automatically strikes me as being relevant context, but I realise it means nothing to Lewis, so I fall back on the classic fact that Toby Aromolaran appeared on *Love Island*. Lewis is no fan of the show, but is at least aware of it.

I make the rookie error of not realising which end Hashtag are more likely to attack. They line up to defend the end we are stood at, so we return to the path above the main stand for a better view of the goal they are attacking. The best vantage points are taken and we have a slightly restricted view, with the stand blocking part of the near touchline. Two kids' teams file into the stand after their mascot duties and start yelling, 'C'mon Coggy.' The unofficial nickname works better than the official one, as

'C'mon Seedy' is up there with me shouting 'C'mon the Arse!' at Arsenal, for attracting funny looks.

Coggy get rid of the ball and it bounces off the roof of the stand, which may or may not cause deadly dust particles to spread our way, depending on whether Lewis's engineering knowledge extends beyond F1 cars. The hosts look to get off to a fast start and the pace of Josh Osude gives his former club some early worries. Lewis gets his camera out and starts snapping. I ask what he's looking for, to get a photographer and novice's perspective. 'Anything that seems like an interesting shot,' he says, capturing duals, spot-the-ball situations where there's an aerial contest, and any form of handbags. There's plenty of this to capture and is what draws many people in. Lewis has tried to watch football on TV, but finds there's too much passing about, so this is more his thing. Perhaps he's a proper football man in the mould of a Big Sam after all. Big Lew dispenses advice on kit I can use to get better action shots on a phone by recording a video and using a still from that.

There's a set-piece situation when the ball goes out for a Hashtag throw. Someone obscured by the stand scurries over and sends it down the line. The ball is held up and fed to Max Cornhill, who spreads it wide to Aromolaran. He hits a first-time strike across the keeper into the bottom corner to make it 1-0. Lew's first game won't be a 0-0. Coggeshall look to respond and force a goalmouth scramble that's better for a photographer than a writer to capture, only neither of us are well positioned to see it. The Hashtag goal remains intact.

Hashtag look to ping it forward. Jermaine Francis finds fellow former Seed Grower Alex Teniola, who holds the ball up and lays it off to Cornhill. He flicks it into the box.

Teniola swivels and shoots, making it 2-0 and celebrates with his trademark 'Teniola time' celebration. No niceties of refusing to celebrate a goal against a former club at this level, which is a good job, otherwise Teniola would have few opportunities given the number of former clubs he comes up against.

The half ends 2-0 to Hashtag. As Lewis is keen to get the full non-league experience, I take him to the kiosk for a molten hot chocolate. We have an obstructed view of a small-sided game between the mascots. The blue team dominate before their number 15 breaks the deadlock. The hot chocolates haven't cooled by the time the second half is ready to get under way. We take up a position behind the goal Hashtag are attacking to get a different perspective and we're in among the handful of Hashtag fans expecting to cheer a few more goals.

Hashtag get in round the back and Lew immediately appreciates the pace of the move. The ball breaks for Cornhill, who drags it wide on to the hoardings. Francis gets in again and pinball ensues in the box, but no change of scoreline. Hashtag continue to press and send a long ball into the box. Coggeshall keeper Tom Middlehurst comes to claim. He spills it under pressure and goes down. A bobbling shot is cleared, but only as far as Eman Okunja. He has the goal at his mercy but scuffs his effort on to the post.

After their reprieve, Coggeshall look to get Osude in. Matthew Wooldridge can't cut out the through ball. Osude is on to it in a flash and away from Wooldridge, before bursting past James Philp in the Hashtag goal and firing it into the roof of the empty net to get his side back in it.

The game becomes a scrappier affair. Time ticks along, slowly for me, wanting Hashtag to hold on; quickly for

Lew, who is enjoying the experience. He compares it to rugby union, which shocks me until I notice a series of long clearances for territory and a few scuffles between players. Lew means the atmosphere in the crowd, where there is no segregation or bad blood. He's taken by the community spirit in the non-league game. Keen to move us away from talk of rugby, I ask him the commentator's staple of which players have impressed him and are in the running for his man-of-the-match award. Like an old pro, he mentions Toby and Josh by first name. He has fallen into the novice's trap of picking the flair players out wide, missing the contribution of Cornhill, who soon has to go off after picking up a shiner that wouldn't be out of place on the rugby field.

We too make a move, returning to the spot we had in the first half, closer to the exit and where the hosts are looking to mount some late pressure. It's Hashtag with chances to finish it off, though. Sub Pedro Carvalho plays a one-two and looks to slot the ball past Middlehurst. It clips the keeper's stray leg and is cleared off the line. Carvalho soon has another effort cleared off the line after rounding Middlehurst. He drags another one wide with the goal gaping. In between these efforts, Coggeshall try to force an equaliser from set pieces. They have one last chance to play in Osude. He beats Wooldridge, and Philp closes him down, but not before Osude slots the ball under him. A recovering defender clears the effort, which looked like it might snatch a point.

The final whistle goes and the Hashtag players celebrate. I allow myself a sigh of relief. The result leaves Hashtag in pole position for the one automatic promotion slot and Lew didn't hate it. Hashtag face second-placed

Sudbury in their next game, but a revisit to the Len Salmon isn't on the cards, as Mrs C seems to think it's more important to pack for our house move and say goodbye to people.

Ground 84

Station View,
Harrogate Railway Athletic

THE WEEK of the move comes, and I make several trips in a rental van up and down the A1. I check Futbology for any midweek fixtures en route, with sufficient car parking to accommodate a long wheelbase Transit, but find nothing worth making a detour for. Two days after the move and the perfect opportunity presents itself to see my new local non-league club, Harrogate Railway Athletic.

If my previous book started as a search for a new team to support and ended with a fondness for groundhopping as much as Hashtag and Clapton Community, then this one about groundhopping may become another search for a new team. In a traditional part of the country, I'm starting by seeing my nearest team. Harrogate Town may be slightly nearer, but as a league club they hold less appeal. I may still go and see them since there are fewer clubs to choose from in the area than in the south-east, which might hinder me reaching the 100 in time.

Harrogate Railway Athletic play in the Northern Counties East Football League Division One, at step six. All the leagues in this area seem to contain combinations of the words northern, premier, east and league. I take a while to work out this league, with a Division One and Premier Division, which feeds into the Northern Premier League East, then on to Northern Premier League Premier Division and then the step two National League North.

I'm familiar with Railway, or the Rail as they are known, from their FA Cup exploits. They reached the second round twice in the last couple of decades. One run included a derby win over Town, before going out to Bristol City. Another cup run was ended by Mansfield. I dimly recall a packed little ground and duly look up highlights of the Mansfield game, where they ran their league opposition close in a 3-2 defeat. Despite playing towards the bottom of the pyramid, the Rail are in fine form, unbeaten in the league since September and firmly in the play-off mix.

The Rail's last fixture, away to champions-elect Campion, fell victim to the weather, much to the chagrin of the visitors who were leading 2-1. Heavy rain rather than leaves on the pitch was the cause. Railway, as the name suggests, were formed by railway workers in 1935 and the club crest contains a beaver, which didn't seem like the most obvious symbol to use. Looking up the reference, I did a double take when I saw that 'beavers were used in the railway industry'. I had images of them cutting wooden sleepers to size with their teeth, until I read the full sentence, 'Beavers were used in the railway industry, as a symbol of hard work.' Apparently, their red and green strip is due to an early version being made from railwaymen's flags.

Tonight's opponents, Nostell Miners Welfare, are also associated with hard work, being one of five teams in the division with obvious connections to the mining industry. In keeping with the mining connection, they could be found deep down towards the bottom of the league table. Much nearer to the surface and indeed my new home was one of Mrs C's old school friends, Martin (only a handful of grounds to his name). He lives around the corner. Rather than go down to the local pub, I suggest we go to the game.

'It's snowing,' Martin exclaims by text just before we were about to leave. 'They'll have an orange ball surely' was my blithe reply. It couldn't be that bad. Martin knocks on my door and great lumps of it are coming down. I have one last check that it's still on and we set off. The game isn't called off in the time it takes to drive to the ground. I park up and we add several layers before leaving the car. Martin dons an extra pair of socks and I remember the ones I keep with some wellies in the car boot.

We pay our £5 entrance and I get a programme for any insights it might provide on two unfamiliar teams in an unfamiliar league. We acquaint ourselves with the ground, walking a lap on the pitch. The near touchline is shorn of the temporary stands erected for Rail's cup games. The main stand is situated behind a goal and reminds me of Margate, sloping from touchline to touchline. It's a mix of seating and standing. A refreshment kiosk adjoins in one corner. The far touchline contains the dug-outs, a modern prefab 50-seater and a few steps of terracing in the corner. Back round the other goal is just a path and corrugated iron sheets in club colours of red and green. The modern clubhouse overlooks from a distance.

We decide to find a spot on the covered terrace. We pass the media office, which is the size of a platelayer's hut, and I enquire about the team sheet. I'm told it's back where I've come from or I can find it online. I do the latter and we pick a spot directly behind the goal, which offers some protection from a spot of last-minute shooting practice. We are in front of the away match officials' section. A few locals eye us warily, but are unlikely to conclude we have any sort of connection to a former colliery team. One home fan asks the linesman, 'Can you make sure you flag them offside when they're up this end, but not us when we're going this way,' which takes him longer than it does for the lino to check the net for holes.

The song 'Papa's Got a Brand New Pigbag' welcomes the teams on to the muddy field, which reminds me of 'Sol's a Gooner' being sung in early season sunshine. We stamp our feet a bit for some warmth and an old boy shouts, 'C'mon Rail', as we get under way. The slope immediately catches Welfare out, with a sideways pass uphill played too short, then a downhill pass over-hit. This invites a robust sliding tackle on the slick surface, accompanied by plenty of shouting between players.

The home side settle in well, exchanging some neat passes. Soon, Kieran Greenway is in and hits the ball across George Bason in Welfare's goal. It skids in to give Rail the lead. Bason isn't best pleased and takes out his frustration on Welfare's defence. 'Get off of it, pinky and perky,' the old boy tells him, referring to his pink jersey, before starting a 'We hate York' chant that doesn't have anyone joining in, so I'm left unsure if I should hate York.

Welfare manage to join up some passes out from the back as they grow into the game, although not without the odd scare. A good old-fashioned long ball in behind Rail right-back Josh Hardcastle catches him out and finds Jack MacGahan. He chips Joseph Wilton as the Rail stopper is caught in no man's land, and the scores are level.

The murky conditions make it hard to see what's going on at the other end. The eagle-eyed old boy is sure a Welfare player had slipped over on a blade of grass when the referee awards a free kick. The shot is fired towards goal. I lose sight of it and of Wilton, wearing grey. A cry of 'justice' from the old boy alerts me to the fact that Wilton has the ball.

It's Welfare with most of the possession, and they play a through ball to Tawheed Ahmed. He squares it to Regan Ward. Wilton is nowhere and Ward has a tap in to make it 2-1. This prompts Rail into action. Greenway makes a good run but his strike is straight at Bason, who parries. Oliver Norman does well to follow up but Bason saves with his feet. This burst of action is followed by a series of fouls until the referee calls a halt to the half.

Martin and I make our way to the refreshment hut. The group in front are told the pies are all sold out, but, 'Of course we still have chips and gravy, lad!' We go for hot chocolate. I query why Martin, as a northerner, hasn't gone for Bovril, but it turns out not all northerners drink it like water and he hasn't tried it. My description doesn't sell it to him either. We do a lap of the pitch to get some warmth into us while waiting for the hot chocolate to cool down to something approaching drinking temperature.

We find a spot on a few steps of terracing near the corner flag at the end Rail will be attacking. 'Bad Moon Rising' plays on the tannoy, and it feels like Brian Glover will warn us to stay off. It is as wild and desolate as the moors on this elevated vantage point at the top of the sloping pitch, which may explain why a group of lads take up a position next to us all wearing North Face attire.

The half gets under way. The ball is sent over the fence into gardens behind us and prompts a dog to bark. Beastly behaviour on the pitch, when a Rail defender ignores a Welfare attack and runs like a man possessed after the ref, who missed a shirt pull. He doesn't miss a crunching tackle to stop the Welfare attack, but the free kick comes to nothing.

The officials come in for some stick from the visitors as well. MacGahan asks the linesman who was playing a Rail forward onside when he was put through. The effort was dragged wide down the slope in any case. The linesman gives a slightly stuttering response, so MacGahan mocks him. Rail sub Prince Attakorah, in turn, teases the Welfare full-back, getting past him before being hauled down. The resulting free kick is punched clear. No blows traded between players, but more fouls and a talking-to for Welfare's boss from the referee follow.

After a brief delay Rail take a throw-in. The ball is played through to Fatlum Ibrahimi, who has charged forward from the back and drills a low shot past Bason to level the scores at 2-2. 'Send in the tank!' exclaims Martin. It certainly was a no-nonsense approach from the big centre-half on a deteriorating surface. Just as I'm saying to Martin that a draw is probably a fair result, Welfare have a shot that appears to have been saved, but Jack Bull smuggles the ball into the net to make it 3-2.

There's more angry shouting from the pitch. I'm expecting to hear someone called a 'shithouse' at any moment. The anger increases when the ref pulls Rail up from the kick-off, as it was taken with a moving ball. There's a sin-binning for dissent in among this to make Rail's task of getting back on terms more difficult.

It takes a while for Rail to regain their composure before they force a series of set pieces. A corner is sent right under the crossbar. Bason claims it and appears to be bundled over the line 1950s style. The goal is given. Greenway has his second, and it's all square at 3-3. Rail continue to press, looking for a winner. A long throw is flicked on and headed over by Ibrahimi. MacGahan is finally sin-binned, putting the officials back in the home supporters' good books. They immediately fall back out of favour when they fail to award a late penalty. Martin and I agree it was never a penalty. We also see that there's a chance for Rail to create one last opening, but a shot is drilled well wide rather than picking out a team-mate free on the overlap.

It ends 3-3 and we shuffle to the exit, glad of the extra layers we donned. We're made to wait for the teams and officials to leave. 'I wouldn't let you ref my six-year-olds,' says one fan as the ref runs the gauntlet. I'm grinning ear to ear, as I've thoroughly enjoyed the game, bad refereeing calls, scrappy play and all. The game had its moments and I feel like I've found my new team to follow, especially now the play-offs beckon. That won't stop me checking out other local teams to see if I can find some more new favourites.

Ground 85
EnviroVent Stadium, Harrogate Town

HARROGATE RAILWAY Athletic are at home again on the Saturday, but Mrs C has the car. It is over an hour's walk into town and I don't fancy the extra distance into Starbeck, where they play. Harrogate Town's ground on Wetherby Road is tantalisingly close, albeit still a fair walk and £20 for League Two football. It beats unpacking boxes, so I navigate the online ticketing system and get an e-ticket, before consulting a map on a more direct route to their ground across several fields. With a small detour, I can also tick off a visit to my nearest brewery, Rooster's, which has a taproom to sample their wares. Beer and football are a classic combination, but donning a pair of stout walking boots and setting off on a five-mile hike across the Crimple Valley is unlikely to feature in many fans' pre-match routines.

I pass Harrogate's rugby union club just outside my village and later learn that the football club, founded in 1919, was an offshoot of the rugby club, whose players decided to play football instead. Having seen rugby players trying to kick a football with all the finesse of Tony Adams on *Strictly Come Dancing*, it comes as no surprise they were playing in the Northern Counties East League until the

1980s. Town were founding members of Conference North in 2004 and reached what had become the National League in 2017/18. Their rise led to various improvements to their ground. The stands were empty when the Sulphurites had their greatest success in 2020, reaching the play-offs on points per game and beating Notts County in the final. A promotion and FA Trophy double was secured with their victory over Concord Rangers in a delayed final, which took place almost a year later than originally scheduled due to the Covid pandemic, by which time Harrogate had spent almost a year as an EFL club having reached the semi-finals prior to winning promotion.

I complete the similarly meteoric rise up the Crimple Valley and sink into a chair in the Rooster's taproom. I have a sampling board of thirds to try out their range. And another in the name of research, before embarking on a further half-hour walk from the brewery to the ground. I time it to coincide with a rain shower. Row upon row of suburban semis would offer great parking opportunities had I been in a car and sorted a residents' permit. Instead, I emerge on to Wetherby Road with mud all up the back of my legs and lank strands of hair stuck to my face. I look like I've just stepped off a farm, should the cosmopolitan away support from Barrow wish to make that observation.

Barrow were themselves in the National League until 2020, winning the title ahead of Harrogate and gaining the unofficial nickname 'Barrowcelona' for their football. The match wouldn't be too far from being the non-league football I was used to, although Barrow could point to 50 years of league football until they were voted out in 1971/72 and were in tenth ahead of kick-off, while

Town were languishing in 21st, only six points above the relegation places.

My programme provides the information on league positions, players who I've not come across before and not much else for £3. There is better value in a Mother's Day bundle on sale, containing a pink T-shirt, baseball cap and some chocolates. I text Mrs C to see if that's what she would like, and she declines my thoughtful offer. I'm then left to ponder whether I queue for a pie or a pint of Black Sheep. There isn't time for both, so I go for a pork pie rather than neck a pint. It's a sensible choice and a decent reminder that pies are the go-to option up north. The accompanying hot chocolate doesn't match it for quality.

I find a spot on the AON terrace, at the hospital end of the ground. The corners are cut off at an angle and plastered with large photos of the team in action against other Yorkshire clubs in League Two, who are now their rivals. To my right, today's rival sets of fans are standing next to each other on the Wetherby Road terrace, which was sold out when I tried to get a ticket for it. It has the feel of a proper old-school terrace. The far end of the ground could do with Arsenal's old North Bank mural to cover up renovations. Those in the main stands to my left are covering their eyes from the glare of the sun, which has now come out.

It's a tidy little ground, holding around 5,000, and has seen plenty of redevelopment over the last 20 years, so it's lost some of its charm and gained sponsors for almost every stand. There's also a loud tannoy, CCTV pointing at the crowd and lots of stewards, which are all deemed necessary at this level. A sign saying 'Please be aware of flying balls' seems somewhat unnecessary, as even Lewis was alive to this threat at Coggeshall.

The first ball does indeed go long, but is of no danger to any supporters, one of whom cries 'Get in!' as Leeds have scored in their game against Wolves. Other supporters are taking their seats in the main stand when a long throw from Barrow is flicked on for Jake Young to volley over. Soon after, Town have a chance when Levi Sutton cuts infield and gets away a shot that cannons off the bar. Some nearby Leeds supporters turn to look for a screen for a replay, but only find a scoreboard. 'Maybe not then. I'm not used to this level,' says one. Neither am I. Scoreboards, names on shirts and seeing a drinks break after very little exertion 20 minutes in are all things I'm unaccustomed to these days.

It's not long before the Leeds fans go for their own drinks break at the Black Sheep bar. This being league football, they can't return to the terrace with their drinks, but they don't miss much. Barrow don't live up to their Barrowcelona nickname, barely keeping possession as both sides hold their shape and chase things down. The only chance of note comes after Town's Josh Falkingham, who has a similar build and presence to Lee Cattermole in the centre of the park, concedes a Lee Cattermole-like free kick. Ben Whitfield's effort is saved by Mark Oxley at a comfortable height on the side of the wall he has covered.

My half-time consists mostly of listening to announcements on the tannoy and reading the programme. So, when early in the second half Falkingham lets fly from the edge of the box, I'm not surprised that a man with eight goals in 255 appearances has his effort palmed clear. Town force a couple of corners and Rory Feely goes down injured for the visitors. 'Get up you soft bastard' comes a shout from the crowd, before realising blood is gushing from a head wound. 'Fair dos,' he concedes.

Town look like they will concede when Josh Kay gets in round the back for Barrow. Oxley parries, but only as far as Billy Waters, who skies his effort with the goal gaping. Chances are few and far between; Harrogate's relegation rivals are all winning, so with a quarter of an hour remaining, the hosts need to make something happen. Falkingham earns a free kick in the centre circle and takes it quickly to Jack Muldoon. He slips in Matty Daly. Daly hits a rising drive that's too hot for Blues keeper Paul Farman, who can't keep it out.

Town lead 1-0 and look to add to that with Southampton loanee Kazeem Olaigbe causing trouble with his pace on the break. It's so much excitement that a teenage fan leaps the perimeter fence and enters the field of play. He's wrestled off the pitch by a steward, then gets chucked back over the fence and scarpers before the steward can climb back over himself. Several stewards turn up on the scene, but the attendance of 2,343, which has just been announced, isn't reduced by one.

Olaigbe is named the man of the match and continues to threaten down the left flank, but can't find a final ball. There has been just about enough entertainment towards the end of the game to justify the price of the tickets, but much like my hot chocolate, it has been bland, overpriced and with the tiniest amount of flavour at the end. I'm pleased to see Harrogate hold on for the win, though. After all their efforts to get promoted, I don't want to see them face a rapid return to the National League. They have lived the dream of many non-league sides in rising through the ranks. I may have missed that and be more interested in their neighbours, but Town may also be worth a revisit, despite it not quite finishing 0-0.

The long walk home gives me time to work out I've now been to 20 of the current 92 league grounds, with relegations and ground demolitions keeping that total down. I'm not moved to increase those figures based on today's experience. Neither will I be walking back from town again anytime soon. I trudge back across a golf course, looking even more dishevelled, carrying a shopping bag with my dinner in it and nearly falling into a stream.

Ground 86
Jan Breydel Stadium, Cercle Brugge

THE PLAN was simple; get the train to Brussels to see my mate Paul (around 30 grounds if we include ones he played at as a junior, where he proved to be the better of our early full-back pairing), watch Royale Union Saint-Gilloise on the Saturday and then the Tour of Flanders cycle race from a cobbled climb on Sunday. As you can see from the chapter heading, we didn't make it to *Les Unionistes'* art deco Joseph Marien Stadium with its open terraces and forest setting. USG's match ended up in the Sunday evening slot, when I was due to be getting a train home. I had a choice of watching Cercle Brugge, KV Oostende, Westerlo or Londerzeel. We plump for Cercle on the basis of the 3pm kick-off offering the best post-match drinking opportunities in the historic old town.

The move up north complicates my journey to Brussels, and it's the best part of two days until I meet Paul at Brussels Midi station. We're soon on another train to Bruges, looking less like a former full-back pairing and more like the characters from *In Bruges*, if in Paul's case Colin Farrell had let himself go, and was on the train beers. In my role as Brendan Gleeson's character, I play tour guide and brief Paul on what I've found out about Cercle. They are matricule number 12, which is a system the Belgian FA introduced in the 1920s to denote the order in which clubs were registered. It gives a relative sense of age and tradition and is something I rather like about Belgian football.

Cercle were league champions in 1910/11, 1926/27 and 1929/30, before falling under the shadow of city rivals and erstwhile groundsharers Club Brugge. A second Belgian Cup win in 1985 was the *Groen en Zwart*'s most recent high point, with time spent bouncing around between divisions. Financial difficulties threatened to overwhelm the club, until Russian oligarch and AS Monaco president Dimitry Rybolovlev bought them. It was a loanee from Monaco who scored the last-minute penalty to secure their most recent promotion back to the top flight in 2018.

Their opponents are another Flandrian side, KV Kortrijk. Matricule number 19 by virtue of taking the older number from a couple of mergers, with the current club formed in 1971. KVK only have a pair of second-tier titles and a Belgian Cup Final appearance to their name. They are owned by Cardiff City's controversial chairman Vincent Tan, mostly known for changing the Bluebirds' kit to a red one. He will be delighted that those are KVK's traditional colours.

I always like to pick a side whenever watching a random game as a neutral and I have a certain amount of sympathy for the underdog in any rivalry, with the exceptions of the north London derby and anything I compete against my younger brother in. Cercle are the underdogs in Bruges, although originally known as the snobs, with Club Brugge known as the farmers. They attracted more sympathy when I read the unveiling of a First World War memorial was marred by a biplane crash, and how a player's injury sustained in a 7-6 win to clinch their second title led to his untimely death and the subsequent death of their chairman, who caught pneumonia at the player's funeral. They had also lost two Belgian Cup finals to their city rivals.

We reach the Jan Breydel Stadium, where the vast expanse of concrete complements the rain clouds soaking us through. The ground is named after a 14th-century Flandrian hero of the Battle of the Golden Spurs. Paul tells me the renaming was to curry favour with the regional government. We find a bar over the road and walk in just in time to see Manchester City take the lead against Liverpool on TV, to the sound of 'oh fuck off' in a Scouse accent. We aren't the only Brits on the outskirts of Bruges for a mid-table Jupiler League clash.

A group of locals query why we're here to watch Cercle. We can't offer much of a justification and they suspect we are investors. One of the group announces they are a Club Brugge fan and won't be leaving the bar to watch them, suggesting the wrong club has the snob moniker. I say we're mainly here to watch De Ronde, which animates one of the old boys and leads to some confusion when they ask if I've ridden it. I have, but not with the pros and somehow I leave the impression that a large bloke who has been getting through several Brugse Zot beers may have mixed it up with your Boonens and your Cancellaras, and is now about to buy Cercle from a Russian oligarch.

We dash across the road, the downpour showing no sign of abating, and get a couple of Jupiler beers from a makeshift bar outside. We take our seats in the second tier of the west stand. The most expensive seats in the ground, but still only €30 and worth it for the roof. Paul nearly got tickets in among the ultras, which would've been fun, but wet in a coat with no remaining waterproof properties. The away fans are tucked away in the upper tier of the far corner of the ground, which looks less fun. Cercle only get 5,000 to 8,000 fans in this 29,000 all-seater, which played host to several Euro 2000 fixtures, so there are plenty of empty seats and most supporters are trying to huddle under any available roof cover. Cercle have plans to reduce the capacity once Club Brugge move into their new stadium and their fans are doing their best to create a bit of atmosphere.

Almost immediately, the team give the home support something to cheer when they win the ball back near KVK's penalty area. A lovely curling finish gives them the lead with only a couple of minutes gone. The players line up to kick off before the referee pauses. There was a hint of a foul and/or offside in the build-up. The referee's finger goes to his ear and VAR swiftly identifies the error and everyone is happy that justice has been done. If only. It works just as badly as it does everywhere else and we wait five minutes before the goal is ruled out for no apparent reason, to jeers from the crowd.

Paul is telling me how to re-waterproof my coat by putting it in the tumble dryer, when the hosts send the ball into the mixer, where Thibo Somers heads home; 1-0 to Cercle and this time it stands. The stadium announcer shouts out 'Thibo' and everyone responds 'Somers', apart from me and Paul, as we're none the wiser who anyone is.

Paul goes to replenish the beers, so I expect something to happen. Somers drags a shot wide before something remarkable does happen. KVK get out of their own half and test Radosław Majecki in the Cercle goal. It's my turn to leave my seat, as my bladder won't last until half-time.

I feel like I'm tempting fate. A cheer goes up as I descend into the concrete bowels of the stadium. It sounds like a free kick. I have enough time to pop to the gents given how long the ref has taken over things. I return in time to see Ayase Ueda dispatch a penalty kick for 2-0.

KVK's rangy Uruguayan target man, Felipe Avenatti, offers the visitors an outlet going forward. He spreads the ball out wide and stretches a leg to get on the end of the return ball, but can't test Majecki. Cercle carry their advantage into the interval. We follow the lead of the home fans down a narrow corridor to reach a lively bar. After Paul chastised me earlier for letting a barman know someone should be served before me (which isn't a thing in Belgium), I have no qualms about us taking advantage of an open goal to add to our tally.

The second half turns more into a pub chat. Paul compares his diplomatic work to me writing up a game. We both go into an event trying to figure out what's going on, often suitably lubricated, and then have to report back something that makes sense. I can report that Cercle's envoys are particularly active, putting together a package of nice moves, often going through Yann Gboho, who I identify as a key figure on the left wing. The moves come to nothing. Abu Francis has impressed Paul in the centre. My notes then descend into something about a Bacardi promotion, number 47 having a shot deflected wide even though there isn't a number 47 on the team sheet, and 'bad pads', which I decipher to be 'bad pass'. I'm not sure how bad a pass has to be to make it noteworthy, as there are a lot of them.

We need something to soak up the beer, so full time is as welcome as the Belgian staple of chips and mayonnaise, which we hide under a stairwell to eat. We dash over the road to a bar, where there's a cheerful post-game buzz, and struggle to concentrate on the Westerlo game on TV, only noting their stadium wouldn't look out of place in League Two.

In the Premier League of bars is the Bruges Beertje, a fine establishment with an extensive selection of beers and glasses to match, all crammed into a cosy, wood-panelled room. We somehow found a bus there, so we can lean on the bar and try more highly alcoholic beer. Just around the corner is the start village for De Ronde van Vlaanderen, the Tour of Flanders. I'm excited to see it, Paul less so. There's a free concert which will almost certainly mean bad Europop, so I use this to lure him out of the bar only to find it rained off. A sausage roll with curry sauce inside it is a decent consolation. It's not exactly world-class dining and is more the culinary equivalent of Arsenal's Rob Holding; it does the job. We agree the day itself more than did the job and we enjoyed the matchday experience.

To complete the weekend away, we're off to watch De Ronde. It's Sunday and we are hungover. For me, it's worth it as De Ronde is my favourite race, one of the five one-day monuments of cycling. It dates back to 1913 and features the *hellingen*, short yet brutal cobbled climbs that whittle down the peloton on the run in to the finish town of Oudenaarde. It may be less well known than races like the Tour de France, but it's one that diehard fans appreciate. I'm hardly a diehard cycling fan, as I toy with watching RSD Jette play amateur football, because their ground has a large crumbling terrace, with a small wooden grandstand. That feels too niche when the Belgian equivalent of the

Boat Race, Grand National and Wimbledon all rolled into one is on. So, we stick with the plan and head to Oudenaarde to see what's going on.

The train to Oudenaarde fills up with cycling fans from the Basque Country and with local supporters at every stop. Unlike football fans in Stone Island, the locals are attired in tiny cycling caps and little earrings. They are noisy, but that could just be because Dutch always sounds loud and angry. We're sat quietly and I struggle to articulate why I like this race so much. It's part the brutal nature of the course, part it's-lesser-known appeal, much like non-league football, and part how the drama unfolds a bit like a title race over the course of a football season. Plenty of different types of rider can win this race and today Mathieu van der Poel, Tadej Pogačar and local hero Wout van Aert are the big favourites. While they're pedalling their way from Bruges at the start of the 270km course, our heroic efforts making our way to the main square in a delicate state will go unnoticed. Paul is just glad to be getting some fresh air when we arrive and is impressed when the cycling fans carry away their empty beer cans.

We almost clatter into the team presentations for the women's race, only realising what it is when we spot the jersey of Norwegian champion Malin Eriksen, who I may have had to look up afterwards. No mistaking the race's permanent museum, with its old team cars out the front. We go into the exhibition and I admire the old bikes and enjoy a spin on a static bike with a VR headset covering the life of the inaugural winner, Paul Deman, including an impromptu, but crucially not vomit-inducing, sprint to evade the Kaiser's troops when he couriered messages in the First World War.

It's carnage as I emerge from the exhibition. Van Aert has crashed, to the dismay of his supporters gathered around the big screens. He has chased back on by the time the race comes past us. It's some spectacle as the riders fly through, on their way out to the *hellingen* backloaded into the last 100km. Paul is more interested in the convoy of support vehicles, including one doing a lunatic overtake on the bend in front of us. The thrill of the up-close experience is what makes any spectator sport special.

We then see women's world champion Annemiek van Vleuten, aided by her rainbow jersey, and last year's winner Lotte Kopecky, aided by a family who excitedly stop her in a side street for a photo and autograph. Paul suggests I ask for one as well, but I can't help think that seeing a hungover old bloke eating a hotdog with all the grace of Ed Miliband wouldn't be the ideal preparation for their 158km race that is about to set off.

Once that's off and running, we find a bar with a big screen to watch the men's race and more importantly work out our Belgian cycling names (first name of the winner in the year of your birth, surname combining favourite Belgian beer and first cobbled climb ridden) so I'm now Michel St Bernardus-Molenberg, and Paul is Michel Orval-Boterstraat. Mr Orval-Boterstraat asks if I wish I was riding. 'Absolutely not,' I reply, recoiling at the memories of being cold and shaken about, while not feeling in any state to ride at the moment.

TV coverage shows roadside fans have adorned barriers with a large quantity of women's underwear, so before my notes end up being another list of partly recalled observations we decide to take a stroll to the finish village, as getting out to a climb means I would miss my train.

149

There's pumping Europop and free cycling caps being handed out by a bank. The caps look suitably silly on us. Less silly is eating more frites and mayo as the women's race passes. We're on Kwaremont beer as the men's race encounters the hill of the same name.

The big favourites make their move and reel in the breakaway. Van Aert is dropped to the dismay of the locals. Pogačar needs to lose Van der Poel on one of the climbs, so he doesn't take him to the line and get outsprinted. The next time up the Kwaremont, he leaves Van der Poel standing. Not literally, he's no amateur like me, who took a breather on a flatter section of this climb, wondering when the battering from the cobbles would end. The men's race ends with Pogačar soloing to victory. We see Kopecky make the decisive move in the women's race at another bar playing Europop versions of Beatles hits near the station.

On the long journey home, I find out Cercle are the best counterpressing team in Europe, which explains how they strangled the life out of the contest. I learn that a challenge route to cycle all the cobbled climbs in the regions is ridiculously long and any future trips won't feature more cycling than football. I also note that I'm probably not doing a terrible job of ticking off most different types of Belgian beer. It's been a great trip, with a good mix of activities, but one that shows I'm not a serious enough groundhopper in allowing cycling to feature so prominently.

Revisit (Part One)

I CONCLUDE the 2022/23 season with some revisits. First up is Harrogate Railway Athletic's play-off semi-final against Horbury. This nearly ends up being a revisit to Harrogate Town, as rugby league Adam went to the wrong ground. He would have gone in if he had been allowed to buy a ticket on the gate, but was refused entry after he was suspected of being a Doncaster Rovers fan trying to infiltrate the home end. Rail's game was decided by two shots off the crossbar. The first is from Horbury's Gibril Bojang, with a perfectly struck free kick going in off the bar to make it 1-0. The second is Daniel Thirkell's second-half penalty to level it, which cannons off the crossbar, hits it again on the rebound and stays out. Later footage proves that the bloke who spent the rest of the half asking the linesman how much they were paying him owes the lino an apology. Town for their part drew 2-2 on the way to securing their place in League Two.

While I'm back in London for work, I hop on a ferry across the Thames and catch Fisher in the SCEFL Premier and see them net a 5-0 win over Sutton, which is a just reward for being up against an opposition centre-back strolling around in rolled-down socks. The Fish finish in lower mid-table alongside Bearsted and Punjab, who picked up a county cup. In Division One,

Staplehurst and Meridian VP also finished mid-table, while Larkfield & New Hythe lost their play-off semi-final on penalties, leaving me and maybe one or two of the Meridian ultras wondering if Frank would have saved them.

Another trip back down south gives me the opportunity to see Clapton Community and the men's first team at the Old Spotted Dog. The Tons had been crowned champions and were waiting on a ground grading decision to confirm promotion to step six. A lot of work had been put into the ground, with the pitch looking in great shape, barriers mended and a 100-seater stand fully open. The team did their bit for the title celebrations with a 5-1 win. Clapton's women didn't add to the club's trophy haul this time round, missing out on silverware in the final of the competition that Mark and I saw them in earlier in the season.

Revisiting the fortunes of the rest of teams I saw during the season, one of my other favourite sides, Hashtag United, were Isthmian North champions. Brentwood and East Thurrock finished well outside of the play-offs. Coggeshall were relegated after losing an Inter-Step Play-Off and Hullbridge were also relegated after finishing bottom. Hashtag will meet Margate in the Isthmian Premier next season, as they stayed up, giving me a possible return trip to the seaside. Brightlingsea won't be there, as they were relegated alongside Corinthian-Casuals.

In the Essex Senior League, Redbridge finished as runners-up and won their Inter-Step Play-Off, which was pleasing to hear about after a fine evening there. They also enjoyed a league cup win. Athletic Newham were sixth, which isn't enough for a play-off place in step five, and Stanway were mid-table.

Also in step five, St Panteleimon may have beaten Leighton Town, but it was Town who were crowned champions in the Spartan South Midland, while the Saints missed out on the Inter-Step Play-Off place, finishing in sixth. Harwich made the play-offs in the Eastern Counties Division One North, a step below, but lost in the final. Both are a long way off European football, unlike Cercle Brugge, who just missed out on a Conference League spot after reaching the convoluted play-off system to fight it out for Belgium's qualification places.

My summer involves trips to Headingley for rugby league and cricket, but I can't find evidence of any football matches taking place on either pitch to justify including this as part of my total. The rugby ground was interesting to see how a League One stadium might look without the requirement for being all-seater. The new south stand is a single-tier cantilevered affair with a large terrace at the front generating a fair bit of atmosphere.

It's the atmosphere of non-league football I most look forward to and the heady aroma of beer and Deep Heat mark a welcome return to Harrogate Railway Athletic at the start of the new season. I take my dad with me to watch a 2-1 home win, with Rail winger Luca Bolini the standout player – so much so that I feel I ought to commit that to print on the off chance he makes it big and I can show off my ability as a scout. Only 44 games to go as someone remarks on the way out with evident enthusiasm for the new season. Only 14 more grounds to go to reach my target, with a few extra to make sure it counts in the eyes of those who enforce a particular set of unwritten rules. Nothing could stop me, apart from a lot of 0-0s or postponements.

Ground 87

Manse Lane, Knaresborough Town

THE CRICKET season hasn't quite finished, and the day starts with me looking forward to a languid spell fielding in some rolling Yorkshire countryside, with a brief flurry of excitement when it's my turn to bat. The weather is better than forecast and the skipper picks up me and Chris, who is also there to make up the numbers. The skipper explains his selection dilemma, in that he is struggling to find 11 players. One of the younger lads is AWOL after a night out, and we would press the 87-year-old groundsman into action. This is all rendered academic when the heavens open.

Our match is off, which presents the skipper with a chance to watch his team, Harrogate Town, away to Doncaster Rovers (and make it 73 grounds visited, more if we include other sports, which we don't). I know local side Knaresborough Town are at home to Frickley Athletic in the FA Cup extra-preliminary round. Either way, I can bag a new ground and get up and running for the season. I perhaps should have taken the opportunity to go to the one furthest away, theoretically offering the higher standard of football, but £20 to watch League Two football in a half-filled bowl that could easily be mistaken for St Mary's or any other identikit stadium didn't do it for me. The lure of the FA Cup is too strong, so Chris and I decide to head to Manse Lane for a fraction of the cost.

We park on a trading estate near the ground, which is a far cry from a rural village cricket ground. The pitch is visible through metal railings, but this isn't such a popular cup tie we would need to peer through them from the outside. We pay our £5 entry fee, pass through the turnstile and find a spot on the small covered terrace set to one side of the goal.

The ground is a basic affair, but meets all of the grading requirements for step five; something I had read up on during the off-season to check whether Clapton Community were likely to have any issues and to see if there were any nonsensical rules. The turnstile we go through is one of a pair, which is double the number needed. The terrace goes towards the required total of cover for 200 people, with the familiar-looking 73-seater prefab stand on the far touchline making up the rest. There are hardstanding concrete paths on three and a half sides of the ground, with one half of the near touchline blocked off by a light industrial building, but this is fine since three sides are all that's required.

I assume the floodlights have the requisite amount of lux, and will probably come into play as it is overcast and threatening more rain. Chris and I express our disappointment at missing out on the cricket. Chris being a Spurs fan (and still a season ticket holder, with 40 grounds visited to his name) no doubt wants to avoid thinking about the football season as long as possible, with the Harry Kane transfer saga rumbling on, and being less keen than I am to see how 'Spursy' Spurs can be. Our fielding reactions are put to the test as the subs take potshots, presumably at the goal, but equally plausibly at someone's car parked behind the goal.

Chris notes that the grass is looking long, which isn't a ground grading requirement. I've not run through these requirements to him in full, in case he thinks I'm far weirder than he's been able to establish from a couple of games of cricket. It would certainly make for a slow outfield and as we contemplate what that will mean for the game, a groundsman remarks that he only cut it on Thursday, but there's been that much rain.

The PA system comes to life, a requirement that kicks in at this level, and I was pleased to note there was a volunteer using it, so I could hear the team news. More importantly, I found out which colours the teams are in, since both are in change strips, Frickley in mint green and Knaresborough at the behest of matchday sponsors in yellow, which Chris cites as another example of money ruining the game.

Since Knaresborough are the more local side, we are nominally supporting them. The club hadn't come to my attention until moving into the area, with the annual bed race being the town's main sporting claim to fame. The Boro have mostly played in regional leagues, of which the West Yorkshire League sounded the most impressive. Under the newer pyramid structure, they have been at step five NCEL Premier and able to enter the FA Cup since 2017/18; their best performance was in 2018/19 when they reached the second qualifying round.

Frickley had a more impressive history, reaching the highest level of non-league and the fabled third round of the cup in the mid-1980s, but are now at the same level as Boro. This accounts for their more impressive ground, which I had noted may be worth a visit for its characterful 490-seater grandstand and a vista of a landscaped former spoil heap.

We are still talking about money spoiling the game when the first incident of note happens only two minutes in. The hosts are awarded a soft penalty that neither Chris nor I can say 'I've seen them given' about, as the merest hint of a push is enough for the referee to point to the spot. Danny Edwards steps up and makes no mistake, sending the keeper the wrong way to put Boro 1-0 up.

Boro have a chance to double their lead soon after, as the ball is pulled back to Ewan Gregson. He cuts inside but has his effort blocked. Frickley are soon down the other end and have the ball in the net. The linesman's flag goes up to the relief of the home supporters, but it takes a while for the visiting fans congregated on the far side to notice. They are gathered in line with the penalty box, avoiding any cross-hatching that should be painted in front of the main stand as per the regulations to stop people blocking the view.

Frickley block a chance in their box and a defender gets a boot to the head for his troubles, so it's a free kick to the visitors. They clear, but lose possession and Boro send the ball back into the area. It loops up to Danny Edwards on the edge of the box and he sends a Trevor Sinclair-esque overhead kick beyond the stricken Callum Bradbury for 2-0. 'I hope someone had a camera on that,' remarks a fan; it was the sort of finish that deserves to end up on a compilation of the season's cup highlights.

Only 11 minutes gone and some Frickley subs are sent to warm up. Chris notices they are in builders' high-vis vests rather than training bibs, which seems like classic non-league improvisation until I realise they are branded with Toolstation logos – the sponsors of the NCEL. From the matchday programme it's also possible to read about the visiting team in their own words, which reveals the players' nicknames. The Hawk gets on the ball as Boro lose possession from their own corner. His attempted chip doesn't soar into the net and is as wide of the mark as some of the other nicknames. Lewis 'El Binno' Binns, Michael 'The Clash' Jones and Jack 'Tailor-made' Burton being the standout ones when Binnsy, Jonesy and Burtony would be the more usual choices.

It's a typical hard-fought battle, as Frickley look for a way back into the tie and Boro look to kill it. Jack Emmett nearly does so as he drills a shot low from the edge of the box. It looks to be going well wide, but Bradbury is sufficiently concerned to be down low to make sure of it. Only then do we realise the Perspex in the side of the stand has altered our perspective of the potential chance.

Half-time presents us with the opportunity to check on some more of the facilities required under the ground grading regulations. I assume the changing rooms are the requisite dimensions and don't feel the need to slip down the walkway among the players to check. Instead, we head for the tea bar for a warming hot chocolate, as summer doesn't appear to have made it this far north. With no need to use the toilet facilities we return to our spot on the terrace before a downpour and with it an influx of away fans to watch from the end they are attacking.

The first action of note in the second half is at the other end, as Danny Edwards looks to bag a hat-trick with a shot that skids off the surface. Soon after, it's a case of handbags when there's an altercation over a throw-in, directly in front of the dugouts (meeting the requirement of providing cover for a minimum of eight persons). The away fans aren't happy, while I have to admit 'I did not see the incident', adopting a suitable Arsène Wenger accent. The yellow card dished out to the Boro player adds to their feeling of injustice, before they calm down enough to go back to a discussion about rhubarb growing, which results in more complaints, this time about how stringy it is.

Neither side is stringing together too many passes, as Frickley huff and puff to find a way back into the tie. Boro clear long and Bradbury is caught in two minds as the ball lands just outside of his penalty area. Cameron Bedford nips in, takes it past the keeper and slots into the empty net to make it 3-0. Edwards has a chance to claim the match ball when the hosts are awarded another contested penalty to give them a flattering 4-0 lead soon after. Bradbury makes amends for his earlier error and pulls off a save similar to Schmeichel denying Bergkamp in the 1999 FA Cup semi-final.

Frickley look to mount an improbable comeback and bring on substitutes Joshua 'The Haigh-maker' Haigh and Rieves 'Boocock of the North' Boocock, who combine as Boocock taps in the rebound after Haigh's effort is parried. The Boro keeper is furious to have lost his clean sheet. 'Shut up, you spoilt brat,' instructs a visiting fan.

A couple of innocuous decisions go against the visitors to halt any outside chance of a comeback, which prompts another away fan to rant about the female assistant ref. 'She really ought to be in the kitchen,' he catches himself saying in front of a couple of female fans, before adding, 'and that other one needs to go back to primary school', by way of some sort of balance. His side can only offer an over-hit cross and Boro take their time over the goal kick. 'They'll have played the next round by the time you kick it,' cries the ever-frustrated fan.

There's time for little else and Boro progress to the next round. We leave as a crowd of 268 is announced. No minimum capacity is required at this level and that figure is well short of the capacity required a couple of levels up. The Harrogate match is about to enter 14 minutes of added time, which means I'm almost home before it finishes and am glad to have avoided that nonsense, which is far worse than anything in the ground grading regulations. I'm glad to have caught a bit of the magic of the cup, which is essentially the magic of most non-league games, only brought to a wider audience.

I'm not in the crowd for Boro's tie in the next round, at home to Dunston UTS, where they exit to the Gateshead-based club who garnered some media attention when a stolen hearse was driven on to their pitch and spun round the centre circle during a pre-season friendly. This puts an end to any notion of following the winner of each tie until I reach the final.

On my way to completing all the grounds with a view of Canary Wharf, at the start of my groundhopping journey.

Old turnstiles at Hertford. No more redundant than the new ones on my trip to see St Panteleimon.

Sunset at my first groundhopping weekend and the start of a collection of photos of grounds at sunset more comprehensive than my programme collection.

The Terry Mac is widely regarded as one of the worst grounds in London. Did I find any redeeming features?

I took photographer friend Lew to his first ever game. He failed to capture the ground at Coggeshall, preferring the action on the pitch and any outbreaks of handbags. (Credit: Lewis Walsh)

What's that I can see over the hedge at Calverley's Victoria park? A fenced off pitch? A Saturday game? It must be senior football and count towards my total number of grounds, surely?

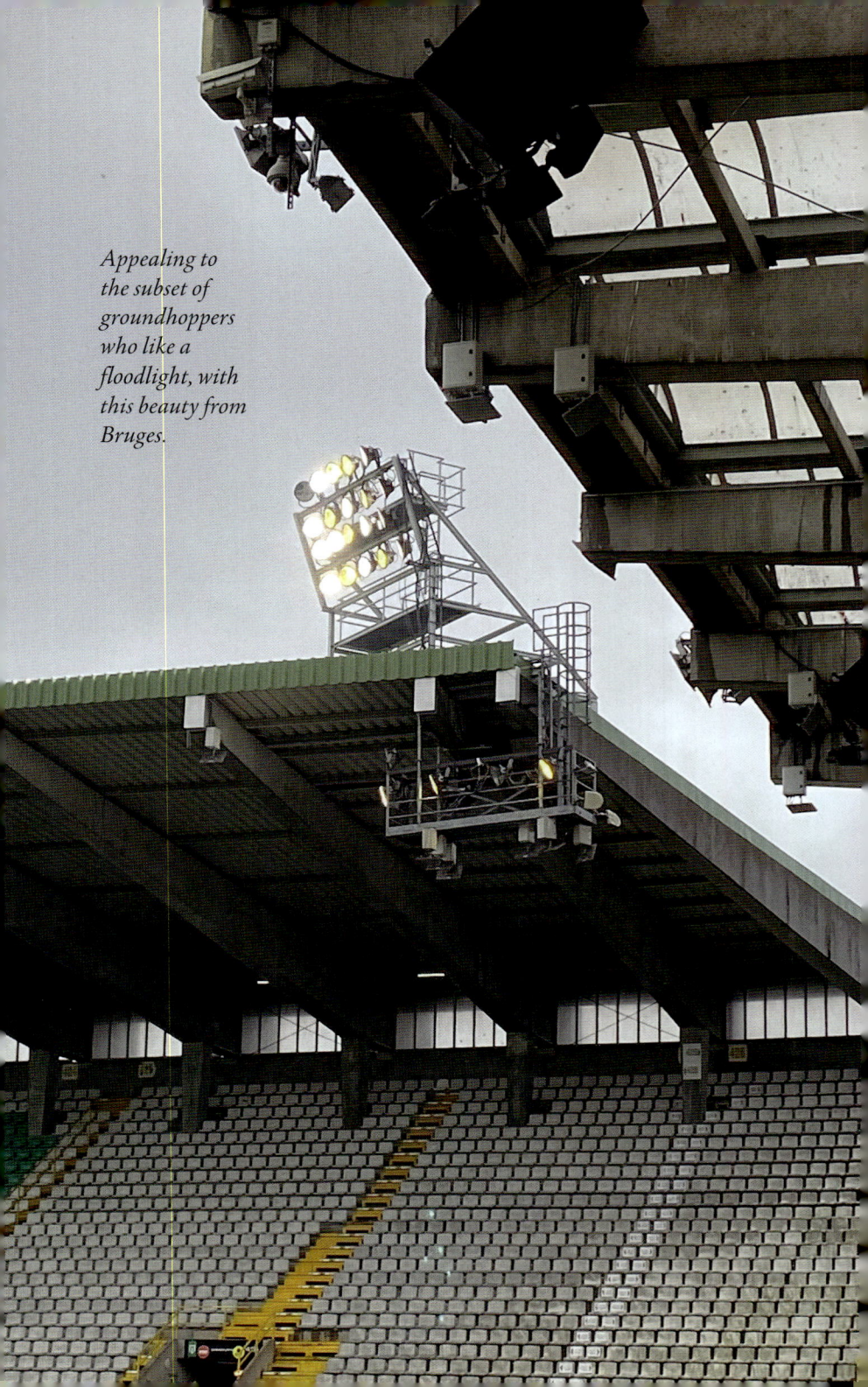

Appealing to the subset of groundhoppers who like a floodlight, with this beauty from Bruges.

A classic tourist's photo from the lovely seaside resort of Whitstable, if you're a groundhopper.

Not watching football in Scotland. (Credit: Trevor Coughlan)

The stand at Albion Rovers looked great with features like these old wooden seats, which I believe were taken from Cathkin Park.

Photographer friend Adam joined me at Emley and he captured these. I photographed their pie. Their succulent steak pie. (Credit: Adam Nash)

My kids wanted to feature in the book, without going to any games. Here they are deciding whether to watch Bradford (Park Avenue) try to end a seven-game losing streak.

Ground 88

Office Interiors Stadium, Silsden AFC

MY NEXT match takes me on a journey to the almost equally romantic destination of Silsden, even if Office Interiors doesn't conjure up such an image, nor does the town's claim to fame as being home to the world's largest onion. Sils' ground on Keighley Road is nestled in the Wharf valley and surrounded by hills. The drive there sees the setting sun make a first appearance of the day and lights up views over lush countryside - the kind that would have most Yorkshire folk make a remark about it being God's Own County. I drop into the town, replete with soot-blackened Victorian buildings, before parking on an out-of-town trading estate.

I attempt a brisk walk since I'm running late, but I'm aching from the previous evening's five-a-side with a group of Chris's friends. After injuring my hand the previous week, putting an end to my cricket season, I made a rare foray outfield. Let the record show I scored twice, including an equaliser, which, since someone had invoked the 'next goal wins' rule, was also the winner, so might as well be a hat-trick. I look longingly at the manicured cricket pitch adjoining the football ground, part of which is being used for youth football while the light holds. I pay my £6 entry and another £2 for a programme and aim to have a quick look round the ground.

I'm keen to get a few pictures before the sun sets, and embark on a lap of the perimeter, hoping to find a water cooler, a photocopier with some copies of the team sheet left on it and see what the hot-desking arrangements in the stand are like. The main stand is 'The Simply Ventilation Stand'. I can confirm it's chilly, but doesn't have someone wandering around asking if anyone has called facilities to turn the heating up. It's a new build, but with an elevated front deck and a bigger capacity than the usual prefabs. I pass a small bar and a covered terrace behind the goal containing a handful of teenage home fans.

I'm stopped in my tracks when there's a minute's applause for Eddie Sessford, a committee man of 20 years who performed many roles within the club, but had sadly passed away. The volunteers who keep the game going are worthy of applause at the best of times, so some discomfort in my bad hand is the least I can do. I take the concrete path on a loop around the dugouts and get a few photos from this side of the ground before the match gets under way. I take up position leaning on the fence alongside the away dugout, hoping for some quotable managerial gems, but expecting extensive swearing.

It's a top-of-the-table clash in the NCEL Premier, albeit with only half a dozen games played. This is the highest level Silsden have competed at, assuming I've not misjudged where old regional leagues were compared to the current pyramid. This seems to be supported by the fact they were forced to groundshare at the Keighley Cougars rugby ground when they started at step six in the new structure, with the redevelopment of Keighley Road, home since 1904, taking place in 2010.

Opponents Barton Town hail from Humberside and their ground has the arguably less scenic view of the Humber Bridge. They may have competed at a higher level in their previous incarnations, winning the Lincolnshire League, which may or may not be impressive. The Swans look to impress themselves on the game early on with a long throw. Sils keeper Kyle Trennery claims it and directs a skidding low kick direct to his full-back's feet. He's closed down straight away and while I might have thought things were fast-paced in our five-a-side, it's clear this is several notches up from that.

A penalty shout goes unanswered, long clearances are momentarily lost in the bright floodlights, a flailing elbow goes unpunished. There are openings at both ends and I'm unconcerned about the prospect of a 0-0. The Barton subs are bibless and can't warm up without them, so a young sub is dispatched to the dressing room to fetch them. His manager's mood isn't improved when a Silsden cross reaches Isaac Baldwin, who catches the ball sweetly and it nestles in the bottom corner. One of the subs then doesn't have a shirt on when needed.

Silsden continue to get forward as Adam Clayton goes on a barrelling run, like one of mine at five-a-side, the only difference being I couldn't find the pass I was looking for. A cute pass finds Kayle Price, who hits it first time with his left foot to make it 2-0. Barton don't give up and Scott Matthews is charging up and down the touchline in front of me as play swings back and forth. Barton try to bundle in a cross. Their keeper slices his kick and Silsden have a potshot hit the bar, before an injury halts play.

Instead of organising their defence against the pace of Price, the Barton bench decide to moan about the female referee giving a free kick. One of them mutters 'daft bint'. I can't decide whether I should register my disapproval when the likely insult for a male referee would be worse. Justice is meted out when Barton give the ball away near their own area and Luke Brooksbank squares it to Price to sweep home for 3-0. The Barton manager walks off to the dressing room.

It's been more even than the score suggests, but in first-half stoppage time Price turns sharply and rockets one into the top corner for his hat-trick to make it 4-0 and put pay to any notion of a comeback. The whistle blows and I head toward the changing rooms in the modern sandstone clubhouse to listen out for the manager's reaction. All I hear are the Barton subs remarking that the quality of distribution between the two keepers has been the big difference. I note Trennery has played at a higher level with Guiseley and Farsley, and wonder what he's done wrong to have fallen this far. I'm also left wondering why there is such a sizeable gap between the goal and perimeter fence at this end.

The bar isn't serving food or hot drinks, just beer and Scotland v England on TV. I check out the smaller bar area next to the main stand instead. It's nice to see three generations of the same family working it, and the eldest instructing the youngest to put a couple of large scoops into my hot chocolate. I foolishly don't take up a position behind the netting protecting the bar from any stray clearances and instead go for where Trennery is aiming his kicks out to Brooksbank. Thankfully, his accurate kicking continues, and the ball evades me much like it did for a large part of five-a-side.

There's little chance of a 7-7 draw here, although Silsden may get close to one side of the equation. Price continues to menace the Swans defence and looks to play in team-mates. Their shooting is as all over the place as the wind swirls around the valley. Very little is visible in the way of views of the surrounding hills now, just a few dotted lights giving away their elevation. 'You should see it when it's all covered in snow,' remarks one bloke to his companion.

The backdrop pales into insignificance as chances come and go, players get stuck in and eventually Casey Stewart buries one, after letting fly from the edge of the box to make it 5-0. Silsden players celebrate, and before long the crowd of 224 can disperse into the night, the majority pleased with the result. I'm pleased to have seen a game in these parts, and there are a few other places known for their setting which might tempt me. I feel like the setting alone isn't enough and after seeing footage of Halesowen taking 800 away fans to a derby game in step three and celebrating a late winner, it has me looking further afield for fixtures.

Ground 89

Alfred Hall Memorial Ground, Eynesbury Rovers

IN CONTRAST to my last match, I find myself in the barren flatlands of Cambridgeshire or, as locals still wedded to pre-1974 boundaries prefer, Huntingdonshire. I'm here for a match in the United Counties League at step five in its Premier Division South, partly to try and cover some of the Midlands – the UCL covers bits of Derbyshire, Nottinghamshire and Leicestershire among various other counties – but in larger part due to its proximity to my parents' house, where I'm staying while I'm travelling around for work.

I take my dad, and on the short drive across town he gives me a potted history of the area where they moved to long after I left home. I assumed Eynesbury was a suburb of St Neots, located as it is down a long road of light industrial units and 1960s housing. Eynesbury is the older settlement, appearing in the *Domesday Book*, while St Neots grew up later around a priory, which contained relics of Saint Neot brought from Cornwall. The only other thing I knew about Eynesbury was that it was the 18th-century home of the Eynesbury Giant, James Toller, who stood at 8ft tall. On a visit to the local museum, I spent an inordinate amount of time explaining to my son that he wasn't like a giant in a fairy tale, he wasn't scary and died some time ago. I hoped Rovers would have a tall striker to make this reference useful.

Back on the topic of football, and I note that the Huntingdonshire Senior Cup must be one of the weakest county competitions in the country, with its most successful sides residing at step five. My dad confirms that there are usually only eight entrants, two of whom are playing tonight, with Godmanchester Rovers the visitors, making it a derby of sorts. Eynesbury are 16-time winners of the cup, while Goddy only have two wins to their name. In the league right now, it is Goddy who have the upper hand, with Eynesbury languishing towards the bottom of the table.

We pull into the ground and follow the bumpy track round the back of the goal and find a space between the five-a-side pitch and some scaffolding covered in tarp, which looks like a temporary stage set up for a music festival, but on closer inspection is one of the stands. We approach a wooden hut and pay our entrance fee. I ask a volunteer if there is a programme. He tells me it's online and laments the passing of printed programmes. We all acknowledge that's the way things are going with printing costs, uncertainty over how many to print and the shift to online programmes. 'Most of them used to just end up all over the dressing-room floor,' concedes the volunteer.

I never do find the programme online, but we do find the snack bar. We pass an on-site boxing academy and an open gate on to fields where one of the teams is warming up, before we enter a squat, windowless building, dating from the late 1970s when most of the current ground was rebuilt. An angry game of darts is taking place, with the participants taking a run-up. I place my usual order and they take no chances of being found wanting under the Trade Descriptions Act, as the hot chocolate is scorching even by non-league standards. A cup holder doesn't stop me juggling it between hands. With the angry darts game continuing and some kids kicking a ball about, I have a quick look at the memorabilia before suggesting we go outside if my dad doesn't fancy a pint.

We take a seat in the adjoining stand dating from the same period. It was a grainy photo of this that convinced me to come here, as it made a change from the prefabs. On closer inspection, it was a lot of breeze block and plywood. The overhanging roof edge with the team name in neat lettering facing the pitch is more patched together from my vantage point, where I'm sat on a bench with a part of a plastic seat bolted on. The chicken wire tunnel completes the look, as Black Cat Radio plays over the tannoy. The pitch is looking pristine. 'C'mon Eynesbury, don't be shit,' shouts a fan as the players come out, suggesting their team won't do the surface justice. I try to see what gloves the goalkeepers are wearing, having just invested in a pair myself for five-a-side. I always used to buy whatever David Seaman wore, but without that reference point I had no idea what I was doing and it came down to a choice between a cheap and cheerful version of the big-palmed, padded classic modelled by the visiting keeper or the fancy, snug-fitting stealthy black pair being worn by the home keeper. I went for the fancier pair as there was more grip when I started lobbing a ball to myself in the shop, to the bemusement of staff. The classic style felt more like giant foam hands in comparison.

It's unlikely this will be the difference between the two teams, but if fans can get excited about boots and jerseys, then why not wax lyrical about my new gloves. My dad didn't share that excitement and I don't think he'll become one of the many shirt collectors out there these days either. Identifying the teams playing today from their shirt colours, a kid in a group sat in front asks his mum, 'We want the reds to win today, don't we?' referring to Godmanchester, who they are cheering on, as an older son is lining up for them at full-back.

The full-back has a comfortable start, mainly as Eynesbury struggle to create anything and the first meaningful chances clear the protective netting behind the goal. The game falls into a pattern of a couple of neat passes, followed by a tackle and hoof clear. Twenty minutes in and the kids in front ask if they can play on the five-a-side pitch. I wish I had brought my new gloves with me and I could have asked my dad if I could play as well, since it would be more entertaining than what we are watching. That is, until one of the managers does some keepie-uppies with a stray clearance while his hands remain firmly rooted in his coat pockets.

Drama is never far away in any game, and a boy runs into the stands and announces, 'Your boy has just broke his leg.' One of the mums hurries away to the other pitch. On the main pitch Eynesbury play a through ball to Rhys Thorpe, who has time to sort his feet and get the ball on to his left. He strikes it sweetly, and his shot clips the post and goes in to make it 1-0. The mum returns having missed the goal, confirming it wasn't a broken leg after all.

That is pretty much it for the half. The teams traipse off, but the kids have the added thrill of high-fiving them as they do so. It's notable that quite a few players ignore them, which disappoints the adults more than the kids, especially as one of them calls the opposition 'fucking dirty cunts' within earshot. The kids are oblivious and head on to the pitch for an impromptu penalty shoot-out.

When the teams return for the second half, there's a hopeful cry of 'Go on, Goddy' as if they have a deity on the bench who will change their fortunes. A trainer gets the visiting team to move in mysterious ways around some cones to warm up before they get under way. Several minutes after the restart, a player emerges from the tunnel and rejoins the game. He hasn't missed anything. When Godmanchester have a shot that bobbles wide, me and my dad can't agree whether it was their number eight or number 11, we are that taken aback by something happening that I might need to write about. It's not dissimilar to my mum waking up on the sofa and asking what's happened in a programme she's been watching. I ask my dad what she would be watching now. 'Quiz shows, probably,' he replies, which is just about worse than what we are watching.

Eynesbury keeper Reece Lewis sends a long kick asking a question of his opposite number. It bounces awkwardly between the edge of the box and the onrushing Thorpe, who finds himself and the ball beyond the visiting stopper, holds off a defender and slots home for 2-0. 'I'm cheering the blues now,' says one of the kids in front.

He then rounds on the full-back, saying he's not very good and he should do what Messi does. The full-back's mum suggests that if he could do that he wouldn't be playing here. They return to a conversation about a recent drunken night out, while other fans are mostly on their phones. I dutifully note a chance for a hat-trick sliced over when the flag was up, a shot dragged wide, Godmanchester appealing for handball and the Eynesbury number six and number eight in the actual positions that modern tacticos describe them as. It's not enough to stir me from my apathy to complain to my dad that number six should always be centre-half. I have to admire tacticos and cub reporters sitting through this sort of dross and coming up with any meaningful analysis.

My dad asks what I will write about for this one. I shrug, knowing most of my notes are fairly pointless observations on the 60s low-rise flats and coppiced trees surrounding the ground, and just how bad the hot chocolate was. Luckily, a bloke shouts out 'David Shin-ola' when there's a miskick that sends the ball into a blind spot behind the breeze block side wall of the stand. With that, the full-time whistle blows. We exit the ground and I manage to make a wrong turn, which does at least take us through the older part of Eynesbury. I haven't been here before. There's St Mary's Church (one of three closely located to one another apparently) where James Toller is buried inside. It's a day of very minor discoveries and an unremarkable game of football - the sort of game that might make me question if I'm really that bothered about reaching 100 grounds.

The following weekend, I visit the village I grew up in, Calverley. I live nearby and the kids are keen to see the set of swings I got stuck in as a chubby toddler, which Granny has told them about with some glee. I'm surprised to see a fenced-off pitch in Victoria Park, which screams senior ground at me. It surrounds the same pitch where I saw my first-ever match. So, does that mean I'm up to ground number 90, or does it just cancel out Tottenham's new ground? There's a game going on, with a crowd gathered on both touchlines near the managers and substitutes. Someone in club colours is running the line.

Before I can establish the game's full senior credentials, I need to show the kids my old primary school and the playground where we played the classic game of Leeds United fans vs Bradford City fans in an unbalanced match of 30 vs 3. It's then time for the playground and Mrs C sees me looking longingly at the clubhouse, a mock-Tudor cricket pavilion, serving beer in plastic cups. 'Go on then,' she says. I go into the smart bar, *Soccer Saturday* on TV, and order an ale from the Ilkley brewery and take it over to a spot by the corner flag.

The team in yellow, later identified as Kellingley Welfare, have lined up a free kick at the other end. It's curled around the wall and beats the keeper, so it won't be a 0-0 I see, regardless of what the actual score is. Calverley United come up the other end and get at the left-back. There's a trip. The referee points to the spot and a home supporter mocks, 'That's your fault 12, rubbish 12.' The spot kick is dispatched for 1-1. Someone walking past asks me what the score is. 'One-one since I've been stood here, but no idea what the actual score is,' I reply. I've no idea what prompts shouts of 'Kick the ball, you fucking nobhead', and 'Get up, ya tramp', but it suggests there's been a certain amount of niggle, with a player responding to the latter with 'Yeah good one' and a sarcastic applause.

Calverley attack down the right, but the final whistle blows and a group of fans celebrate. 'Top of the league and you're fucking shit' another group sings. I've seen about 20 minutes' play before the home team are taking the nets down, bringing in the corner flags and trudging over to the pavilion. In that time, I've enjoyed a decent beer in the late-autumn sun, seen two goals, and felt the competitive instincts of both players and fans. The latter outnumbered those at Eynesbury and really opened my eyes to an even lower level of football than I've been going to.

It turns out I was watching a game in Division Two of the West Yorkshire league, the 13th tier of English football (step nine of non-league, if such a thing exists), in Calverley's first season at this level. The Premier Division feeds into the NCEL and was a path trodden by some current clubs. The depth of the pyramid would continue to amaze me, and there would always be surprising football experiences out there. I'm not minded to look into other grounds at this level or go out of my way to watch it, but it's a more typical scene of English life than cricket on a village green and both are worth slowing down to watch for a few moments. I don't feel the need to record it, especially as this level isn't on Futbology. Of course, if someone adds the league on to the app, that's another matter.

Ground 90
Sandygate, Hallam FC

I TAKE another step back in time as I visit the oldest ground in the world for a must-do tick. The ground dates to 1804 when Hallam Cricket Club started playing on an adjacent field. There's still a cricket ground, but no grand old pavilion, just a brick building with metal shutters and several shipping containers for equipment. The outfield overlaps with the football pitch, with a temporary fence separating the two. The football club came later, but since Hallam were formed in 1860 it makes them the second-oldest club in the world. It's inevitable their first fixture was against the oldest club, Sheffield FC, in a 16-a-side match.

Hallam founder John Charles Shaw was instrumental in agreeing nationally accepted rules with the FA, where the early editions didn't define the size of teams. One notable early rule was that teams should change ends after each goal scored, which makes sense on a sloping pitch like the one at Hallam. Once rules were codified, Hallam won the first-ever football competition, the Youden Cup of 1867. They remained resolutely amateur and joined the Hallamshire League. Indeed, tonight's fixture was in the Sheffield and Hallamshire Senior Cup, the fifth-oldest surviving cup competition, a title Hallam have claimed on four occasions, with the big Sheffield sides dominating.

No tales of dominating amateur competitions either, as the Countrymen have a relatively modest honours board. Their claim to oldest ground, unlike similar ones for oldest pub, is uncontested. Northwich Victoria once laid claim to the Drill Field as being the longest continuously used ground, but it was demolished in 2002. A nomadic period for Hallam in the 1930s and 40s may have allowed other claims to arise. Their landlord at the time decided to lease the ground to other teams as Hallam supporters weren't providing enough bar takings, which is ironic since every other person in the ground tonight appears to be holding a pint.

Further landlord issues in the 1980s nearly put an end to Sandygate's long run, as protracted negotiations to extend the lease meant Hallam were unable to commit to ground improvements required under the newly formed NCEL. This was resolved, and floodlights were added in 1992 and further improvements made in 2012. The team remained in the NCEL and are well established in the Premier Division at step five.

All of this gave me reason to make a detour on another drive south to stay at my parents' ahead of meetings in London the next day. It didn't matter that it was a county cup fixture against Worsbrough Bridge Athletic from the division below. The visitors may have been in their centenary year, but it was Hallam, Sandygate and their long history that drew me through endless Sheffield suburbs. I pass Hillsborough, which looms large and, in an era of modern concrete bowls, has more charm than I thought possible when I visited in the early 90s. The satnav sends me on to some charming, but clutch-burning, country lanes, before dropping me into a warren of 1930s semis near the ground. I pass the ground, and go so far beyond it looking for somewhere to park that I have to turn the satnav back on again.

Eventually, I pull up round the back of the ground. There's no entrance, but someone is having difficulty padlocking a set of gates. I ask if there's a way in. He says yes, so long as I go and pay, and he lets me in. I approach the turnstile from the wrong direction and there's a queue, so I ask a programme vendor if I can pay and get a programme. I can and thinking I've saved everyone involved any hassle, I create a queue for programmes while the lad tries to find the right thing to put into his device.

Once that's sorted, I can take in the scene. The slope from the Sandygate Road end down to the other goal is most striking. Immediately you can tell the topography hasn't changed and similar to Harwich you can get a feel for a bygone age, plus I like the random factor a sloping pitch adds to a game. The modern buildings are congregated on the one side and I make use of the refreshment kiosk.

I'm in the mood for pie, mushy peas and gravy, but I'm shocked to find only Cornish pasties are available, albeit with mushy peas and gravy. I know I'm further south, but this seems ridiculous. The programme confirms that hot pork pies aren't really a thing in these parts, with a fan's review of an away game at Silsden remarking that they were on offer and are a divisive topic among Hallam fans. I go for a plain pasty and a hot chocolate that's notable for actually tasting of chocolate. The volunteers are all clad in T-shirts referencing the club's history, which is clearly a matter of pride even if they source their pies from outside of Yorkshire.

I take a seat in the main stand, at the end furthest downhill, which seems like the equivalent of a seat right on halfway at a more level ground. The announcer reads out the teams and I learn Worsbrough is pronounced Wzzbruh, before he exclaims, 'Let's get ready to go at the world's oldest ground.' Hallam are looking ready to put their lower-division rivals to the sword as they are shooting downhill in the first half. Wzzbruh make a swashbuckling start and battle uphill, but the ball rolls tamely to Hallam keeper Jordan Douglas. Wzzbruh retreat to the edge of their own box and Douglas clears to his opposite number, Brett Souter. Wzzbruh decide to play out from the back and start battling uphill again and win a throw-in. 'He's done fuck all there, good stuff' comes a quiet voice over the tannoy, which hasn't been muted.

It looks like the grass hasn't been cut as short in the bottom corner, so the ball holds up. There are the first signs of the surface cutting up, the non-league equivalent of Japanese micro-seasons tracking slight changes in the natural world. It's the start of the coat-wearing season at games. Wzzbruh themselves are straitjacketed and as soon as they lose possession in midfield, they are under pressure. A ball into the box finds Scott Ruthven, on as an early substitute, who loops a header over Souter to give Hallam the lead, as the man he replaced leaves the ground on crutches.

Another concern to the Hallam bench is expressed. 'Don't let them play through you!' comes the shout, which is heeded and Wzzbruh are allowed to play round them instead and put Harley Holt in on the overlap. He wins a corner. Hallam clear and charge down the hill like they are chasing a Gloucestershire cheese. A deep cross is headed back to Jamie Austin who takes it away from the keeper and a covering defender, before sliding it past someone on the line to make it 2-0.

Hallam nearly have a third before Wzzbruh look to get forward again. A studs-up tackle from Jamie Matthews leaves a visiting player in a heap. The referee calls Matthews over and, fearing the worst, a Hallam fan shouts, 'It's a contact sport, help him lino.' That's true, but no hacking is a law as old as the club. Matthews gets away with a long talking-to. I wonder what Uriah Rennie would make of the decision, as he walks past, receiving cheery greetings from home supporters as their club president. I can't recall any decisions he gave against Arsenal, so I've no reason to give him a less cheery greeting. In fact, his most controversial decision seems to have been to send off Alan Shearer, which didn't happen often enough. My reaction to seeing a former ref involved with a club is the sort of surprise normally reserved for spotting an old school teacher down the pub.

Openings come thick and fast, as Wzzbruh look to pull one back and give themselves a chance in the second half, while Hallam seem keen to finish their opponents off. A Wzzbruh free kick doesn't clear the wall, and another chance is straight at Douglas. Hallam are soon down the other end and have it in the Wzzbruh box. They pass it around in a triangle before Ruthven bags his second on the stroke of half-time, turning a dangerous 2-0 lead into a comfortable 3-0 one.

At the start of the second half, Hallam make light of playing uphill and Wzzbruh continue to struggle with clearing their lines. Iren Wilson profits, drilling low past Souter, who crumples to the floor, suffering from some sort of injury he's picked up. The ball inevitably makes its way back down the slope after the restart. It finds its way to Kane Swinburn, who swivels and shoots. The shot creeps in between keeper and post to make it 4-1, much to everyone's surprise. The ball is soon returned downhill and is slipped into Swinburn again. He squeezes a shot past the onrushing Douglas, which rolls in for 4-2, this time generating some applause in acknowledgement.

Just as an unlikely comeback might be on the cards, there's a shout for a penalty in the Wzzbruh box. It's waved away before a second trip sees a penalty given. Danny Buttle converts to restore Hallam's three-goal advantage, not that most of the 361 in attendance seem unduly worried about a comeback. The Hallam defence is equally complacent as they give the ball away to Holt, who squares for Swinburn to complete his hat-trick and make it 5-3.

I'm glad I've been keeping notes, as I have to double-check the score, and it feels like Wzzbruh are right back in it. Holt charges into the Hallam box but only manages to ease a defender into a collision with Douglas, for which the winger goes into the book. The stoppage takes some of the momentum out of the game. After the restart, Hallam mount an attack and a low cross is swept in by sub Alex Palmer to make it 6-3.

Even a nine-goal thriller can have its quieter moments, and I use one to edge towards the gate as full time approaches. Hallam can't add to their tally, but progress to the next round. The majority of fans can leave happy and so do I. The game could have been as poor as the Eynesbury one and I would still have felt buoyed by this historic venue and grand old club proud of its history. The fact it was the highest-scoring game I had been to (if we don't include the heavy defeats I used to be on the end of as a player) was a bonus. Not arriving at my parents' until gone midnight when I had a 6am start the next day was less than ideal, but this tick was absolutely worth it.

Ground 91

SCEFL Groundhop Weekend (Friday)

ANOTHER EVENT worth the extra travel is the SCEFL groundhop down in Kent. After the success of last season's hop the league was keen to hold another one, and I was just as keen to be there. I put up with a faulty alarm going off in the car for the three and a bit hours it takes to get there from a meeting in the west country. The event is sufficiently niche that I'm not stuck in Friday afternoon traffic and make it to Martyn Grove, the home of Lordswood, over an hour before kick-off. The car park is almost full, and the organised coaches are already there.

I pay £10 entry and £2 for a programme and then queue at the refreshment kiosk for my dinner. I use the time to read the programme, which has a nice summary on the two teams fighting it out in the SCEFL Premier at step five. Hosts Lordswood were founded in 1968 and started out in the Rochester and District League, playing at several grounds until they teamed up with the cricket club to purchase the current site. They reached the SCEFL in 1995 and currently sit in 14th place. Their prominent club motto of 'no battle, no victory' suggests they will get stuck in against third-placed Corinthian tonight.

Corinthian were founded in 1972 by Mr R.J. Billings (snr) with the motto *pro omnium beneficio* (for the benefit of all), although whoever wrote their potted history appears to be keen to point out they are no pushovers on the pitch and would be 'hard, but fair'. They stepped out of senior football for a while to focus on youth development, but on their return made it as far as step four, from where they had been relegated last season.

The burger is as standard as the small prefab stand, but various barriers, boards and bits painted in the club colours of orange make the ground more appealing. A tall, shaky-looking camera gantry also stands out, and it's not clear if players are taking potshots at it, as they're certainly not shooting towards the goal. Younger age group teams are playing on the pitch and a girls' game is taking place on the five-a-side pitch behind the goal. I can't do a full lap round the ground as the far end doesn't have a path and my way to the nearly full main stand is blocked by some increasingly wayward shooting.

I try to work out where to stand behind the goal that isn't likely to see me hit by a potshot or a ricochet off the high metal fence behind me. Another fan has a similar dilemma, which is how I get chatting to Bryan (303 grounds visited, but his first groundhop weekend). Bryan is a former Southampton fan who now volunteers with fan-owned Hendon. He's drawn to supporting Corinthian because of their similar green and white colours, but likes the 90s Hull City look of Lordswood's shirt as well.

Lordswood start as brightly as their kit and keep play at the other end while Bryan and I talk about groundhopping. Despite his 303 grounds, he still has a long bucket list, including classics such as Matlock, Belper, Gala Fairydean (all of which I'm familiar with even though I've yet to visit them myself), Aveley (which we've both inexplicably not been to, despite the number of teams that use it, which also applies in my case to Coles Park) and Inverurie Loco Works (which hadn't been on my radar, but turns out Bryan has a penchant for oddly named teams, which is why West Allotment Celtic and Harrogate Railway Athletic feature on his list).

I managed another trip to see the Rail between the Hallam match and the hop and they were admirable for the way they were committed to playing out from the back in a 4-2 win. Lordswood are looking to do the same and we note how it's one of the better things to have trickled down from the top level of the game. Bryan is less impressed when players insist on cutting holes in their socks, which costs Hendon a small fortune. Lordswood nearly count the cost of a wayward pass near their own goal, but get away with it.

A more presentable chance falls to Corinthian as defender Sam Fitzgerald, who I remember being a threat coming up from the back during his Fisher days, hits the post after connecting with a cross. Lordswood battle to stop the visitors getting in front and go some way further than their motto when Joel Odeniran hauls down a Corinthian forward who has been played in over the top. It's only the fact the ball wasn't under control, to make it a clear goalscoring opportunity, which prevents Odeniran from being sent off. A crowd of Corinthian players insist the referee has a chat with the lino, not quite living up to the Corinthian spirit.

Any sense of grievance on Corinthian's part is soon dispelled when Jamie Billings steps up to curl in the free kick to make it 1-0. I'm checking the name of the scorer in my programme and ask if Bryan is a collector. He says he doesn't need a programme to prove he was there, but does have a collection of club mugs, until his other half put a stop to it, and now he settles for fridge magnets instead. I admit my programme will probably end up in the recycling at some point.

The half drifts on like the wait between fortnightly recycling collections. Bryan says the enjoyment for him is just to zone out and forget about life's ups and downs. I admit the same, and feel if there were some Japanese or Scandinavian word for it and I could spin out a self-help book, then watching non-league would become even more popular. Bryan is yet another person I've met who fell out of love with the professional game. Non-league is full of nice people, he says, although when pressed he isn't so sure about a few of the referees who have officiated Hendon's games in the west country now they have transferred into the Southern League.

Half-time arrives and with it there's another chance for Lordswood's youngsters to get on the pitch, as they queue up to take penalties against the reserve goalkeeper. They are notably more accurate than the first team during the pre-match warm-up, or at least they don't lift any over the perimeter fence. This allows me and Bryan to discuss all things groundhopping and Hendon uninterrupted. It's great to find out more about a club I didn't previously give a second thought to seeing play an Arsenal XI in a friendly.

They are three-time FA Amateur Cup winners, European Amateur Cup winners, and winners of the Isthmian League, London League and London Senior Cup. Their Claremont Road ground fell prey to developers in the 2000s. A nomadic period ended in 2016 when they moved into Silver Jubilee Park in a groundshare with Edgware (another club who lost their old ground). Bryan was full of praise for the new landlord, who had invested in facilities, but the club struggled to make money, relying on a hardcore of 150 or so supporters. They couldn't open the club up for investment as the landlord was keen they kept their fan-owned status. The need for facilities to comply with exact measurements and the possibility of having to provide separate changing facilities for female referees meant he had a less sympathetic view of some of the ground grading regulations than I had.

We both agreed that an artificial pitch was a boon for clubs like Hendon, who had only lost a single fixture to the weather when fog descended. Another fixture was lost when red mist descended and it was called off due to fighting, which Bryan blamed on the more agricultural stylings of the Southern League, preferring the Isthmian. Although he noted he didn't like Wealdstone regardless of the league they were both in. He also wasn't a fan of Margate, who I professed a fondness for. His reason was they had dumped Hendon out of the FA Cup a couple of times and the money for that made all the difference, with players being released once they exited.

The players exit the dressing room here at the Grove and Lordswood start on the front foot. Chances continue to sail over and a couple of those disturb a men's five-a-side game on the court behind us. Another break in play allows me to ask Bryan which ground he would most want to revisit. 'Besides the Dell, I would have to say Villa Park.' Even though both of us had drifted towards non-league football, we can't help being drawn to the Premier League, despite all its faults. Bryan recalls another ground on his bucket list is Anfield.

Former Liverpool keeper Jerzy Dudek has a lot to answer for in the next key moment in our game. The hosts win a soft penalty for what may or may not have been a trip on the far edge of the box. The Corinthian players go in hard on the referee and linesman, but not exactly fairly expecting the linesman to overturn the call from the other side of the pitch. After some delay, during which Billings is sin-binned for dissent, and the linesman repeatedly tells Hoops keeper Nathan Boamah to stay on his line, James Jeffrey lines up his kick. He goes low to his right, but so does Boamah, who saves. He had stepped forward, as several hoppers videoing it and watching it back can testify. It was hardly Dudek being well off his line to save several Milan penalties, but after that incident the rules were changed and a retake is awarded, which always feels harsh. Boamah makes his feelings known and boots the ball toward the linesman.

At the second attempt, Jeffrey sends it the other way. Boamah, who has to stop himself naturally falling forward, can't react and concedes the equaliser. Bryan notes he hasn't seen a fight since the one leading to a Hendon abandonment and says, 'I know everyone says we don't like to see that sort of thing, but we all secretly do and it might kick off here.' Indeed, the Lordswood bench are up on their feet when the linesman doesn't flag for a foul in front of him. Bryan admits he's done a full 180 on Lordswood and is cheering them on, after initially going for Corinthian. In the end, we agree a draw was a fair result in front of a decent crowd of 324. Bryan tells me that Hendon had tried to arrange a few Friday night games themselves to boost attendances, but to no avail. I would certainly be on the lookout for one of their fixtures when in London, as I add them to my long list of grounds to visit.

Grounds 92–93
SCEFL Groundhop Weekend
(Saturday)

THE NEXT day, I ought to have made my way to Rochester for their 11am kick-off against Faversham Strike Force to open the day's proceedings. My priority was to tick off another parkrun course. I go to Sheerness for parkrun number 219 at my 79th different course. It's a flat out-and-back along the seafront and I try to follow a pacer to get my time back under 25 minutes again. I slowly fade in the headwind on the return, but post a better time than I've managed in recent weeks, which is pleasing. In fact, it's nearly impossible to be unhappy at a parkrun. There's the same level of friendliness you get in non-league and I get chatting to the bloke I beat in a sprint finish. 'Whatever floats your boat,' he says when I explain why I'm down here, as if I've just said I'm doing competitive flower arranging in the nude, and not overdosing on the world's most popular sport.

I'm back at the hotel in enough time to make the Rochester game. A true hopper would grab a McDonald's breakfast and hotfoot it there. I prefer a more leisurely morning in Faversham, ahead of the Faversham Town game at 3pm. Too often my travels for football see me nip in and out of a place and I'm keen to be a flâneur around town for a change. It's a crisp sunny day and I bag a decent parking spot well before the match. I spend the morning drinking artisan coffee, wandering past the mix of chic florists, a record shop pumping out Dr Feelgood, discount stores, market stalls, and tempting Shepherd Neame pubs, with smartly painted exteriors and hops hung above the bar.

I stumble across, as opposed to stagger into, a small second-hand bookshop, which is covered floor to ceiling with piles of books in every nook and cranny. I find the sport section and bump into Eric (over 1,000 grounds visited). He's here on the offchance of finding an edition of the Rothman's non-league directory, where Deal Town's entry listed directions as 'drive to the centre of town and ask someone'. He tells me he supports Spurs and Deal, but moved to Vancouver and is back visiting. He's off to the rest of the games this weekend, including the Deal game on Sunday.

He's written an article for the programme, which he shows me, and I learn that former Southampton player and one-cap wonder Danny Wallace played six times on loan for Deal in the 1980s. Eric tells me how the Saints used to hold their pre-season camp nearby and talks fondly about the club and how their facilities have improved. He mentions friends who have been groundhopping for some time and is looking forward to seeing some old faces, before remembering he has a lunch booking.

I don't have a booking anywhere; there's no need for one at the bakery I find, which appears to have installed its fittings in the 1980s and not felt the need to change them. Several people have to be told the sausage rolls will be 20 minutes while they make my order. I would normally go for a local delicacy as well, but I've tried gypsy tart before and I'm not in the mood for a slab of sugar.

I wouldn't usually be in the mood for a craft fair either, but I've exhausted things to do and can only hope the Rochester game finishes goalless as I'm kicking myself for not going. I get a small gift for Mrs C, since she's once again allowed me to go off on a jolly and I'll have the luxury of quietly reading the old hardbound copy of *The Cricket Match* by Hugh de Selincourt I picked up at the bookshop.

I head towards Faversham's cricket ground, although I'm not going for a look at it, as I've not forgotten I'm there to see the neighbouring football club at the Aquatherm Stadium on Salter Lane. I go through an old turnstile and to my right is a covered terrace, all uneven steps and tin roof. There's a bar taunting me like the pubs in town. Along one touchline is a whitewashed bunker containing toilets and changing rooms, outside of which some young autograph hunters are obliged by the home players. I continue my lap on a newly laid tarmac path beside the 3G pitch until I reach the ground's main attraction: a low-slung stand running the length of the other touchline with a corrugated iron roof and a nameplate picking out the individual letters of Faversham Town in metal, painted white. There's a tea bar and a couple of temporary bars to deal with the expected crowd, which includes visiting supporters of Hollands & Blair who have tied their flags to the hoardings, showing the Blair Army are in town and hopefully have some sort of tap-dancing routine prepared.

It took an army of volunteers to get the ground back up and running, after the club stopped playing in the early 2000s. The matchday programme is diplomatic about the reasons relating to the previous regime, but pulls no punches when it describes the state of the vandalised and overgrown ground. A comeback saw the Lilywhites get as high as step four, from where they were relegated last season. There are plenty of murmurs about them being big spenders, as they top the league with a few former Gillingham players.

Their history is more modest, with a smattering of county titles to their name, including the forerunner to the league they are in now, but the club dates back to 1884 and the ground 1948. Opponents Blair were only formed in 1967 out of a toolmaking factory and would hope to put a spanner in the works of their hosts' table-topping form. In the clubhouse, I'm keen to see Spurs' early season form dented by Luton, but the other Lilywhites come away with the points as a committee man walks past with a board displaying the line-ups.

Team sheet photographed, I find a seat in the main stand, noting the decent quality of the tannoy as the line-ups are read out by an excitable announcer. There is early excitement in the game as Warren Mfula bursts behind the Blair back line. He doesn't back himself to shoot and the square ball fails to find a team-mate and elicits groans from the crowd. It's not clear whether that's from a sizeable home contingent or hoppers ruing an early chance to put to bed concerns about it ending 0-0. Mfula then contrives to miss another presentable chance from close range.

A hopper near me doesn't seem too concerned. He is passing on the parish news to a friend and, since I'm in earshot, me. I hear about dubious player trading arrangements between a couple of non-league clubs and expensive stewarding requirements at another. The Blair defence cannot prevent an interloper in their penalty area and Kieran Campbell cuts inside to drill past Dan Ellis for 1-0 to the sound of the home fans banging on the hoardings.

Faversham continue to press, looking to switch play to Campbell. A corner is headed on to the bar by Connor Essam and other chances come and go. In the meantime, conversation has turned to Chesham United, sponsored by the TV show *Taskmaster*, with comedian and co-host Alex Horne a club director. He recounts the rules introduced for a charity game, where both sides had a set number of uses of a hooter, which, when blown, signalled the opposition had to lie down. A spill from Ellis doesn't hit the same comedic heights.

Mfula is played through and appears to be offside, but the linesman must have adopted the Horne rules where all offsides must be 'well offside'. He's denied by a defender. The corner, which under Horne rules would require the goalkeeper to come up for it, fizzles out. Another Faversham corner sees another Essam header hit the woodwork. The ball is recycled and a cross to Stefan Payne is taken on his chest and volleyed in for 2-0, which is greeted by widespread applause. This isn't enough for an old boy nearby, whose only words are 'poor half'. It's not clear whether introducing 20ft plastic ducks would improve it for him.

At half-time, the entertainment consists of a crossbar-hitting challenge from the edge of the box. The contestant milks it for all its worth by carefully choosing his spot, then lofting it gently over the bar, so the result is in doubt for a moment. I go for another wander round and bump into Bryan. He tells me the Rochester game was more entertaining than it sounded, with plenty of chances and a bit of controversy, before a last-minute winner. There's nothing controversial about a Faversham penalty early in the second half, which Payne converts.

Mfula struggles to convert several chances and I feel I can boldly proclaim he couldn't hit a barn door. There are equally bold claims from the Faversham defence that a forward was offside (he wasn't) and that the ball has gone out of play (it hadn't). Blair play on and the cut-back finds Dean Grant to reduce the arrears. Blair find some renewed energy and look to charge down Essam. Despite the linesman's repeated calls of 'no foul', Essam is cut down. His assailant protests on the basis of 'look at the size of him'. Bryan agrees with the Blair man and thinks it was soft. I can't help wonder whether the linesman should be saying no foul. Surely the players should know the rules and it doesn't need the officials to provide a running commentary.

I continue to see if I will invoke the commentators' curse by pointing out that Mfula has missed another presentable chance, while the announcer reads out an attendance of 563. We move to the end Faversham are attacking, so we're nearer the exit for the dash to the next match. Faversham carry the ball up that end as we do so. A cross is swept in by Ashley Miller for 4-1, to the delight of the young supporters nearby.

The youngsters cheer Jefferson Abangbee's every move, as he looks dangerous having come on as a substitute. Another substitute, Ollie Gray, comes on when Faversham win a corner. His first touch is a bullet header to make it 5-1. He wheels around to high-five the youngsters and gets a telling-off from the ref for his trouble. The game is restarted soon enough and Blair go down the other end and the ball appears to be bundled in among a melee of players, which leads to the inevitable tussle to retrieve the ball.

The announcer confirms Grant has bagged his second, but it's Faversham looking to add to their healthy goal difference. Mfula has a shot blocked. He's then in on the keeper but shoots straight at his legs. 'Go on, let him score,' says one fan, feeling sorry for him. The match ends 5-2, so the home fans and hoppers can move on happy to have seen a high-scoring encounter. The announcer reminds those parked in the car park to let the groundhoppers' coach out first, as Bryan and I scuttle off to the side streets we have parked in.

I see the bus again as it pulls into a road leading to Whitstable Town's Belmont Ground. I ignore it and the convoy of vehicles following to park near the seafront. There's time for a stroll as the sun sets. I'm too late for the shack selling crab sandwiches to be open, and I don't have enough time to queue for fish and chips, so I make my way to the ground to see what they have on offer. There's no queue for their burger bar when I arrive. They serve chipshop chips and a passable burger.

Once dinner is out of the way, I can take in my surroundings. There is a classic pitched-roof grandstand, with the club name painted on the corrugated iron roof. The whitewashed walls and red seats all look immaculate. An announcement comes over the tannoy saying, 'Wander where you like, but not on the pitch obviously.' I take that as my cue to do a lap of the pitch. I go into the bar to find the toilets. There are booths with people inexplicably watching rugby union, and a scrum for the toilets. A volunteer mentions there are more in the far corner. 'They're not as nice, but there's no queue,' he says apologetically, and that's how I get chatting to Dan, who is the 50-50 ticket seller today.

Dan asks how Faversham got on in their earlier game to see how he's done on a sweepstake between friends on three local matches. He admits they have some good players there, but not as good a 3G pitch, with this one being more forgiving from his experience playing on it. A more unforgiving, hard midfielder is lacking from this Whitstable side, he informs me. The Oystermen currently languish in 15th place and are facing Bearsted in eighth, who are once again cast in the role of team I won't be rooting for on a groundhop weekend.

I continue my lap as Dan continues to sell tickets. I pass a covered terrace adorned with flags. The newly tarmacked path follows a cut out round the goal, reminiscent of the old Goodison. The main stand is lit by the setting sun, but the best seats have been taken. Fans and hoppers stream through the other set of turnstiles on this side of the ground, and there's a hum of activity by the corner boardroom. I head to the old gasworks end, where flats have now replaced the old gasometer. A photo in the programme shows it in all its former glory. I decide to stand here under the old cover, so the grandstand is in my eyeline. Eric from the bookshop walks by and we get chatting again until some more wayward shooting practice has him scurrying for the relative safety of the touchline.

I take up a spot on the perimeter fence and look forward to the evening's contest. This ground, dating back to 1886, is one of the main reasons to attend the hop, being a really smart facility, with lots of old features like the main gates and old stand but with newer additions that all fit together neatly in club colours of red and white. There's a friendly feel to the place and a deep sense of sadness when the club marks the sudden passing of under-14s manager and volunteer Matt Milne.

Groundhoppers may just be passing through, but it's always heartening to find clubs that are key parts of a local community, bringing people together and offering a wider welcome, even if some of the programme notes for groundhop games barely disguise their bewilderment at why people would go to random games across the country. What brings most of the crowd together is the sight of Josh Oliver being slipped through early on and the Bearsted stopper, Frankie Leonard, being unable to keep it out, to put pay to any worries about it being 0-0 with only three minutes on the clock.

The half continues with plenty of bright play, lots of industry and mixed range of passing. Whitstable twice hit the woodwork and have another knuckleball shot dip just wide. Bearsted create a couple of half-chances from crosses. The blokes nearby are locals. There isn't any interesting non-league chat to tune into and the only line I pick up on is 'bird in Ibiza'. The game washes over me and is finely poised at half-time. An attendance of 682 is announced, as the blokes nearby offer equally loud approval of the later kick-off and then their opinions on all things Premier League, including an unprintable story about a former player they once bumped into in a boozer.

I bump into Bryan again and we wax lyrical about the ground, although he is less impressed by the digital scoreboard, which he sees as showing off, knowing how much other upgrades will cost Hendon, chief among them additional changing rooms for female officials. We see the scoreboard change early in the second half, as Harvey Smith has a dipping shot from the edge of the box, leaving Leonard rooted to the spot. It's 2-0 to the hosts, but no two-fingered salute in celebration to pay homage to his namesake.

There follows an important announcement over the tannoy, 'Pin badges are available from the club shop,' which will be important for some of the crowd. Perhaps of more relevance is when the Bearsted goalscorer is announced as they reduce the deficit, which rather worryingly I didn't actually note down. I'm forced to pay attention late on as the Oystermen are on the back foot after being comfortable and having chances to restore their two-goal advantage. Through a crowd of players at the other end of the ground, the ball ricochets back off the post and Bearsted win a corner. Leonard comes up for it deep into stoppage time. A defender gets a big head on it and the game ends 2-1 to the hosts.

There's a danger when going to so many matches in quick succession that they blend into one and lose some of the magic that comes with a week's build-up and, while this was by no means a bad game, it will be the ground that lives long in the memory and I end my weekend there contented.

Ground 94

The Scottish Ground

SERIOUS GROUNDHOPPERS don't limit themselves to stadiums in England. Rural grounds in Wales appeal to many. Northern Ireland and Scotland have plenty of grounds with wide-open terraces and vintage grandstands, but the nearest I got to one of these was on a bus past Glentoran's famous Oval. I needed to find a classic venue north of the border now that I wasn't such a long drive away.

The Dumbarton Football Stadium, commonly known as 'The Rock', leapt out of my *Remarkable Football Grounds* book. Situated beneath the eponymous rock, on the Clyde estuary, it appeared to be in an idyllic spot. I was about to plan a weekend here until I realised the scenic photos had all been taken from above, and the rock was behind the lone grandstand, so the view would be of Scottish League Two football, a fence and some housing beyond.

I search around for another well-situated ground with some classic features, looking at Queen of the South, Arbroath and Ayr, before settling upon Greenock Morton's Cappielow. I'm also keen to sample some corporate hospitality and treat my dad for his birthday, so I invite the family. I'm joined by my mum (12 grounds visited, including at least two in a corporate box) and my brother Simon (52 of the 92 league grounds visited, about 70 going down to step two and another dozen below that, which by my reckoning is less than my current tally, so I can chalk that up as another result in my favour).

Morton's offer looks like great value. For £110, we would get matchday tickets for a Scottish Championship fixture, a three-course meal and, most appealing of all – a free bar. It would be like a wedding, but with football replacing the boring bit of the ceremony. I suspect we would feel like guests who tenuously knew the couple through work, while everyone else spoke a foreign language. But, there was a free bar, so that didn't matter. There would also be a Cappielow legend we could meet and have photos with.

For all this, I would not be put off by a cancelled train, several more cancelled trains, getting turfed off a train in the middle of the Pennines and getting on a packed train that made it about a mile down the line before stopping for a fallen tree. Then, after this was cleared, managing to lean on the passenger alarm, which mercifully didn't add any further delay and see me get lynched. I reach Preston three hours later than planned, to get a lift from Simon another three hours to our hotel.

On the drive he asks why on earth we were going to Greenock Morton anyway. It comes down to a single picture, showing open terraces at both ends, a giant crane behind one of them, and another covered terrace down one side. In a word, it's gritty. The fact Morton are fan-owned and had a very tempting corporate hospitality offer only added to the appeal. I ask Simon if he has done his research on Greenock Morton legends, so we might have some idea who we will be meeting. He had looked, but hadn't heard of any. The mugshots from their hall of fame might as well be from an episode of *Crimewatch*. The only one I had looked up was Jimmy Cowan, who was capped 25 times for Scotland as a goalkeeper and, legend has it, wore his Morton shirt underneath his national jersey. Cowan died in 1968, so it wouldn't be him.

We wouldn't be seeing any Morton players, legends or otherwise, as I see the news that the match has been called off. The Scottish FA and police made the decision on the basis of it being unsafe for visitors Inverness to travel as Storm Babet wreaked havoc on the east coast. Fans were annoyed that their own game in Glasgow a few weeks previously had not been called off when they, and one of their players, could not get out of Inverclyde in similar circumstances. My reaction was to do what all groundhoppers would do in the same situation and find some alternative games. Partick Thistle and Albion Rovers jumped out and not just because of their team colours. Hamilton Academical was a sensible 3G backup, but not the most characterful ground, and several games were taking place in the West of Scotland Cup likely to escape the worst of the weather.

We left a final decision until the morning and settled into our lodgings right under the flight path to Glasgow airport, with the bar having just closed before our arrival. We hope tomorrow will be better. To get off to a good start, we drive into Glasgow for parkrun, stopping en route at Clyde's old Shawfield Stadium. Clyde vacated the ground in 1986, but it was used until recently for greyhound racing and is now threatened with demolition. It is a sad sight in the grey early morning light. We embark on a lap of the ground and can tell how it held a record attendance of 52,000.

It didn't look like we would see much other than external walls, which could have belonged to some derelict industrial buildings were it not for the floodlights. One wall has the telltale narrow slits of a turnstile entrance and we are greeted with some gaps to hold our cameras up to and get a glimpse of the pitch and far stand. There's a certain buzz in finding this viewpoint. Others had clearly been more adventurous and we notice various patched-up bits of fencing where urban explorers had broken in. A lone Clyde scarf is tied to some railings along with tributes to former player and national team manager Craig Brown.

After this lap we do three hilly laps of Queen's Park for parkrun. It was my 220th at an 80th different location. Parkrun are keen to point out it's not a race, so I won't dwell on mine and Simon's times and simply point out he has only run 76 times at 16 different locations. On the drive back, I spot the famous bowls club on the site of the first Hampden Park, so we pull over to look at the mural boasting the result from an early contest between two other auld enemies.

We pop back to the hotel to change and then pick my parents up near St Mirren's ground, which has all the architectural merit of the New Den, and head off on a family outing. I'm not sure how many families would go to Cathkin Park, the famous abandoned ground once home to Third Lanark, but we were unlikely to go to any of the more obvious tourist destinations. My parents had spent 13 hours the previous day on a return train journey to Mallaig, out of choice, to look at a bit of scenery and see the Harry Potter viaduct. This wasn't just a must-do tick for groundhoppers, regardless of personal rules, it was somewhere that captures the imagination of even the most casual fan. And for my mum it was a pleasant walk in the woods to see the autumn colours.

We wander around the sections of terrace without trees and take in the elevated views of the pitch, which is marked out for youth matches. There are a few park benches on the far side where the main grandstand was situated. It's all familiar to me from photos I've seen, but it's worth the detour to experience it in person. I found my feelings towards the loss of Shawfields were stronger, as you could see what might still be. The overgrown terraces at Cathkin have a certain beauty in their current state and while it would have been better for the club to have hung on and either be playing at a run-down version of this sizeable bowl or groundsharing somewhere, it stands as a monument to what happens when clubs are mismanaged and how clubs and their grounds should be cherished.

While we were in the area and had time to kill, we check out Hampden Park. The modern stadium evokes very little in the way of feeling. Only the vast footprint hints at its former glory, accommodating up to 130,000 fans on its expansive open terraces. Next door was Lesser Hampden, which had been subject to an even less sympathetic makeover. The adjoining farm cottage, regarded as one of the oldest buildings in world football, had been replaced by an ugly stand with what looked like very few actual seats. An old Queen's Park club crest set in brickwork nearby was the only redeeming feature before a spot of lunch cheered us all up.

Our mood nearly sours when I check if Albion Rovers are still on. I see 'closed' and 'high winds' before I make out it was just the east terrace that would be out of action, so the match against Berwick Rangers in the Lowland League is still on. We head to Coatbridge, which from what I can tell is a mix of soot-blackened Victorian buildings and giant unwelcoming flats with a pagoda-style addition to the rooftops that wouldn't look out of place in North Korea. We park up right outside the main entrance of Cliftonhill, which has the appearance of a repainted 1980s B&Q. The Reigart Stadium, as it's also known, after its sponsors, a demolition firm, has a slightly forlorn air about it. It was their relegation play-off defeat against Spartans, which saw them fall out of the Scottish league after 120 years, that brought them to my attention. The gritty appeal of an old ground, left largely unchanged, came across in the coverage I had seen of their demise.

We wait outside for the gates to open an hour before kick-off as some Berwick officials are let in. The Wee Gers suffered the same fate as the Wee Rovers back in 2019, having been a stalwart of the Scottish league, despite hailing from the other side of the border. This was a fact that had us contemplating which side we ought to support today. A look at their playing staff on Wikipedia revealed they had a single Englishman on their books, so we stuck with the tradition of backing the hosts. First, we pay £35 for the four of us and then get some 50-50 tickets from the friendly seller who points out where everything is.

There is no mention of a bar and Simon casually tells me they don't have them in Scottish grounds. Indeed, alcohol hasn't been allowed anywhere inside Scottish grounds, besides corporate hospitality, since 1980. I'm forced to settle for a programme and a look around. We check out the club shop in a portacabin. It's not quite cold enough for us to buy hats and scarves, but it is cold enough for me to have borrowed a jumper from my brother earlier. It looks like the sort of thing Jimmy Greaves would have worn on *Saint and Greavsie*. I make a mental note not to laugh too loudly at any poor Scottish goalkeeping on display.

Looking around the ground, there is a semicircular retaining wall holding a grassy bank at one end. There's evidence of a cinder track, from the ground previously hosting speedway and greyhound racing. The far terrace is closed off and in places looks in a not-dissimilar condition to Cathkin. The small east terrace, closed today, is newer and cuts off the original oval shape. We spot the fence panels that have fallen and then take in the ground's highlight, its main grandstand.

Seating is on an elevated deck, with standing below. The seats themselves are old wooden ones, which look great, but I suspect aren't at all comfortable. A group of lads have bagged the single row of plastic seats near the back on halfway. Stairwells and walls are all painted in club colours, with alternating red and yellow showing it off in all its glory. The pitched roof has an ugly newer extension, but one that's offering the terrace some cover, so it can be forgiven.

We check out the offering at the refreshment kiosk. The scotch pies are very tempting, but very unnecessary after a big lunch. Irn-Bru is less tempting, but every other group who gather around us on the terrace seems to come with a plastic cup full of the stuff. Less numerous are shots on target in the pre-match warm up. 'Dog shit' is Simon's verdict. Berwick are no better and their players get some stick off the Wee Rovers fans near the tunnel. I could do with subtitles for the insults, but I suspect even then they might say *unintelligible pelters*.

The match gets under way to muted applause and the gentle murmur of the crowd. Players have time on the ball and the Rovers midfield can knock it around in what some might consider the traditional Scottish style. It's not long until there's a jarring tackle and a Berwick player lets fly with a shot to give one of the ball boys something to chase. There's an anguished cry of 'C'mon Rovers'.

Both sides continue where they left off, with some wayward shooting and more hopeful through balls going astray. Members of the crowd pipe up: 'Get the fucking ball on the floor'; 'Ah fuck off.' I check the scores of the games elsewhere, noting all the other games in contention for a visit today have seen a goal. The thought dawns on me that after all this I could end up with a '0-0 revisit required' situation. Another move breaks down and the shout of 'fucking ... just fucking talk to each other' is the best that can be offered. That doesn't bode well.

There's a flurry of action before half-time, with Albion in the ascendancy but unable to create any clear cut-chances. My mum's verdict, clearly not wanting to say anything too outrageous I might quote her on, is 'it's a very bitty game', which adds as much insight as Alan Shearer in his early years on *Match of the Day*. I ask my dad if it's worse than the Eynesbury game we saw. He says it's a close-run thing. The match is not a ringing endorsement of the Scottish fifth tier, comparing unfavourably with the tenth tier of the English game thus far.

Me and Simon join a queue for the tea bar. A group of kids in front politely make room for a blind away supporter and ask him what he thinks of the game. 'It's been tight, but you've edged it,' he says before he predicts the home side will win 1-0. I'm about as confident in that as my ability to finish a pie, so we settle for £6 worth of warm brown liquids for us all.

Albion pick up where they left off and my mum suggests it's 'because they've been told off by their manager'. She then decides she needs to go to the toilet. 'They'll probably score now,' she says. I resist the temptation to say she should've gone before they kicked off. As she leaves, Bright Prince bursts through for Rovers. I've had no problem with this part of his game, but his wayward finishing has led me to provoke the football gods again following my lack of comeuppance at mocking Faversham's Warren Mfula. Prince lashes a shot across the keeper and it nestles in the corner for 1-0. It's his seventh of the season, the same as Mfula had bagged.

Dismissing non-league strikers based on being hit and miss isn't as bad as a Chelsea-supporting friend writing off Lionel Messi on the basis of not scoring against them. The home side are inspired by their goal, admittedly not to Messi level of skills, but Joe Bevan does bring the ball forward to murmurs of appreciation from the crowd. These efforts come to nothing and Berwick try to find a foothold. 'For fuck sake, Rovers' comes a shout from a man nearby who sounds like the comedian Kevin Bridges, when Berwick defender Jamie McCormack sidefoots a corner just wide.

I miss something myself as there's an altercation involving McCormack, which he gets away with after apologising to the linesman. Bridges launches into some stand-up. 'Sorry. You're a shitebag lino. Sorry. It's all right, I said sorry.' The home fans are getting nervous about their slender lead. A punch is thrown in the crowd, which is from me defending myself from a sliced clearance and does my recovering hand no favours. The crowd are more pensive, with Bridges making nervous remarks. Clearly, we are at a level where the result will make or break people's weekends.

Niyah Joseph has a chance to seal it. He steps inside to shake off a defender but shoots straight at the keeper's legs. The crescendo of noise leads to sounds of exasperation. Joseph is then named the man of the match, which leaves Bridges speculating that the admin just wants her photo with him again, as various other names are offered unconvincingly as alternatives.

Some unconvincing defending from Rovers gives the visitors a free kick on the edge of the box late on. The crowd can sense what is going to happen next as Bayley Klimionek lines up a shot. He curls it over the wall but the Rovers keeper helps it over the bar. The corner is seen away and McCormack gets away with a foul. 'You're a dick, number five,' shouts Bridges. The centre-half looks over. 'Sorry, you're a dick. Don't hit me, sorry,' he adds, returning to his routine, before saying to his mates, 'I can outrun him anyway.'

Time gets away from the visitors chasing an equaliser, and the full-time whistle blows to the relief of most of the crowd. 'The second half got a bit frantic,' says Mum, remaining as uncontroversial as a former referee asked to do TV punditry. It was a better experience than Eynesbury, but we all agreed a run at a free bar would have markedly improved things. We settle for the Shilling bar in Glasgow for drinks afterwards, where Simon watches England lose a rugby World Cup semi-final and I watch it through the expression of the Scottish fans cheering on South Africa, which is more entertaining than rugby union. Their relief is similar to mine that the Wee Rovers game hadn't been 0-0 to add groundhopping insult to groundhopping injury.

Ground 95
The Mystery Ground

AT GROUND 70, I learned that Saint Panteleimon was the patron saint of lottery wins and it is something similar that brings me back to see them at their latest groundshare with Potters Bar Town. Adventurer Alastair Humphreys ran a competition, 'coolest adventure idea wins a bike', and while I can never lay claim to being cool, I could latch on to someone else who was. My entry was that I would deliver the bike anywhere on the UK mainland to the person with the coolest idea.

This led me to Charing Cross station to meet Keith, who had kindly donated a new adventure bike for the competition. Photographer friend Soren (eight or nine grounds visited, having mostly watched the home games of FC Copenhagen and then Fulham) had come along for the day and snapped me getting ready to set off. In among all my faffing, I remember to check whether the match I planned for us to watch was still on (part of my entry mentioned various side quests, one of which was to watch a game of non-league football).

Peckham Town was to be my match of choice. They had suitable hipster credentials, being inclusive, serving craft ale and looking like I could take the bike inside the ground. There was the added novelty of them having the smallest stand in the world, which bears a resemblance to a hunter's chair you might find in the woods. Unfortunately, a 10am pitch inspection deemed the pitch too wet to play on, so I needed to track down an alternative. I left a Twitter poll running to decide where I should go.

The options were Wembley FC, which I liked for the fact they were in the FA Vase that would conclude at the more famous Wembley Stadium down the road, but would be a pain to cycle to; Cray Valley Paper Mills, who had taken Charlton Athletic to an FA Cup first-round replay, but were in the wrong direction having found out I needed to ride the bike to Somerset; London Lions and St Panteleimon, both on the way to my parents', where I had a bed for the night and I could worry about heading west another day.

St Panteleimon were in the lead after we had gone for coffee and spare inner tubes, while navigating our way around the Lord Mayor's Show. We retraced the steps of Dick Whittington and headed north, past the Emirates where fans were already gathering, and eventually out of the metropolis into Hertfordshire. Today's visitors, Mildenhall Town, had travelled further still, from Suffolk, for this FA Vase last-64 tie.

This time I can't just walk in, so I pay £8 and take the bike in through a side gate. There still isn't a programme or printed team sheet, but there is a clubhouse, covered outdoor seating and a couple of catering options. The main stand is a brick base with a crimson-coloured metal roof. There are an assortment of other stands and it's one of the more basic grounds at step three where landlords Potters

Bar play. For step five it's more than enough, although a band of away supporters are less than impressed and taunt 'We've got more fans than you' and 'Your club is Mickey Mouse'.

The ref shouts, 'Matt?' and gives me the thumbs-up to check I'm ready for kick-off, or else that's also the linesman's name, and we get under way. Almost immediately Saints' Dwayne Clarke cuts inside and curls a shot past Josh Pope, but is denied by the upright. Somehow the rebound is put wide and the brother of England keeper Nick Pope is forced to retrieve the ball from a hedge.

Mildenhall have a chance from a corner but a free header can't be directed on target. From these early exchanges, I fall back on old stereotypes from my playing days and expect the side from nearer to London to try to play a bit, have a few tricks and want the ref to give everything, while the team from out in the sticks will be more agricultural in their approach. A shout of 'just kick it anywhere' does little to dispel this belief as Mildenhall go long, before some neat interplay puts Saints' Javarn Bernard through, only to be denied by Pope's fingertips.

Mildenhall have a chance flash across the goal and are on top when they have a goal rightly ruled out for offside, which is a good job as the linesman had already had some stick from the players for not telling them exactly where to take a free kick from when his flag was clearly pointing to the spot. 'Who would be a linesman?' sympathises a fan. I feel confident enough to taunt the football gods again and say, 'I can feel a goal coming.' Callum Anderson duly obliges for the visitors, finishing from a tight angle, and the away fans' celebrations aren't cut short this time. There don't seem to be many home fans around to mind, as quite a few of those around me have Potters Bar hats or scarves on.

I find a reason why so many Potters Bar fans are watching their lodgers when I try out the seafood van at half-time. My usual experience of food at football is that it's often unnecessary with a game falling between lunch and dinner, or it's a bog-standard burger. The Footie Scran Twitter account has had cause to show the game's culinary offerings, with the likes of Avro serving some tempting dishes, although not enough to justify a trek over the Pennines. The Thai soft-shell crab here was worth the journey, and Soren was impressed with his squid. Hot chocolate from the other van is nothing to write home about but is at least warm, as the temperature drops and shadows lengthen across the ground. I'm left thinking I might have to break out my thermal sleeping bag before full time.

Full time gets further and further away as stoppages rack up in a bitty second half. Soren has to leave to get a train home, having probably witnessed the match highlight and sampled the gastronomic highlight. I feel duty bound to tease him that under arbitrary groundhopping rules he can't count this as ground number nine or ten, but as he'll be on a warm train well before me I don't think he minds.

St Panteleimon try to move the ball around and create an opening. They are thwarted by a well-organised defence and a grass pitch that is cutting up and looks a little bumpy, which deters them from making a riskier pass. There are fewer chances this half, but more supporters, as several people turn up asking who is playing and what the score is. Someone confirms it is straight to penalties if it's a draw, which keeps me interested until the end. Even when

Mildenhall go looking for the corner flags, all it would take is a quick break upfield, an untimely slip or a potshot. A nearby supporter is less convinced, 'They've played some nice football, but they haven't worked the keeper.' Nor do they. Mildenhall see the game out and you can see what it means to the players being a step closer to Wembley, as they celebrate.

The fans celebrate as well, singing 'C'mon the Hall, c'mon the Hall'. They ask some home fans if they will go to the final when Mildenhall get there. They seem bemused by the question. I check who else has gotten through. Wembley went out on penalties after drawing 3-3, London Lions went through on penalties, while Cray Valley Paper Mills won their league game 3-0. Another FA Vase tie was abandoned following an injury to a linesman. Who would be a linesman indeed?

Before the next round, I had the small matter of delivering the bike to Somerset. I plotted a route that took me most of the week, stopping off in Towcester, Stratford-upon-Avon and the Cotswolds. Unfortunately, I couldn't find somewhere cheap to stay near Stroud to watch Forest Green Rovers and try some of their famed vegan chips or the more likely option of non-league Shortwood United, who were nearby and had a small wooden stand on a grass bank on their Futbology listing. I made it to Wells, with just the odd bit of flooding to wade through, headwinds battering me, and pub accommodation in the middle of nowhere where the chef had just left them on a free transfer to have a shot at fine-dining glory. It was an otherwise delightful time of year to see the autumn colours and find a nice pub for a well-earned pint at the end of the day.

It was exactly the time of year when I like to be in the elements watching football. It didn't matter that I hadn't seen the landlords play. I felt I had the experience of a game at Potters Bar, which was mainly about the catering anyway. Sometimes going to a game can be about what happens around the football and it was good to combine the match with a bit of cycling and an unplanned adventure.

Ground 96

Postponement Bingo

NOW I'M into the final five grounds in my quest, I feel I should give some thought to which ones round out my 100 and plan some trips accordingly. The ones I've enjoyed visiting most have been those steeped in history like Corinthian-Casuals, Hallam and Harwich, were part of an event like a groundhop weekend or trip away, or featured a team I was interested in, like Clapton, Hashtag or Harrogate Railway Athletic. More opportunistic ticks have been a mixed bag, with Redbridge a pleasant surprise, while league football at Harrogate Town and the game at Eynesbury were the biggest disappointments.

I have a lengthy list of grounds I would like to visit, but I will not manage them all this season. I like having plenty of gems to look forward to while keeping an eye on those that might fall prey to property developers. I'm also into the part of the season where #postponementbingo starts appearing all over my Twitter feed. So, it is with a certain inevitability that my next game succumbs to a waterlogged pitch, with Sheffield FC and their Sheffield and Hallamshire Senior Cup tie called off.

Sheffield FC are the oldest club in the world, formed in 1857 and not to be confused with United or Wednesday.

At one time they played at Bramall Lane, in the days when it was also a cricket ground. They had an itinerant history, not dissimilar to Corinthian-Casuals, taking in several grounds around Sheffield. They now found themselves in neighbouring Dronfield, but the Home of Football Stadium wasn't due to be their home for much longer. Plans were afoot to move into a new 5,000-capacity ground shared with Sheffield Eagles rugby club as part of a multi-sport facility.

I was keen to see The Club (which is their official nickname), but the current ground had only been home since 2001, with Norton Woodseats its previous occupants until they folded. It seemed to go against the spirit of focusing on the grounds more than the clubs, so I put my visit on hold. In looking into their history, I found an answer to my question of who did they play if they were the first club? It was a series of inter-club friendlies, sometimes married men against single men, which is essentially a training game. If there had been groundhoppers around at the time, many wouldn't deem this worthy of a tick. Their first game against Hallam would be of more interest, and I've already seen one of those teams.

If I've ticked off age and history, then an alternative presented itself with novelty and the almost irresistible combination of brewery and non-league ground; one described as a ground in a brewery. Tadcaster Albion's Ings Lane ground is located behind the John Smith's brewery and they were originally named John Smith's FC. Less is written about whether they were a no-nonsense team and had a penchant for 'aving it clear into the river Wharfe. Their adverts were more memorable than their beer and in the end I decide to stay indoors and watch Arsenal on the round of fixtures I could see on the Amazon Prime subscription we still hadn't gotten round to cancelling.

This was the proof I needed that the Saturday 3pm TV blackout was a good thing for the wider football pyramid, as the convenience of watching a game on television could trump getting out to see one live, particularly in the colder, wetter months. So, much like forcing myself out for a winter ramble, where I know I will enjoy it once I get out there, I resolve to get to a game the following week. This leads me to The Citadel to watch Farsley Celtic.

The Citadel is the nearest senior ground to where I grew up in neighbouring Calverley, when the ground, which dates back to 1948, was called the Throstle Nest. It may not have the history of Sheffield FC, but it felt like one I ought to visit. The Celts are one of the highest-ranked sides in the Leeds area, playing in National League North. This is after a turbulent recent history, which saw them reach the National League only for financial difficulties to lead them into administration, starting back up again in the NCEL Premier, before returning to step two. During that time the club went through something of a rebrand with the classic crest and ground name making way for something more like a Super League franchise in rugby league. The traditional colours also went from blue to green and white hoops, as they made more of their Celtic suffix.

Tonight's opponents had their own nominative novelty in their prefix, with Curzon Ashton being so named following the merger of Curzon Road Methodists FC and Assheton Amateurs FC in 1963. They hailed from the wrong side of the Pennines, in Ashton-under-Lyne, of which the only thing I knew was that it was the birthplace of World Cup winners Geoff Hurst and Simone Perrotta.

The Nash's team bus was parked up in the pothole-riddled car park when we arrive to bag one of the few remaining spaces. We being myself and cricket skipper Sam, who joined me for a sport marginally less sensitive to heavy downpours. I tiptoe round one of the small lakes that has formed from a week of near-constant rain and we approach the main gates, adorned with a *Game of Thrones*-style image of a medieval citadel. The accompanying street art leads Sam to ask me if I've been to Billericay, which allows us to compare notes on our favourite elements of their unique approach to decor.

It's £15 entry, and then some rustling around for change for a programme after we click-clack through the turnstile. The teams are warming up on the pitch, which is getting more and more cut up after the recent wet weather. We are after something warming ourselves and go to the Nest food kiosk. I've held off having dinner, so I could go for the classic meat pie, peas, chips and gravy. It doesn't disappoint, but as a man more accustomed to a matchday pie following Harrogate Town, Sam would like more gravy.

I'm on the lookout for more northern stereotypes as we wander round the ground. There's been no cause to shell out for new seats, with the old blue plastic ones bolted to the terrace behind the goal. We pass through a metal cage that can segregate the crowd at higher levels. The visiting supporters have taken up position here on the terraced section of the covered end. The far touchline has several steps of uncovered concrete terracing, with netting to catch any stray clearances. We complete the loop and stand next to a small band of home supporters.

'You're in the wrong shirt' comes a shout laced with bitterness from someone standing nearby, indicating the presence of former players in the Curzon line-up. Sam is trying to work out if there are any former Harrogate Town men on display. Clayton Donaldson, the one name I recognise as a staple of *Soccer Saturday* match reports from the lower divisions, is just sticking to managerial duties in his player-manager role for the Celts. He won't be happy with the way his side starts the game, with an early chance for the visiting winger, allowed to cut in from the right and get a shot away. It's over the bar, but serves as a warning to defenders and those supposed to be taking notes rather than chatting about the heights we've reached on *Championship Manager*, the depths of non-league and the even deeper level of our Monday night five-a-side.

If this had been a game of *Championship Manager* (my point of reference being the 1997/98 version, where it was more Harry Redknapp-style wheeler-dealing than the endless admin more complicated than my actual job in later editions), then there would have been breathless updates in blue text on a pink background, representing the visitors' change strip. Header by Spencer. Tipped over by Leban. Corner for Curzon Ashton. Cleared by Atkinson. GOAL FOR CURZON ASHTON!, which would flash in alternating blue on pink, then pink on blue.

Seeing that text in game would prompt more anger and frustration than seeing George Waring redirect a cross back past Žan-Luk Leban for the opener. The visitors deserve their lead. What the text commentary wouldn't note is a home fan inadvertently juggling the ball when he tried to return a clearance, but twice hit it into the perimeter fence to ironic jeers from those nearby. Nor would it note that the Celts' Ryan Watson was lucky to escape with just a yellow card after lunging into a tackle.

I go in studs-up on Sam when he describes himself as a groundhopper, knowing he has only visited 75 grounds. I point out the arbitrary figure of 100 grounds that I'm working towards ought to be the entry criteria. He tries to argue for the inclusion of other sports, all of which he has on a spreadsheet, which takes him over 100. He has already ruled out my justification for Spurs' new ground when I told him I'm on 95 or 96. We're both keen to bump our own stats up but to not allow the other to do so. It's utterly pointless one-upmanship between friends that's ultimately harmless. Unlike the tackle, which, had it been a red, would have significantly harmed Celtic's prospects. The victim eventually gets to his feet and Sam too arrives upon a definition of a groundhopper that I rather like. 'It's someone who is happy to go by themselves to watch two teams they don't support,' he concludes.

We can also agree that Celts debutant Michael Coulson is well offside and his frustrations with the linesman are unwarranted. 'He should have been looking along the line,' we concur, as if we don't find ourselves goal-hanging at five-a-side. After a brief interlude, where Nash's Miles Storey clatters a left-footed shot off the angle of post and bar, Coulson is in again. He has Dylan Youmbi square with the goal at his mercy, but chips it tamely to Nash stopper Cam Mason, to the disgust of Youmbi and ourselves, as even our games wouldn't see such greed when you might expect it.

Warmth rather than greed is on our minds approaching half-time, as we conclude our lap of the ground before returning to the tea bar. We pass the main stand. Someone shouts, 'C'mon liner,' a more northern expression of frustration than the 'farking hell, lino' you get down south.

I'm pleased to note the seats are old wooden ones that have been repainted in alternating strips of green and black. It's a surprise given the new brick and metalwork. The hot chocolate is surprisingly good and we find a spot on the far terrace in line with the 18-yard box for the second half.

This is the sort of spot Sam would hunt out for Town games. He recalls their time at this level and a previous visit. He's not a fan of the street art on the metal fence panels behind us, which, given he is a teacher, doesn't surprise me. He shows an enormous amount of self-control early in the second half not to shout, 'It's your own time you're wasting', when the referee halts the game to ask Mason to adjust something strapped to his arm. There is further delay as Mason has to put his gloves back on, which leads a home fan to suggest the ref gives him a booking.

That this incident is the most notable action tells you all you need to know about what continues to be a poor game. Celtic get forward a little more, but fail to register a shot on target. We return to a discussion about which grounds hit the mark for us. Sam is keen to visit Matlock for its setting. I ask what's wrong with the 1980s housing and Lidl sign we can see here. He's also keen to see Goodison Park while he can, even if it won't help him complete the 92 in the long run.

I wonder if Goodison should be on my list. It's exactly the sort of characterful old ground fast disappearing from the game, the sort I will look at photos of in years to come and wish I had visited. Yet I wasn't inclined to get tickets. There was something I preferred about being stood on a sparsely populated terrace on a cold winter's night, able to wander around, the odd song or passage of play punctuating any quiet contemplation or, in our case, a conversation about why people in the grandstand seemed to prefer the black seats to the green ones.

There's some mild amusement in the game itself, when Adam Barton is booked for the visitors after throwing the ball away in a hissy fit following an obvious trip. Nothing resembling an effort on goal results from this Celtic foray forward, and we decide to take in another vantage point behind the goal, joking that we will be in the right place for a big finish. Instead, we can just about make out some wrestling between players, pinball in the Celtic box at the other end, and yet another foul.

'C'mon, they can't play football' comes words of encouragement for his team-mates from Mason, as Celtic skew a through ball out of play. It's a fair assessment, but there's still time. Sam claims that if they do score, he's running over to them to join in the celebrations. Celtic play a hopeful ball forward that's knocked on to Chris Atkinson, who finds himself one-on-one versus Mason. With a flick of the outside of his boot, he slots it home to level with Celtic's first attempt on target in 94 minutes of play.

Celtic sense there is still time for a winner; Coulson bustles past a defender and swings in a cross. Watson flings himself at it, but can't make contact. The Nash are suddenly under pressure. They half-clear but the ball finds its way back to Coulson. He takes on Waring but is upended. Waring gets a second yellow for his trouble and, after a brief delay, Coulson lines up the free kick. Right-footed, he curls it high over the wall. It dips into the top corner, giving Mason no chance. Coulson has bagged a 97th-minute winner on his debut. He runs to the bench rather than to the two of us celebrating more enthusiastically than you might expect for neutrals, not realising that Sam would

221

have joined in. Coulson tries to rip his shirt off but it gets stuck on his head.

The two late strikes turn the game on its head and move Celtic clear of the relegation places. The result has given me another local club to keep an eye on, with the manner of the turnaround giving me a whole different feeling about the evening. We leave buoyed by the late drama in a way that a turkey of a film couldn't be saved by a twist at the end, nor could a poor gig be saved by its encore.

That's the magic of the game. Even as a neutral, you can get drawn in. I may have to visit again given how there are some relatively big-name clubs at this level, with seven former league clubs by my reckoning. I might even find out why they are called Celtic. It's not an original moniker, relating to founders with Scottish roots as with Stalybridge Celtic. Maybe someone just liked the sound of it in the way you find Sportings, Reals and Inters in grassroots football.

I would like to see more Daring clubs, in homage to Daring Club de Brussels (matricule number two), which is now only represented by the D in RWD Molenbeek. Daring Club Farsley probably wouldn't work, but the daring end to their game did it for me. When I get home Mrs C asks, as she always does, 'Was it a good game?' 'Well, it was a good bit of stoppage time,' I reply, not wanting to display too much euphoria in case the kids have been difficult at bedtime.

Ground 97

The Fantastic Media Welfare Ground, Emley AFC

MRS C is integral to the next ground I visit, since it's the one closest to her parents. After a couple of excitable bedtimes for the kids around Christmas, I'm here for the Boxing Day clash between Emley and Penistone Church. This was the same fixture I missed last year that finished 4-4, so I was naturally concerned my 83-match run since my last 0-0 would be under threat.

Football in Emley has been under threat in recent years after the original club moved to Wakefield and became Wakefield & Emley, before dropping the 'Emley' and their reserve team who had continued to play at the Welfare Ground. This led to the current club being formed in 2005. The Pewits made their way via a promotion and a Covid-era points-per-game elevation to find themselves in the NCEL Premier. The history and records of the original Emley were returned when Wakefield FC were wound up in 2014 having played at the level above this. Emley AFC, as they are now called, are riding high in the table going into this derby in second place, with games in hand over table-toppers Campion.

I'm given a lift into the village by Mrs C, who drops me off in among the cars ditched around the remains of the ancient market cross. I follow a sign down a narrow lane to the ground. This always used to be a scruffy hand-painted notice that belied the fact the club had once made the final of the FA Vase, and played an FA Cup third-round tie away to West Ham in 1998. I assumed from driving past on those early visits that it was just a recreation ground used by a Sunday team, given the size of the village.

I emerge into the club's already full car park and see a more substantial main stand than I've been used to at this level. It's been freshly painted, while keeping some old Emley signage, although it's the refreshment kiosk round the side that captures my attention. Despite the festive excess, I was ready for pie, peas, chips and gravy and it didn't disappoint. I was tucking in when rugby Adam joins me (16 football grounds visited). He couldn't contemplate eating anything else, so we make our way to the covered terrace at the transmitter mast end. I don't think this is the official name, but it should be as it dominates the surrounding area.

Quite a few fans have been pulled in from the village and beyond, as the main stand is full and we squeeze past those stood in front of it before finding a spot. We're next to a group of younger fans with a drum, and some slightly older fans with cans of Stella. Adam is telling me about how they had to station extra police in the village to deter burglars when everyone decanted to London for the West Ham game, when he's approached by someone who knows him from rugby. I tell him afterwards I would be more impressed if anyone remembers him from his handful of appearances for the club.

A couple of older fans look like the sort who might have an encyclopaedic knowledge of every player past and present, but they are engrossed in the game. It's a typically feisty local derby with challenges flying in, including one rather literally, in the manner of Nigel de Jong. There's little of the quality Adam recalls from one of his games when a team-mate scored from a bicycle kick on the halfway line.

Emley work the ball towards the end we are standing at, where our sight of goal is a little obstructed, but not as much as the Pewits' James Walshaw. He is bundled over by Church skipper Danny Howes, who uses his shoulder and enough nous to stay on the right side of the official's decision. Howes is soon on the wrong end of a robust Emley challenge. The bumper festive crowd are more animated by that than some crowds are for a goal.

At this point I conclude the rule of revisiting a ground because of a 0-0 is a nonsense. If you've experienced a competitive game, with a crowd around the usual attendance mark and been able to appreciate the ground and its offerings (in this case the pie, the magnificent steak pie), then that's good enough. A 0-0 at Layer Road was far more memorable than the countless Arsenal games the Futbology app reminds me I went to down the years, which might have some hoppers deducting another ground from my total since I can't revisit. I don't think I missed anything from the occasion seeing how the fans celebrated a goal. Maybe if it were Boca Juniors scoring at La Bombonera, that would be integral to the experience, but by that logic a 1-0 away win should require a revisit as well.

I feel like I'm seeing the Welfare Ground at its best as the team push for an opener but are denied by Harry Ambler in the Church goal. Going back to thoughts about ticking off Goodison, my best bet would be a youth match, but that wouldn't be the same as a game where the team are battling relegation and the fans are protesting. It then dawns on me that my trips to St Panteleimon's shared homes go against this logic as well, but I feel I got a good look at Hertford and sampled the chief attraction of the seafood van at Potters Bar.

It's half-time and we return to the bar for a warming drink. The other touchline adjoins the cricket ground, so we're unable to complete a lap. Adam laments that Emley should be 3-0 up; not quite a cricket score, but the standard score that most fans aggrieved at it being 0-0 plump for. The xG is probably nearer 1.37 at best. It's been a decent contest, though, even if it's lacked an overhead kick from halfway, or just a ball bundled in from a goalmouth scramble.

The second half gets under way and Emley continue to press forward. Adam nips behind the goal they are attacking to get some photos. In doing so, he misses the chance to photograph the main incident, when a supporter in just a Burberry shirt and his socks runs the length of the pitch. He dives head-first over the barrier in front of where Adam had been standing and ends up with his arse in the air, before untangling himself and scurrying back to his mates. And his trousers.

Church's defence is exposed again, but Walshaw sends a shot well over, so another old chap is sent off on a run to retrieve the ball from someone's back yard. It feels like only a matter of time before Emley open the scoring. Church do get the ball forward to Nathan Keightley, who takes a bobbling ball past the keeper and it slots it home against the run of play. A sizeable away contingent celebrate, but surely it's only a minor setback for an Emley side unbeaten in 17 games.

I join Adam behind the goal Church are defending, as the Pewits set up camp outside the visitors' box. The game becomes a blur of claret-clad Emley players sending the ball into the box, to be met by a wall of black-and-white-shirted defenders. Church struggle to clear their lines and Emley look for an angle to get a shot away. Chances are blocked. Snatched shots are dragged wide. Ambler makes a few saves that a bloke next to me approves of. He doesn't approve when a couple of kids fight over the ball rather than give it straight back for another Emley corner. There are deflections, there are blocks. It's thrilling to watch, expecting a late turnaround like the one at Farsley.

At the same time, it's a nightmare trying to take notes. Every move looks like it might be the one that leads to an equaliser. The ball is flying around and the game has a timeless quality to it, seeing the exertion of both sides, the pitch getting heavier, with expectant faces looking on from the packed stand. I manage to note that those faces are part of an attendance of 681, which is announced late on. Emley can't force a late turnaround like Farsley, so most of the crowd are left disappointed when the referee blows his whistle for full time. Players slump to the floor, the away bench breathes a sigh of relief and the band of visiting fans celebrate. Adam concludes he must have been a bad-luck charm, and while I felt Emley deserved to be rewarded for their efforts, I could still enjoy a defeat where they dominated, in a way that's not possible when it's your own team. Emley are still well placed for promotion and Adam's car is well placed for a swift getaway, being one of the worst offenders for abandoning his car in the village.

Adam resolves to go more often and I've found something to like about a trip to the in-laws. This is less a setup for a Les Dawson gag and more to do with there being no central heating and the amount of times I've fallen ill when visiting their bleak, windswept farm. The grandstand, the pie and the impression of an old-school bombardment of the opposition goal makes an impression on me, although for some it was the streaker who was still being talked about as we made our way back to the car.

Ground 98
Southwood Stadium, Ramsgate

NEXT UP is another match I expect to write little about, but hopefully won't involve nudity. I'm down in Kent again for a game on my birthday weekend. It's an excuse to get together with my Essex-based mates. Kent has the appeal of being easy for them to get to, yet somehow feeling slightly more exotic with a better selection of seaside towns and its micropub scene. I'm not sure many people would describe Thanet as exotic, but for me a game at the seaside in January beats going to a far-flung location for some winter sun, as I develop something of a rhythm to my own personal football season.

I'm joined in Ramsgate by birthday-weekend-at-the-football-in-Kent veterans Phil and Mark, along with Big Sweaty Martyn (think secret love child of Neil Ruddock and Ange Postecoglu, who prefers to watch Spurs on *Super Sunday* in a pub with a pint of cooking lager - he's only been to eight grounds, a kind of anti-groundhopper, even turning down the chance to visit Spurs' new stadium), Dom (a dead ringer for Alan Brazil, but with the accent of Jamie Carragher, and like both pundits always up for an argument – I would not allow him sneaking in to watch a training session in Siena, or a stadium tour in Munich to bump his total above 56), and Dom's former workmate Big Al (with the not-so-big total of 13 grounds visited).

We assemble in a micropub near the ground. Big Al has already arrived and is waxing lyrical about how resinous the IPA is. A couple of old boys are sporting Ramsgate scarves. Martyn, unfamiliar with actually going to a match, asks if they are going to the game. One scarfless member says he isn't, and affects a camp voice to say he prefers hockey and netball. He then switches tone, à la Frank Lampard, to announce he's off home to watch a John Wayne film. Because he likes to see people get shot.

We mosey on over to the ground before our posse is stopped in its tracks. We can see 'cash only' notices on the turnstiles. While we rustle around for some change, one queue clears enough to reveal a 'cash and card' turnstile. We emerge behind one of the goals, separated from a curved terrace by an expanse of tarmac, which hints at the ground having once had a dog track (later research suggests not). The terrace is wonderfully undulating. 'Beautiful,' I remark. 'Scary,' is Big Al's retort.

We head straight to the clubhouse in a corner of the ground between the terracing and main stand. I briefly notice the stand's slightly barrelled roof, held up by concrete supports, giving it a classic postwar look. The announcer hopes we will enjoy 'some free-flowing attacking football'. I'm more impressed when I find Gadds' No 5 is flowing from a polypin. We return pitchside and automatically head towards the main stand and it's me, the one supposedly here to enjoy the ground in all its glory, who suggests we shouldn't stray too far from the bar. The addition of a cage for youngsters to play panna at the other end of the ground is of limited use to us anyway.

We find a spot in front of the scoreboard, a row of terrace houses backing on to the whitewashed wall behind us. It's a nice place to be with a pint in hand, even if we wouldn't otherwise contemplate standing around in a beer garden in this weather. It falls to me to explain that Ramsgate are top of the step four Isthmian League South East division, reached the FA Cup second round earlier in the season only to lose to AFC Wimbledon, and the main threat up front is Joe Taylor (which I only know as I'd seen him play twice for Lewes at the level above). I tell Martyn they are playing in red. As for the visitors, Burgess Hill Town, all I know is they are in mid-table and are from somewhere in Sussex.

The game gets under way, and it doesn't take long for it to provoke Dom to launch into some misty-eyed nostalgia about when he used to play. It's all Ron Manager 'jumpers for goalposts' stuff until Big Al reminds him of their old works team and how they conceded a goal while their keeper was leaning against the post, smoking a fag and flicking through a porn mag. Either keeper could probably get away with such antics here, as the game is slow to get going.

There's only one course of action that will prompt something noteworthy to happen on the pitch, and that is to return to the clubhouse to use the facilities and get another pint. I just about make out Ramsgate keeper Tom Hadler getting dispossessed on the edge of his area. Defenders recover and hold up play. The Hillians get a shot away, but Hadler recovers and makes the save.

This prompts the Rams to flock towards the other end and get a shot away, but it's straight at the keeper. It also goes straight into my notes, which prompts Martyn to exclaim 'and Martyn was a legend', so that also gets recorded. More noteworthy events follow as a deep cross falls to Hill's Dan Perry. He's in on Hadler, who appears to have done enough to make the save, but it loops in to give the visitors the lead. 'Goal for Burgess Hill, number nine, Dan Perry,' adds the helpful announcer, which prompts Phil to enquire, 'Den Perry? From *Phoenix Nights?*' before launching into an impression which turns into Sam Allardyce, and Phil heading to the bar to see if they do wine by the pint.

Everyone is back in time for the next notable passage of play. Hill's Kieran Rowe collects the ball and runs at the Rams' defence. He slaloms round a couple of them and slides the ball past Hadler, which has Dom exclaiming, 'That was just like Messi.' It's less clear how that made Martyn the legend in this situation, but it was a wonderful goal to give the visitors a surprise 2-0 lead.

We expect a reaction from the league leaders and they soon have a corner. Lee Martin swings it in to the far post for Craig Stone to head home and reduce the arrears. Not long after the restart, Joe Taylor bundles his way past a defender and slots home, but the flag is up, so Dom can continue to insist that my one to watch is a bit of a carthorse. Very few carthorses can turn their man when shepherded towards the byline and square it to a team-mate, which Taylor manages, as he lays on an assist for Medy Elito to level things up going into the break.

There's no question of doing a lap of the ground to have a closer look at the main stand, far terrace or fence running along the other touchline. We retire to the warmth of the clubhouse, where discussion focuses on the finer points of how cold it is. Mark offers the sort of in-depth analysis normally reserved for an article on The Athletic during a quiet week. The only tactical discussion is whether we should stay in the bar for the second half.

It's not entirely clear how we end up back on the terrace, joined by a sizeable home following who have swapped ends to be behind the goal Ramsgate are attacking. The first action is at the other end as Dan Perry sweeps in a low cross, only to be denied by the linesman's flag. No flagging among our group, as some of us take another trip to the bar and refreshment kiosk. In among the beers, an excessively smoky griddle and an average burger, I spot Taylor hold the ball up, swivel, play someone in and the net bulge. Bode Anidugbe emerges from the celebrations as the goalscorer, while Phil emerges with a Bovril and soon regrets it.

With the Rams 3-2 up, I see one of the old boys from the pub walk past clinking a couple of empty whisky miniatures like castanets. Most of the sizeable 1,044 crowd are in a celebratory mood and expect to see a few more. There's a goalmouth scramble from a corner which has Dom saying, 'That's the non-league football I remember!' A thirst for more goals remains unquenched. We have no such issues and return to the bar, where I remain to keep Mark company. He's shaking more than the visiting defence, who I can just make out have allowed someone beyond the keeper. The net bulges. Fans bang on the hoardings and players' arms are aloft. Tijan Jadama wheels away as he makes it 4-2.

Now the result is settled, my mates are keen to retire to a nice warm pub. I recall I am here for groundhopping purposes and offer the feeblest of counter-arguments that it won't count if we don't watch it to the end, which they all mock. We head for the exit and some home fans chant, 'We can see you sneaking out.' Phil isn't happy and approaches one of them to remonstrate. He either corrects them to say he supports Leyton Orient and not Burgess Hill, or that he is striding out of the ground to the pub and not sneaking. As a result, we get to see a few moments more of play before sneaking out.

We don't exactly sneak into the pub as we loudly take over the pool room. I get to witness another sport at the equivalent of non-league level, albeit with Martyn's legendarily bad play, making it far worse than the relative level of football we've just seen. I liven things up by introducing an 'ice bro' into proceedings, whereby a Smirnoff Ice is presented to someone to get on one knee and down in one, provided they can't present one of their own back and make you drink both. If Neville and Carragher were to analyse the events around our subsequent performance on *Monday Night Football*, it's likely this moment would be highlighted.

More pubs ensue and we cover the important issues in the game. Dom quizzes us on every league club's official nickname, and I ask the lads to come up with their best XI of animals. Mark jumps in with Ruel Fox, before I clarify I mean real animals, so octopus in goal, that sort of thing. Dom goes for a blue whale in goal, as no one is scoring past that, before being berated for Mourinho-style parking the bus, and letting a player die for a clean sheet. He then offers Billy the Fish, before I suggest he might struggle if the opposition field a brown bear. This continues and takes in other types of XI and has some sort of drinking game appended to it.

We eventually meet up with Mark's wife and Mrs C, who have spent the day drinking cocktails. Mark leaves early, reduced to tears, either by the size of the tab they have racked up or because the cold has finally gotten to him. Martyn adds to his legendary status by drinking too much cherry-flavoured rum and losing the ability to stand in a kebab shop, going down like Harry Kane in the Arsenal penalty area. It's hard to draw too many other conclusions about the ground but it will be remembered fondly, like a cosy backstreet boozer.

Ground 99

Horsfall Stadium, Bradford (Park Avenue)

AFTER MY trip to Kent, it's time to take things more seriously and do some proper research into the next ground I'm visiting – really getting to know the club and city they hail from. I spend much of my time looking at old pictures of a stadium I won't be visiting, since it was demolished in 1980, but it is what drew me to Park Avenue.

The old ground on Horton Park Avenue was a thing of beauty. A triple-gabled, Archibald Leitch-designed main stand, with a slate roof. It was double-fronted, also serving the cricket ground that played host to Yorkshire. A covered terrace adjoined at one end and at the other was the 'doll's house', a building similar to the cottage at Fulham. In its heyday it was considered a finer venue than Valley Parade, which now dominates the city skyline following its redevelopment.

Park Avenue holds a similar place in my football consciousness to that of Third Lanark, being one of those famous old names that folded several decades before that became a much more common occurrence. They reached the top division in 1914, before a steady decline resulted in Avenue failing to be re-elected in 1970. Avenue struggled on for a few more years before being liquidated, with a new club re-emerging, first as a Sunday league team, then entering the non-league pyramid. During this time they played at McLaren Field, the same rugby ground where I watched Bramley. If I use the same logic, by which I included the new White Hart Lane, that would make this ground number 100, which doesn't feel right. Maybe there just needs to be leniency in how you count the ground of rival teams you have a particular dislike towards. After all, it's not like I want to get tickets in the Spurs end or would qualify for tickets in the away end.

There's not much chance of watching football at the Horton Park site either. A sports centre and cricket nets have been built over it. All that remains are some outer walls with bricked-up turnstiles, the entry price still faintly visible, and a section of overgrown terracing. You can see the steps up to the terrace, and the remains of a toilet block. It was possible to get in, but I would not see what I wished were still there and, besides, I'm a terrible climber. Even if the original club had clung on, it's likely that the timber in the main stand would have caused it to have been demolished anyway.

My research even goes so far as to visit a local museum in Bolling Hall, which is somewhat better preserved. My daughter Ruby indicated she would like to come along to a game. She wasn't interested in increasing her number of grounds visited, but wanted to get her picture in this book. It led to a family day out with something to keep everyone happy. In the museum we learn about the tongueless boar that features on the city's coat of arms, which came about when a bounty was placed on a boar that terrorised locals in medieval times. A man named Northrop killed the beast, but the head was too heavy to carry on foot, so he took the tongue to claim the reward. Another man came across the severed head and took it by horse. He arrived before Northrop and was about to be given the reward only for Northrop to arrive and prove he killed the porcine pest. The head also features on Avenue's club crest. We then spend far too long doing a treasure hunt activity, which is analogous to Avenue's struggle to amass points this season.

Avenue are in the relegation places, some way adrift of safety and facing a second successive relegation from the Northern Premier League down to step four. They face Lancaster City, who are just outside the play-off places and play at the wonderfully named Giant Axe, which is a ground I've had my eye on visiting. The only other thing I know about them is their nickname is the Dolly Blues after some sort of laundry product that was once made in the town. I'm expecting the game to have a similar feel to the drudgery of household chores, given Avenue's poor form. It feels in keeping with the spirit of groundhopping that sometimes you expect the game to be shit, but go anyway.

Ruby isn't keen on watching the game, so we reach a compromise and I take a photo of my kids looking like they are queuing to get in the ground, which has the stewards asking to search Mrs C's bag. I explain it's just me going in and the badly staged photo is just part of the admission cost. The actual cost is £15, and a queue forms when the card machine stops working. 'It's half two, and it's not been busy,' remarks the man on the gate. 'Seven defeats in a row will do that. I'm only here because it's a nice day,' replies the bloke in front. I give up and pay cash, keen to have a look round.

The ground is built into the side of a hill, but is level in order to house a six-lane athletics track, immediately making the venue more sterile. A tired-around-the-edges 1930s pavilion does its best to cheer things up. It's guarded by a security man, as it contains the dressing rooms. Next to it is a forlorn 29-seater stand, where the view is almost entirely obscured by the perimeter fence and team benches. It's made even more superfluous by the large main stand opposite. Brick steps run the length of the pitch, with the middle section covered and containing seats taken from Lord's cricket ground after a renovation there.

I end up back at the clubhouse, which is one of several portacabins and has the feel of a builder's yard – one based next to a signwriting company, as there is an abundance of freshly printed signs labelling everything in capitalised green text on a white background. Inside are framed shirts for the West Bowling rugby league team, who share the stadium, some photos of the old ground I hadn't seen online, and hidden behind a projector screen showing Maidstone beating Ipswich in the cup is an exhibit on Len Shackleton.

I look online and find out that Shackleton played for Avenue early in his career, before more famously turning out for Newcastle and Sunderland. He's the sort of player that a certain generation of fan will fall into a dewy-eyed reverie for, but the only footage I can find of him makes him look like Charles Charlie Charles from the Harry Enfield sketch. The famous blank page in his autobiography for the chapter on 'The Average Director's Knowledge of Football' has aged much better.

The beer in the clubhouse is in decent nick too, and it's tempting to remain in a spot overlooking the pitch. Instead,

I go to the main stand and wonder if I'll overhear any old boys reminiscing about the glory years. Naturally, I end up in front of someone who has more of a propensity to moan about the current state of affairs. 'You might as well be playing for them,' he opens with as Avenue struggle to clear their lines from the off. 'For God's sake, get it forward,' he implores as the ball keeps being played backwards with Avenue hesitant in possession.

I find myself thinking a Lancaster goal might not be a bad thing to avoid a 0-0. Not because goalless draws are as bad as some groundhoppers make out, but it might lead to Mrs C questioning my choices this afternoon. Avenue respond and finally get the ball into the Lancaster box, but only from a hoofed clearance. Soon after, they have a genuine attempt on goal, but it's curled well over to ironic cheers from the visitors. One of their number can't chip the ball back over the perimeter fence while holding a pie, and is on the receiving end of a chant of 'sign him up, sign him up, sign him up'.

Lucas Odunston looks to get forward for Avenue from right-back. He cuts in from the flank and runs into a crowded penalty area and goes down. It's a soft penalty, but raises the prospect of a better game if the hosts can convert. Jordan Preston sends Andre Mendes the wrong way to make it 1-0. The stadium announcer notes that Preston is sponsored by Margaret O'Shea and the 'thank you very much' makes it sound as if she paid for the decision as well.

Lancaster remain calm and confident on the ball, while Avenue snatch at opportunities to get forward. The bloke behind isn't happy with Edy Maieco. 'Bloody Nora,' he exclaims, which has me thinking what other classic Yorkshire expressions I might hear today. The stadium announcer is much more effective than the team, with a crowd of 332 announced before half-time and thanking us for our support, perhaps expecting that's as good as it will get.

The visitors are piling on the pressure with a series of corners which Avenue somehow see off. They can't keep hold of the ball, though. Maieco is deemed a waste of space, and Justin Iwobi also comes in for some stick from the man behind, 'He couldn't hold up a bank, that fella.' His one-liners fall apart just as easily as Avenue's play, as he follows this up with 'seven, you're a lump of wood' and 'stop dicking around with it'. Not wanting players to overelaborate must be a trait of Avenue fans, as Shackleton apparently got a fair bit of stick from the home crowd.

The away section vents their frustrations with a series of anti-Yorkshire songs, which makes me feel less bad that I didn't visit any grounds in the red rose county for this book. An unsavoury chant about Jimmy Savile is met by one bloke shouting, 'He's from Leeds, you dickheads.' The stadium announcer also shows a no-nonsense, matter-of-fact approach when he calls out the raffle numbers as soon as it's half-time.

I take a stroll around the running track to warm up. One old boy has broken into a jog and kids engage in running races and impromptu matches. Running tracks are usually out of bounds, but this gives it the feel of an Italian *passeggiata* as the sun sets and clear skies turn chilly. I suspect my kids would have found it all far less entertaining.

The second-half action gets under way and Odunston threatens again with a burst through the middle. He plays in Preston, whose cross finds Odunston continuing his run.

The right-back's effort is saved before Justin Iwobi tucks in the rebound to the delight of the home crowd, not to mention the surprise of the bloke behind me who had been berating Iwobi only moments earlier. He cautions, 'There's still a long way to go.' Sure enough, Nic Evangelino turns in a Lancaster corner at the near post to reduce the deficit almost immediately afterwards.

Lancaster bombard the Avenue penalty area, and the hosts do their best to clear their lines. A ball goes out for a throw and the Lancaster captain says he will time the ball boy, using the old parenting trick to encourage him to retrieve the ball quicker. Once back in play, the visitors have a strong shout for a penalty. 'That's more of a penalty than the one we got,' concedes the bloke behind, while the ref doesn't yield to a swarm of yellow-shirted players incensed at the decision.

Avenue are allowed to break. Maieco bursts forwards and beats his man. He gets a shot away. It's saved, but falls to Iwobi. He slams the ball past the keeper and off a defender on the line. It ricochets off the bar and doesn't cross the line. Somehow it remains 2-1. 'That's the two players I've moaned about. Just goes to show what do I know?' admits the bloke behind. Despite this sudden bright spark, I think we all know where this is going now.

Avenue continue to hang on. A ball into the Avenue box leads to an innocuous clash between keeper and forward which is given as a penalty. It's both a surprise, in that keepers are usually allowed to get away with far worse, and inevitable that Lancaster have a way back into the game. Samuel Bailey dispatches the kick to level the scores. 'Bloody hell fire, this has 3-2 written all over it,' sighs the bloke behind.

The home side do their best to repel a string of crosses, but what happens next wouldn't trouble the eponymous *Question of Sport* round, as Dominic Lawson heads home what will surely be a late winner. 'Gordon Bennett!' exclaims the bloke behind, before getting frustrated that Avenue still end up playing it backwards in the few remaining minutes. The final whistle blows to signal an eighth defeat in a row, leaving Avenue nine points from safety. If the Bolling Hall ghost reputedly saved Bradford during the Civil War by urging the Earl of Newcastle to pity poor Bradford, it might need a similar intervention to spare Avenue a second successive relegation.

'See you in two weeks,' the bloke behind says to his companion, as everyone shuffles out of the stand. I make my way back to the bar while I wait for Mrs C to come and pick me up. I have a pint and stare contemplatively at the old photos, half expecting an old boy to come over and regale me with tales about the good old days. Instead, I receive a few suspicious looks before I realise I'm lurking near a donation bucket and look like I might be about to make off with it. I then spend far too long trying to work out if it's for a worthy cause supporting the club or the lost cause of funding the playing squad, and whether I should put some spare change in.

Ground 100
LNER Community Stadium, York City

MY 100TH GROUND needs to be something special to celebrate the milestone, so I decide to push the boat out. After missing out on corporate hospitality at Greenock, I look for something closer to home and find that York have a very reasonable-looking package for a shade under £60.

Their new ground was also the most recently built in the top five divisions of English football at the time of writing. It was entirely appropriate to celebrate an arbitrary milestone (that some may contest) with the prawn sandwich brigade in a modern stadium.

While new-build, out-of-town grounds are one of the ills of the modern game, another such issue was the topic of conversation in the run-up to the match. My parents and brother were coming along, and this time my nephew Sam (12 grounds) was joining us. Sam was recently released from the academy of a Championship club at the age of eight. The young age at which clubs recruit players with little chance of making it is another aspect of how cold and calculating the beautiful game has become. I ask my brother what he made of it all as a parent.

Simon tells me Sam had some amazing experiences playing at venues that children his age don't ordinarily get to play at, and will give him memories that last a lifetime (a few of these training grounds are probably on Futbology, so ought to be added to his total). During his 18 months in the academy the coaches were always open and honest about his progress. He received two nights a week of coaching and a match at the weekend (Simon was delighted about him getting five hours of football for free), he got to pull on the kit, play with talented players and improve his skills.

Simon was less effusive about the atmosphere surrounding kids' football, namely some of the other parents. Some would pay a small fortune to the companies springing up promising academy football. It all created pressure on children to perform, or be considered a failure at such a young age, when the odds are stacked against them. It took the fun out of the game, with some kids having to choose between playing grassroots football with their mates or playing for an academy. Some of this was plainly ridiculous and Simon was none the wiser how anyone could tell who would make it or not at that age.

Sam has taken this all in his stride and if he doesn't make it as a player, he could have a future as a sports journalist doing Q&A features for matchday programmes if the conversation in the car is anything to go by. I'm grilled on my head-to-head record against his dad at various sports (surprisingly good if it doesn't involve too much running), my favourite ground (Highbury), favourite player (Thierry Henry), favourite goalkeeper (David Seaman, whose name I once threw into a pub conversation about England's best keeper, and had my closest brush with football violence when Mark lamped me in his staunch, but misguided, defence of Ray Clemence) and my most embarrassing moment (letting a through ball bounce on Burnham Ramblers' rock-hard main pitch and see it loop over me into the goal).

We arrive in the sizeable car park adjoining the stadium, which is convenient, but is seldom something you hear hoppers laud as a feature. I would prefer the trickier journey into the city centre for their old Bootham Crescent ground, as hoppers appreciate a certain old-school charm. It would only exist in my mind as footage of York's famous FA Cup win over Arsenal in 1984: a frozen solid pitch, John Lukic in jogging bottoms, Keith Houchen dispatching a penalty and fans packed on to the terrace celebrating.

This historic result was a bit before I started following football, so didn't leave any lasting trauma. Besides, a more recent League Cup win over Manchester United in 1995 gave me a fonder feeling towards the Minstermen. Other than that, York had been a league club from 1927 to 2004, before relegation into non-league, a brief return in 2012, and they were now back in the National League and looking nervously at the relegation places below them.

We approach the stadium, which is barely distinguishable from the other entertainment facilities on site, with an endless glass and steel frontage. My parents are waiting and were particularly impressed by the large Marks & Spencer located opposite. For Sam the club shop beckons, so we enter the complex to be confronted by a swimming pool, library and shops for both the football and rugby league teams who share the ground.

Souvenirs stowed, we walk up to the desk for corporate hospitality, but not until half our party exits the building, in order to re-enter and sashay down the roped-off red carpet.

Our names are checked off and we are given wristbands so we can ascend past an outpatient facility to the lounge. We're given a cheery greeting and asked if we had a good journey from Maidenhead, as our accents don't suggest we are local. We clear up any misunderstanding; I've only ever seen the Magpies' York Road ground from a passing train, and we are shown to our table.

The lounge has a hotel conference suite feel to it, but with Everton v Spurs on TV, a brief appearance from Yorkie the Lion and a decent local ale from Brew York on tap. We are served steak stew, which is at the level of a decent gastropub, and that is far less derogatory than if I said their players were of pub standard, which some home fans might argue they are. The chocolate torte is almost as delicious as seeing Spurs concede a late equaliser.

Ahead of the pre-match Q&A with York City legend Steve Tutill, we realise we ought to think of some questions. I think of something to do with grounds and tell Simon he should ask whether he would rather fight one horse-sized duck or 100 duck-sized horses. The compere asks no-nonsense defender Tutill about various moments in his career and his brilliantly deadpan answers typically start along the lines of: 'We lost 1-0 and I gave away a penalty.' We don't have a chance to ask him a question, but Simon turns to me and says, 'He would definitely take on the giant duck.' I can be fairly sure that any attempt I'd made to find out about a favourite away ground wouldn't have led to any reminiscences about a rickety old League Two venue, given how fondly he spoke about his schoolboy appearances at Wembley or his part in the League Cup upset at Old Trafford.

Players clearly value the quality of playing facilities and scale of the venue over a twee grandstand that might draw in a groundhopper, which is fair enough as I prefer to work in a featureless glass and steel office over a barely converted basement of a Victorian workhouse. A current player walks past with a protective boot on his leg and fields the worst question any player past or present is likely to be asked today, when someone enquires, 'Are you out injured?' I fail to ask the obvious follow-up of whether his injury means he would prefer to use the boot to stamp on some tiny horses rather than face up to a giant duck.

We head to our padded seats near the halfway line to watch his more mobile team-mates. It's not the worst new build I've been to. The mixed pattern of different-coloured seats partially hides the ground being half full and the stands are at least different to each other. Simon is less impressed. 'Architecturally, this is the worst ground I've been to. If I'd given George [my other nephew; three grounds visited] some Lego, he would come up with something better,' he concludes. One flaw that may be specific to the time of year is the low sun in our eyes, which looks like it will take all half to dip behind the giant grey wall behind one end.

One fan is keen to see something else away from the field of play. 'Put him in the stand,' he shouts as play gets under way. It's reassuring that it isn't just the fans to our left, singing along to a drummer, who are backing their team vocally. The away supporters have their say with the ever-original 'shit ground, no fans', which is a bit rich given there's only 72 of them.

The fact I'm spending a lot of my time shielding my eyes as I look towards the end Maidenhead are attacking suggests they are on top. Sure enough, they burst into the York penalty area and cut it back for Ashley Nathaniel-

George, who slams the ball into the roof of the net to make it 1-0. York are less incisive. Their build-up is laboured and when Dipo Akinyemi releases Will Davies for a one-on-one with the keeper, he can only fire it straight at Craig Ross.

There follows a backheel to no one in particular and a poorly worked free kick. York get a second bite at this and send a better ball wide to Scott Burgess. His deep cross eventually falls to Akinyemi, who is denied by Ross, only for a Maidenhead defender to slam the ball into his own net. Simon and I burst out laughing at seeing such a wayward clearance. I won't name the scorer, less to spare him his blushes and more because various sources credit Davies with the equaliser. We question what we witnessed. Just to add to our sense of disorientation, Sam performs the traditional role of grandads at the football, and offers around his sweets. My mum then comes up with a comment I can't argue with as she says, 'They keep fannying around with the ball and losing it,' which goes to show those criticising female pundits that they should be given time to grow into the role. Although I'm not suggesting Sky Sports get on to the phone to my mum just yet.

Half-time comes around and we return to the lounge and our pre-ordered drinks are waiting at our table, just like at the theatre. There's enough time to quaff a very quaffable offering from Brew York until I realise the match clock on the opposite stand is counting on from 47 minutes. So, like the very worst patron of Club Wembley, I make my way back to my seat after the half has started.

The Minstermen are less sluggish and start on the front foot. Akinyemi cuts in from the left and lets fly with a strike that crashes back off the post. The number nine is less incisive when played in soon after. He checks his run and looks to cut it back to someone rather than shoot, so the chance goes. We think there might be a chance when a loud shout goes up for handball. A Maidenhead defender goes down and nothing is given, leading to boos from the home fans and Sam, who is getting drawn into the contest. A bloke nearby remonstrates, 'He's hurt his hand, ref!'

Another stoppage for a head injury is my cue to pop to the gents. I'm surprised there are several people who have remained in the bar, where the curtains are drawn lest someone drink alcohol in sight of the pitch. The announcer uses the break in play to let us know we're in a crowd of 4,667, also confirming the total number of away fans we had been getting Sam to count.

Sam and some of the other young fans nearby are chanting for a penalty soon after I return to my seat. This is more out of desperation for another goal than anything untoward. Both sides have chances, with York the more eager for a winner. I hold off on confirming to Sam my pick for the man of the match, expecting to be swayed by a late winner. Sam boos the official selection and no one can make a telling contribution before the final whistle blows.

The verdict from my parents is that the game cleared the low bar of Eynesbury in terms of entertainment and they enjoyed the surroundings more than Albion Rovers. It comes as no surprise that the creature comforts of a new ground are preferable to the more spartan delights of Cliftonhill for them, as they do like a house on a new-build estate. For me, those sorts of developments, along with city-centre motorways and out-of-town shopping centres, are a dispiriting aspect of modern life. I would sooner be walking back to the station from the old ground, past rows of terraced houses, rather than sitting in a queue of traffic trying to get out of the car park. It makes a mockery of what was billed as 'green football weekend', along with other games involving teams travelling by plane and late kick-offs making fans miss the last train home.

The corporate hospitality was good, but all it really does is give you the glimpse behind the curtain you used to have in days gone by, and still get at lower levels. It's a decent money spinner for clubs, and you have to trust that these sorts of ground moves are done with the club's best interests at heart. The drive back has the timeless sound of football commentary on the radio, but if you listen carefully, it's newly promoted Sheffield United unable to compete at the top level as Aston Villa rack up the goals.

Ground 101

The Real 100th Ground

IN CASE anyone reading this has been deducting a ground off my total for my claim to the Tottenham Hotspur Stadium, I thought I ought to make up for it with a bonus ground. In other words, this is my official ground number 100, as recorded on Futbology. It needs to be somewhere special, befitting of the occasion. I toy with Wembley FC, for a terrible road to Wembley pun, Barnsley for their Archibald Leitch stand and game against Orient, only for Phil to be less keen on the nightlife than Georgi Hristov was, or Hashtag United women's trip to face Halifax in a cup semi-final at Liversedge, only for the kids to prefer National Trust hopping (30 of their 500 sites visited).

I fit in a revisit to Emley for their FA Vase tie at home to Whickham. The pie is just as good as last time and the team get a better result, as I watch from an elevated position in the grandstand. There is a sense of getting a diminishing return from going back to a ground without having much of a connection with the club. A spirited contest in testing conditions makes it worthwhile, but I'm more enthused by what I have up next.

I expect my next excursion to be worthwhile regardless of events on the field, which is just as well as it's a six-hour round trip. I'm off to Galashiels to visit Netherdale, the home of Gala Fairydean Rovers. I think long and hard about which ground I most wanted to tick off my bucket list and it comes down to Rovers and Great Yarmouth Town. In the end, a *Terrace Edition* article on the Peter Womersley-designed brutalist masterpiece swings it in favour of the Lowland League side.

The anticipation builds as I exchange emails with club secretary Robert Fairburn. I try to avoid making too many requests of busy club officials, but for this trip I make an exception. I ask what sort of impact groundhoppers have on the club: 'Each home game, we normally get a handful of people who are there just to look at the architecture of the Historic Scotland A-Listed stand. We don't normally get many groundhoppers, although for a recent midweek home game someone had driven up from near London and was going to watch an SPL game the following day. Back in 2014, we hosted a groundhoppers weekend game, so we got them all at once and they have ticked our ground off their list. There were more than 100 if I remember rightly.'

On the costs of maintaining the stand: 'When the stand was closed due to crumbling concrete and safety concerns, it was established that although Gala Fairydean and Gala Rovers built the stand in 1964 at a cost of £27,000, the ownership falls on to Scottish Borders Council as they own the land, so therefore they are responsible for the maintenance of the stand and they fronted the £1.45m renovation programme. If it had been established that Gala Fairydean Rovers FC were legally responsible for funding the repairs programme, it is doubtful whether it would ever have reopened after being closed for four years. The cost would have killed the club financially.

'The uncertainty of the ownership of the stand and the legal wrangling was perhaps the biggest challenge of the renovation. Being closed for such a long time killed the atmosphere at home games and the closure was a difficult period for the club. Historic Scotland and Scottish Borders Council vowed to return to the stand to its original 1964 condition, which meant all advertising boards had to be removed from the back of the stand and the glass installed to give the appearance of a floating roof. It looks quite remarkable from a long distance away.'

On how architect Peter Womersley got involved: 'Peter Womersley was friendly with a man called Jimmy Walker, who in the early 1960s was the treasurer for both the Fairydean and Rovers. They both lived in nearby Gattonside. He persuaded Peter to come up with a revolutionary design which would hopefully boost Fairydean's chances of being elected to the national Scottish Leagues. Sadly, it hasn't worked so far.'

Robert concludes by saying, 'Netherdale is always worth a visit. We run a friendly bar and the cafe sells delicious butchers' pies. Opinions are divided [on the stand]. Was it really built to cope with a Scottish winter? But we at the club are proud of the stand.' The team themselves are standing less proud in 16th place out of 18 teams. Visitors Broomhill are only marginally better off in 14th. Watching a potential dead rubber, with neither side in danger of being relegated, is of little concern in this instance, though.

I pull into the car park next to the ground and admire the striking stand before me. The roof does indeed appear to float. I get a closer look and take in the full effect. My photos don't do it justice and there's a lighter feeling up close to the edifice. The concrete, despite its imperfections, allows the structure to have an airy, modernist and uplifting feel to it. I spend far too long staring at concrete before realising there are still two hours until kick-off.

I'm wandering around the site when I notice another ground next door, playing host to rugby union. The stand is less obviously stunning, but isn't without its charm. It's a little reminiscent of photos I've seen of Chelmsford City's former New Writtle Street home, backing directly on to the road, claret-coloured woodwork and an elevated seating deck, with some standing below. It also has an open gate, so I sneak in, with the scoreboard showing the hosts trail 17-21. I snap some photos of the ground as I find my way to a seat. Luckily, my photos are all of the stand as I soon establish I'm watching an under-16s match.

The lack of burly forwards explains why I'm seeing both sides attempt some running rugby rather than something about as entertaining to the casual observer as the Eton wall game. The strong tradition of sevens rugby in the borders is also likely to be an influence. It's back-and-forth stuff, with the hosts edging in front, before potential controversy strikes. I've no idea what's at stake, and the finer points of the rulebook are lost on me, but it appears the hosts had done enough to earn a line-out with some last-ditch defending. Yet the visitors are given a scrum in their favour, from which they build a platform to go over for the winning score.

Rugby's typical gentlemanly acceptance of the referee's decision leaves me none the wiser whether it was the correct call. It means I'll face making the obvious contrast with the reaction to any dubious calls later, although at least I'll have a chance of understanding whether or not it was the correct one. The match was an entertaining diversion, which I rarely say about union. It also allows me to compare whether the football stand is noticeably colder.

I still have time to wait until kick-off, so I warm up in the car, admiring the stand before me. The PA system is pretty impressive too, as I can hear the 90s indie music while I wait for the turnstile to open. I see people go into a door for the clubhouse under the main stand and decide to follow suit. It's marked members only and once at the bar I'm asked if I'm part of the Broomhill committee. I wonder how far my pale complexion and ginger hair could carry me if I decide to say yes, but since I can't take advantage of any free booze, I say no and order an Irn-Bru.

I walk round to the turnstile and am again asked if I'm with Broomhill. I explain why I'm here and am told I could have a press pass if I want, before being introduced to a committee member. It's just as well I decline the pass as I fail the most basic journalistic tasks of noting down anyone's names or anything they say I could use as a quote. Instead, I fall into a friendly conversation about the Lowland League (a tough league to get promoted from, but easier to fall out of, with ambitious clubs coming up and spending decent money), the involvement of B teams from Hearts and Celtic (to my surprise not seen as a bad thing) and former Scotland international John Collins (who grew up nearby and is an ambassador for the club).

I'm shown around the boardroom, where there is a shrine to Collins, but the man himself isn't there. This at least prevents me from telling him how I unceremoniously ditched him from my Monaco save on *Championship Manager* in favour of the much cheaper Tommy Svindal Larsen, in lieu of recalling any matches I must have seen him play for Everton or Fulham against Arsenal.

The Broomhill committee are now in attendance, so I'm unlikely to have been able to blag so much as a sausage roll. Besides, the pies came recommended, so I head to the catering hut. I order a hand-sized steak pie, similar to the ones I saw at Albion Rovers, and it's the perfect football snack. I bump into club secretary Robert and thank him for the recommendation. I can't exactly blame him that I've burnt my mouth in my eagerness to scoff it down.

Next up, I want to devour the view from the stand itself. I find a spot on one of the bench seats at the back, not quite on the halfway line, so my big ginger bonce doesn't obstruct the Veo camera setup. In front of me is the 3G pitch (helpful for avoiding postponements and community use throughout the week), a small 100-seater stand with one person in it (useful when the main stand was being renovated, and if you want to look at the main stand from afar rather than experience its elevated views), and beyond that are several other pitches and the faint outline of the hills marked as Scott's View on Google Maps (after Sir Walter Scott, who lived locally).

The match gets under way and Gala would have done well to have held in mind the Scott quote, 'Success – keeping your mind awake and your desire asleep', as they start the brighter of the two teams, but opt for a couple of speculative efforts when there might have been a pass on. Broomhill are able to 'look back, and smile on perils past' as they grow into the contest.

Another Gala injury interrupts proceedings. It's another insofar as committee members and volunteers have all mentioned them being a feature of their season. Soon after the break in play, Broomhill cross low for Josh Jack to sweep home on his debut for 1-0. I've avoided a 0-0 again, but in this case I wouldn't have minded an excuse to revisit. There's nearly another soon after when Jack is denied his second, as the game becomes more frantic. 'Stop passing *aboot* at the back for no reason' comes a cry from the stand.

The Gala defence is impervious to any quotable advice and allows Corey O'Donnell to wriggle through and get away a shot across the keeper for 2-0. Ryan Kidd, in goal for Gala, is called into action again to deny Jack, and then presents him with a tap in for 3-0 when he spills another shot from distance. Both sides exchange further efforts from distance, before Gala fail to clear their lines once more and Scott Roberts has time to place one left-footed in the bottom corner for 4-0.

The half-time whistle draws a dispiriting 45 minutes for the home supporters to a close. I can at least be cheered up by another pie. I go for the mince one this time, which is not to be confused with the ones you get at Christmas. It's second best to the steak, but not by as big a margin as the team have been second best. I go for a lap of the ground so I can get a look at Gala's star attraction, the main stand, from another angle. As I return to my seat, I realise I'm blocked from doing a full lap, so I climb through a fence and find myself in the media area behind the dugouts.

It's a good job I don't linger, as any slight journalistic credentials would have been undermined when I lose track of the score early in the second half. Broomhill add to their tally before Gala pull a couple back. The way one of the Gala scorers fetched the ball from the net and hurried back for the restart suggested things were closer, only for someone in the crowd to confirm it was now 6-2.

No one can agree on whether a late challenge from a Gala player deserves the red card he's shown, which puts pay to any slim hopes of a comeback. Broomhill take advantage of the extra man, hitting the woodwork and having efforts blocked, before finally bundling home a seventh. It ends 7-2, which is disappointing for those involved in such a friendly club.

I've had a warm welcome and enjoyed speaking to those who keep things running off the pitch. I've not even found the stand to be that cold and, if it was I could have followed the lead of someone sat nearby and grabbed a blanket from the car. It's a fitting way to end my quest to reach 100 grounds, for which I get a little digital badge on the Futbology app, and the warm glow of the memories I've had along the way. It's been more than just about the numbers. It's been great to get to know more football clubs, visit some charming places and occasionally see some entertaining football.

More Grounds for the Purists

I REALISE that some readers, for whom it is all about the purity of the numbers, may be less keen on that conclusion and refuse to count reserve games I've seen at Barnet and Welling, a youth-team game at Colchester Community Stadium, or a friendly at Portsmouth. There may be others expecting me to somehow revisit Layer Road following a 0-0 there or see the main tenant at various places. And because it's not as if I'm going to stop going to new grounds at the end of this project, I thought I should capture those I visited in the rest of the 2023/24 season.

I watch Sheffield FC, not at the Home of Football Stadium, but at Bracken Moor when they use Stocksbridge Park Steels' ground while they are forced to play home games at other less waterlogged venues to complete their fixtures. This might be a no-no for some groundhoppers, but given their itinerant history and losing income from playing nearly an hour's drive away from their usual home, it feels both appropriate and worthy to be supporting the club, in a crowd of only 105. The team duly reward us with a 4-0 win over Winterton Rangers. A tight first half is mostly notable for the high quality of heading, which would have impressed fans over a century ago. It's a header that sets up a goal in first-half stoppage time before Sheffield run away with it after the break. The ground itself is worth a visit, although the hard, wooden seats with minimal leg room in the Jamie Vardy Stand were more irritating than if the player himself celebrated a winner right in front of me.

My next games are a celebration of completing this project, as I book a return to Brussels with vague plans to see Royale Union Saint-Gilloise. For a second time that plan falls apart, as I pick the Tour of Flanders weekend before the play-off fixtures are settled. Instead, Paul books three games, in three days, in three different countries. First up is NAC Breda v MVV Maastricht. All the trains run smoothly, so we have time in Breda for some beers at the superb Frontaal brewery. The barman assures us we are going to watch the team with the most drunken fans in the Netherlands, and it will be the party of our lives if they win.

It's not clear how sober those coming up with the NAC prefix were, since it's a blend of two abbreviations that translate as 'never give up, always persevere, pleasant for its entertainment and useful in its relaxation, combination'. There was reason to celebrate not long after their formation, with a league title in 1921. Only a KNVB Cup win in 1973 has followed, with the club bouncing between the Eredivisie and Eerste Divisie in recent years, currently finding themselves in the latter.

NAC moved into their 19,000-capacity Rat Verlegh Stadion in 1996 and we take a taxi through the Breda suburbs to arrive in time for kick-off. Paul uses the journey to practise his Dutch and the tricky 'gh' sound in Verlegh, which sounds like he is clearing his throat. He has booked us tickets in what he believes to be the ultras' end, and we are the only people not wearing Stone Island. We order beer and find some available seats. It's far from looking like it's about to kick off, but neither is it the civilised environment of the Premier League. The graffiti on stadium walls, banners being more prominent than adverts and blokes drinking and smoking in the stands makes it feel far less sanitised, and it's all the better for it.

The football itself isn't great and early chants soon turn to the murmur of pub conversation and one bloke doing what sounds like an impression of Pingu, as he bemoans another poor passage of play. MVV have a shot deflected on to the woodwork and we take that as our cue to hit the bar ourselves. On our return, the home support tries to rouse their team. Paul translates it as 'Who are we? Yellow and Black.' It has little effect on the team and the game enters the break goalless. We return to the bar to sample the local cuisine. The plastic texture of the burger slapped into the bun is alarming, but slathered in curry sauce turns out to be just what we needed alongside another beer. We're determined to enjoy ourselves, even if the team aren't going to get the party going. They are helped on their way when an innocuous cross shot is deflected in, to give NAC the lead soon after the restart.

MVV respond almost immediately, attacking the end we are standing at. They burst into the box and Tunahan Taşçı slams the ball into the roof of the net to make it 1-1. It's not clear what this means for NAC's play-off hopes, since you can't simply equate their league position to how many slots there are, as some are taken by bottom sides from the Eredivisie and others by winners of the mini-season-within-a-season *Nacompetitie*, but not those in automatic promotion or relegation positions or B teams. We can only assume winning is desirable. So, when MVV work the ball over to Taşçı, who is free in the box, and slams it home for 2-1, that's not a good thing.

Pingu and the ultras are unhappy, so much so that one bloke with goggles in the hood of his coat calls out to a NAC player going off injured, 'You're a *fooking* wanker,' in a perfect northern accent. Although, I suspect this is more of a misappropriation than malice towards the player being applauded off. There is little else to give the home fans a reason to clap, and the game ends in defeat. On the way out of the ground there is an unlit corridor next to the toilet block, which I speculate must lead to some sort of sex club. Paul investigates and informs me it's just another bar. We order more beer and the mood is not unlike being on a stag do unwillingly sitting around a strip-club bar. We are not going to have the best night of our lives here, so we get a taxi back into town.

The next morning, I'm awoken by Paul blasting 2 Unlimited from his phone. I have a vague recollection of going to several bars in the delightful old town, culminating in somewhere playing what can only be described as the sort of music you might expect to hear in a Portuguese circus, which I have a video of Paul dancing to. I'm not feeling too spritely and am in no state to do parkrun, which is just as well because groundhopping trumps that hobby, and we have an early train to catch.

We arrive in Aachen in time to see Alemannia Aachen v Fortuna Köln in the regionalised fourth tier of German football. Aachen are nailed on for the title and promotion. When we see the size of the Neuer Tivoli ground on the approach from the long, straight road out of the town towards the stadium, it's clear they ought to be playing at a higher level. Indeed, they have had two spells in the

Bundesliga, finishing runners-up to Bayern in 1967/68 and spending a single season there as recently as 2005/06.

The 'potato beetles', as Aachen are called because of their yellow and black strip, are creeping back up the leagues after bankruptcy saw them fall to this level. They have the support of a near-sell-out crowd, who are in fine voice, led by an ultras group behind one of the goals. We have seats up in the gods and it feels like we could be in a World Cup venue. Fourth-tier football soon dispels that notion. Fortuna cede ground in midfield and defend their penalty area, forcing Aachen wide. Aachen lump balls into the box and, despite having a physical presence up front, they can't find the target.

The ultras sing, drum and wave big flags throughout, including one adorned with the image of Charlemagne, a former gaffer in these parts. During the odd pause in songs, a small band of Fortuna fans up in the far corner make themselves heard. None of this is in response to events on the pitch and a drab half draws to a close.

We make our way to the bar and the catering operation is about as effective as either team at creating chances, making a mockery of supposed German efficiency. We don't move, so with the second half about to kick off we use what little hungover energy we have to ascend all the way back to our seats. Paul rations out an old packet of nuts he finds in his pocket, as Alemannia's forwards look for scraps in the box. Anton (pause for fans to shout his surname) Heinz prods home after an initial effort is saved; 1-0 to Aachen. The fans hum the intro to 'I Will Survive' and swirl their scarves in unison.

Aachen hold on for the win and the home bench empties on to the pitch. We slip away from the celebrations and get a currywurst to fuel the walk back into town. We're held up by fans getting their deposits back on plastic cups before we finally get to have this classic matchday staple. After walking back into the old town, we're ready to get back on the pilsner, only with more restraint than is evident among the home fans.

We have another early start the following day as we hop across the border into Belgium, and the city of Liege. It's then a bus out past Standard's ground and the rusting hulk of an old steelworks to the suburb of Seraing. A couple of visiting KV Oostende fans tuck their scarves deep into their coats, clearly concerned about their surroundings ahead of this relegation six-pointer in the Belgian second tier. We wander obliviously into a local bar with a small band of Seraing ultras and, more importantly, a TV showing the Tour of Flanders cycle race. It's the long attritional run up to the cobbled climbs, as we lay down our own steady base of sub-six per cent beers.

The nearby ground is hidden among rows of terraced houses. Once inside, getting a beer appears equally obscured, with prices advertised in 'Jetons'. Paul establishes we can pay in cash and not just these mysterious tokens. We're in French-speaking Wallonia, and he only gets us small Gallic measures of lager, though. Once in our seats, we spot the group we had seen earlier in the bar, who start the 'allez, allez, allez' songs. It's a sparse crowd, with the open terrace behind one goal closed. The other end houses a few corporate boxes, and in the stand opposite there's plenty of empty bench seating on show in the home end, with a lively away contingent crowded towards one side.

I notice a pleasing slope to the pitch, so I feel at home. It's my kind of place after a couple of newer, larger grounds.

The original Seraing club carried matricule number 23, but bought the rights of another club to swap places and now carry matricule 167. They are also facing a second successive relegation. Oostende (matricule 31) test any sympathies toward the home side, as they are an equally venerable club, facing a second successive relegation of their own. They start the brighter of the two sides, but go a man down to a questionable red card.

I would question the penalty Seraing are awarded soon after as well, but that's mainly because I feel goalkeepers should be allowed to flatten opposing strikers with impunity when challenging for a loose ball. Pape Moussa Fall converts the spot kick to break the deadlock not long before the interval. We check out the local cuisine at half-time and the French influence is noticeable with one of the finest bread rolls I've ever had, combined with whatever offal was shoved in it.

Paul joins the queue for beer and misses the start of the second half. Mohamed Berte is played in for the visitors and slots through the keeper's legs to level. The Oostende bench pour on to the pitch as it restores their advantage in the league table as things stand. Paul returns having managed to get large beers, which end up being the only notable item of quality during the rest of the half.

It ends 1-1 and we return to the local bar, only to find we have missed Mathieu van der Poel's race-winning move and the sight of most of the peloton being forced to dismount and walk up the sodden cobbles of the Koppenburg. The football may have been poor, but it was preferable to getting drenched on the roadside of the race route. Groundhopping once again proved to be a little window into somewhere we wouldn't otherwise have visited.

I'm tempted to extend our groundhopping adventure and head across the city for an evening kick-off at RFC Liege (matricule number four), but I haven't developed the dedication of more serious groundhoppers and take the next train to Brussels. Here I can admire the decor of Café Verschureren, with its nameplates of now-defunct clubs adorning the walls. I also have time the next day to look at the art deco frontage of Royale Union Saint-Gilloise's ground. It's as fine as Highbury or Craven Cottage, but with more of a faded grandeur.

On my return to England, I go to a far less architecturally appealing venue for Peterborough Sports v Farsley Celtic in a National League North relegation six-pointer. The ground is nothing to write home about, so I won't. The contest is a tight affair. Celtic keeper Žan-Luk Leban keeps his side in it with several saves, but the Everton loanee can't prevent his side succumbing to a 1-0 defeat. The evening was mostly notable for a conversation with an old boy in an Umbro overcoat, the sort of which every youth coach I ever played for seemed to own. He tells me about who one stand was named after, how a player is the son of the deputy dean at the cathedral, and how when he returned to his car parked in a nearby church he was offered drugs and replied that he's already on plenty of medication already. When I mention I'm here mainly for groundhopping, it was gratifying that my tally impressed a proper footballing man.

I fail to notch up any more grounds before the end of the season, missing play-off matches, county cup finals, one of Colne's dozen or so games crammed into April after a series of postponements and a random dead rubber at nearby Northallerton. These can wait for another season.

It's far from anticlimactic, as I follow the fortunes of several teams I've seen and start looking at next season's potential fixtures as promotions and relegations are confirmed.

Revisit (Part Two)

THERE WERE revisits during the season to Clapton Community, Chelmsford City and Harrogate Railway Athletic. The first-ever Clapton derby was a must-watch game that tempted me back to London and was as good a footballing occasion as any I'd been to. The Rail's matches were less of an occasion, but it was always nice to get along and see how they were doing. They fell well short of the play-offs this time around, so will once again miss out on games against Knaresborough, Silsden and Hallam, who all finished mid-table in the NCEL Premier. Emley were promoted as NCEL Premier champions to the step four Northern Premier League East, where they will face Bradford Park Avenue, who were relegated despite a decent run of results following my visit. Emley, like Mildenhall, exited the FA Vase the round after I saw them. Although it was worse for St Panteleimon, who folded before the season's end.

Elsewhere in step four, Ramsgate finished second and lost in the play-offs. Of the other Kent sides I saw, Faversham also came second and missed out on promotion, losing their play-off semi-final. Whitstable finished just outside the play-off places and Lordswood finished mid-table, so the trio remain at step five.

The other step five side I saw and have less fond memories of, Eynesbury, appear to have offered little excitement during the rest of the season, finishing second bottom, albeit avoiding relegation. More Saturdays are likely to have been ruined in Coatbridge, with Albion Rovers only finishing mid-table in the Lowland League. Gala Fairydean finished third bottom, but can look forward to hosting Lowland League football next season in their fine ground, hopefully with a shorter injury list.

The Lowland League would benefit from an automatic promotion place and extended play-offs to maintain interest, reward ambitious clubs and stop it from becoming such a graveyard for former league clubs. Opening up more promotion opportunities has improved the National League, south of the border. York City weren't a beneficiary of this, being at the wrong end of the table, but at least clung on to their position in the division. Farsley also survived relegation on the final day of the season, a step below.

At the furthest ends of the footballing spectrum, Kellingley Welfare confounded the group of Calverley fans singing 'Top of the league and you're fucking shit' by winning Division Two of the West Yorkshire League, and NAC Breda were promoted to the Dutch top flight. NAC made the play-offs despite finishing eighth. They beat Roda JC, whose fans had been on the pitch erroneously celebrating automatic promotion. They followed this with wins over FC Emmen and Excelsior, almost blowing a 6-2 first-leg lead to win the final 7-6 on aggregate. How drunken the celebrations were is unknown. Seraing finished adrift of KV Oostende in the relegation places, but were reprieved when Oostende became the latest Belgian club to go out of business. Aachen, bouncing back from their own troubles, sealed promotion to the third tier of German football.

My ability to scout players able to step up in levels remained as stubbornly poor as some of those league positions. Joe Bevan secured a move from Albion Rovers to Burnley, while I only noted that he made one decent run. Various other strikers I questioned all registered positions in the top scorers charts. The most remarkable story of all was Richard Kone, who featured at the very start of this book for Athletic Newham. He secured a move to League One Wycombe Wanderers, having initially come to England for the Homeless World Cup as a teenager in 2019. Kone finished the season with four goals in 20 games for Wanderers.

It's striking how groundhopping makes it possible to shape your own football journey throughout the season, unshackled from the drudgery of following a single team. From games full of early season optimism in late summer sunshine, preliminary rounds of the FA Cup through to midweek fixtures when you need to wrap up warm, putting on a beer coat at a seaside ground for my birthday, and finishing up following promotions and relegations unfold. It's great to see these stories play out in different settings.

Looking back on the grounds I've visited, I feel the same sense of adventure and discovery that I might get from going on holiday. There have been memorable sights, where grounds haven't been swept away in favour of new stands meeting ground grading requirements at the lowest possible cost. There's always been a utilitarianism running through stadium architecture, but seeing those with little flourishes, combined with a warm welcome from storied clubs and some form of entertainment on the pitch has made this a worthwhile exercise.

If I were to build my ideal ground, I would take the brightly painted main stand from Albion Rovers, although I might have to budge it along a bit to squeeze in the stand from Gala Fairydean. I would place the scaffold terrace from Clapton Community behind one goal, with their can bar and fusion food stalls conveniently next to it. Whitstable's main stand and scoreboard would go on the other touchline, which would leave some room for the beach huts from Lewes. Behind the other goal, I would have Margate's sloping stand, but with the clubhouse containing the sort of memorabilia from Corinthian-Casuals and some decent beer from just about anywhere else. I would need to find room for the Potters Bar seafood stall. I'd then take Hallam's sloping pitch and place it all in a valley like Silsden's.

Admiring the grounds teams play in is another way of appreciating the game. Football isn't just for the lads, lads, lads, banter merchants. I may have started out by describing groundhoppers as the footballing equivalent of trainspotters, which could sound disparaging, but the game needs occasional fans to add to the gate, and give wider prominence to issues facing individual clubs. Groundhoppers may not be incentivised to return to a club, but many will, and they often care deeply about the health of the wider game. I was surprised by how few grounds many of my old group of friends have been to, when they profess to be football fans. It's easy to take the pyramid for granted or get too wrapped up in one club's fortunes. At the other end of the spectrum, it's also easy to get too wrapped up in the numbers, completing leagues and collecting memorabilia. Most people I spoke to just treated it as another hobby. I did still have a nagging feeling that I ought to have been to more grounds by now and at least ticked off a whole league.

I seek the views of veteran groundhopper Laurence Reade (2,531 grounds visited in 28 different countries). He tells me he got into it 'by watching Oxford home and away, then when I couldn't attend an away game, I did a local game. I enjoyed it, and it slowly grew from there.' I ask how much the numbers matter to him: 'The higher the number gets, the less important it becomes.' He still has grounds he wants to go to and lists Cliftonville's Solitude, Linfield's Windsor Park and Lancaster City's Giant Axe. I wonder if it can feel like a case of diminishing returns after a certain point: 'No, there's always a corner to look around, or another town or country to visit. Knowledge isn't a finite commodity.'

Laurence adds that groundhopping 'makes you more sanguine about your own club. You soon understand there's more than just that little world.' He's happy to 'look for two teams, two goals and a game' and doesn't get drawn into whether a ground needs to be enclosed, issue a ticket or programme, nor any of the other quirks groundhoppers might deem necessary to enjoy the experience. It's a case of 'each to their own', and like many other pursuits, it's harmless fun, a diversion.

Does this all mean I'm a fully fledged groundhopper now I've reached 100 grounds? Well, does playing in goal at five-a-side make me a goalkeeper? The answer to both must be 'yes'. I may not be any good at either endeavour, but so long as it's enjoyable, then it doesn't matter. It's been great to immerse myself in this world, racking up grounds over the past couple of years, and since there isn't a groundhopping equivalent of me clattering opposition forwards with a slide tackle well outside my penalty area, then it's all good. Groundhopping is another way of enjoying the beautiful game in beautiful and not-so-beautiful locations, or the Belmont Ground and the Terence McMillan Stadium to name two notable examples.

I will continue to explore new grounds near and far when there's something to make a trip worthwhile, whether it's a vintage stand, a vocal following or a big game with something riding on it. Even a ground with little obvious appeal can have its charms, so I won't rule anywhere out. I suspect I'll most probably follow in the footsteps of a bloke I heard on the way out of the Silsden game, who said to his mate when asked where he was off to next 'I'll probably just float around different non-league teams round here.'

Appendix I

Full list of grounds visited
(correct as at May 2024)

Club	Ground	Visits	Notes
AC Milan	San Siro	1	A bucket-list ground for many, but an underwhelming atmosphere for a Champions League knockout tie when I visited.
Albion Rovers	Cliftonhill	1	Some lovely old features in this classic Scottish venue.
Alemannia Aachen	Neuer Tivoli	1	Good atmosphere, inefficient catering.
Arsenal	Highbury	272	I don't feel like I miss this fine stadium too much having been lucky enough to go so often. In fact it might even be 273 visits as my mum recalls taking me in a downpour, which doesn't tally with any of the games I recorded.
	Emirates	168	Losing some of its lustre, but decent sightlines and I can lay claim to having played and scored on the carpet in a five-a-side tournament there (not included in total visits).
Aston Villa	Villa Park	3	The classic FA Cup semi-final venue and should host one every year.
Athletic Newham	Terence McMillan Stadium	1	Widely regarded as one of London's worst grounds but wasn't that bad. Still not great.

Barking	Mayesbrook Park	1	Saw some old turnstiles.
Barnet	Underhill	1	Demolished, much like Arsenal's reserves were on my visit.
Bayern Munich	Olympiastadion	1	Roof looked fancy, but offered little protection from the elements.
Bearsted	Otham Sports Club	1	Rural setting with a paddock, an actual paddock of horses and not an old terrace.
Billericay Town	New Lodge	1	The infamous mural is shorn of its full glory, but upgrades from the Tamplin era make it one of the better venues in Essex.
Borussia Dortmund	Signal Iduna Park	1	Lives up to expectations.
Bradford (Park Avenue)	Horsfall Stadium	1	Someone went to town with green on white signage.
Brentford	Griffin Park	2	Three of the four corner pubs are still there, but it's not the same without a classic old-school ground in between them.
Brentwood Town	Brentwood Centre Arena	1	Plywood main stand, scaffolding and tarp behind the goal. Decent parking.
Brightlingsea Regent	North Road	1	A smart ground, even with a stand bought off eBay.
Bristol Rovers	Memorial Stadium	1	Felt like the rugby stadium it was, so it was entirely appropriate we brought in a hip flask to keep drinking throughout.
Burnham Ramblers	Leslie Field	4+	Horrible memories of the surface embarrassing me in goal. No memories of the various 18th birthday parties I attended in the clubhouse or actual games watched, but I did get Steve Tilson's autograph there once.

Calverley United	Victoria Park	<1	Probably doesn't count for several reasons, but opened my eyes to park football. Nice clubhouse.
Canvey Island	Park Lane	1	Below sea level and below freezing when the wind whips in from the Thames. Didn't see a ship sail past, so revisit required.
Cercle Brugge	Jan Breydel Stadium	1	Ersatz San Siro.
Charlton Athletic	The Valley	4+	Fond memories of putting five past David Seaman here. Don't recall it? Just watch the video of the preseason friendly from the very start and you might spot them in the warm-up.
Chelmsford City	Melbourne Stadium	6+	Deserves its nickname of the Gulag.
Clapton Community	Stray Dog	1	Just a pitch with a bit of scaffolding, but Clapton brought the atmosphere.
	Wadham Lodge	1	Again, my assessment is swayed by the famous Clapton atmosphere, but a decent enough facility for the level.
	Old Spotted Dog	3	Oldest senior ground in London. Best atmosphere in non-league. A unique club who saved the ground. Lots of reasons to visit.
Coggeshall Town	West Street	1	Clubhouse out of *TOWIE*, stands made out of corrugated metal.
Colchester United	Layer Road	1	Everything I liked about an old ground: cramped, quirky, atmospheric.
	Colchester Community Stadium	1	Everything I hate about new grounds: sparse, identikit, soulless.

Corinthian-Casuals	King George's Fields	1	Remarkable club, unremarkable ground, apart from the banners and memorabilia.
Dartford	Princes Park	1	A great example of how to do a newbuild: erect a massive wooden statue in the main stand.
Dulwich Hamlet	Champion Hill	1	Doesn't cope well with its recent influx of hipster fans. Decent food and beer.
East Thurrock United	Rookery Hill	1	Future of the ground up in the air, which is a shame as it's a decent facility.
Emley AFC	Welfare Ground	2	Who rates all their pies? Who rates all their pies? This fat bastard!
Enfield Town	Queen Elizabeth II Stadium	1	The exception that proves the rule that all grounds with a running track are bad. Lovely art deco grandstand.
England	Old Wembley	10	Dreadful sightlines and either a dreadful experience (usually watching England) or the best day out in football (if your team won).
	New Wembley	2	Better sightlines, but less fond memories of the actual games.
Eynesbury Rovers	Alfred Hall Memorial Ground	1	Struggling not to allow the match I saw bring down my view on a perfectly adequate ground.
Farsley Celtic	The Citadel	1	Guest opinion: too much graffiti, not enough gravy.
Faversham Town	Aquatherm Stadium	1	Nice old stand on one side, a few quirky older bits, and a smart bar, but let down by a massive changing room/toilet block bunker on the other side.
Fisher	St Paul's Sports Ground	3	A midweek favourite when I'm down in London. Views over Canary Wharf, good pubs nearby, decent beer in the ground as well.

France	Stade de France	1	Looked tired within a decade of opening, but I'm mostly haunted by Henry's miss.
Fulham	Craven Cottage	1	The façade on Stevenage Road is the best bit.
Gala Fairydean Rovers	Netherdale	1	A must visit ground, and well worth the journey. Stunning.
Gillingham	Priestfield	1	Seemed to be mostly scaffolding.
Hallam FC	Sandygate	1	World's oldest ground, a sloping pitch, a club proud of their history. Loved it.
	Len Salmon Stadium	7	Ball-swallowing forest on one side, housing estate from which a firework was once launched on to the pitch on another, fairly standard non-league ground in the middle.
Harrogate Railway Athletic	Station View	4	My new local, so I'm growing to love its quirks and finding a favourite vantage point for each half.
Harrogate Town	EnviroVent Stadium	1	Built piecemeal as the club rose through the leagues, so there's a mix of characterful terrace and bland seating. Good pies.
Harwich & Parkeston	Royal Oak	1	Classic grandstand.
Hashtag United	Chadfields	2	Breeze blocks and decent burgers.
Heybridge Swifts	Scraley Road	1	Nothing wrong with the place, but nothing to recommend it on.
Hornchurch	Hornchurch Stadium	1	Saw athletics at the same time as the football, with some young urchins vaulting the fence to get in (and get back out again). The athletics track just got in the way.
Hullbridge Sports	Lower Road	1	Extensive catering options; just made the mistake of choosing Bovril.

Ilford	Cricklefield Stadium	2	Only six lanes on the running track, so it could be worse.
Ipswich Town	Portman Road	1	Near the station. Thought it was a bit of a dump when used to going to the Emirates. Suspect I'd like it a lot more nowadays.
Knaresborough Town	Manse Lane	1	Meets ground grading requirements.
KV Mechelen	Achter de Kazerne	1	Modernised since my visit. Glad to have caught its old-school charm.
Larkfield & New Hythe	Taray Group Community Stadium	1	Smart setup for the level.
Leeds United	Elland Road	1	Nothing smart about this one.
Lewes	The Dripping Pan	1	Possibly the best ground in non-league – beach huts, decent beer, natural bowl, evocative name – love it.
Leyton Orient	Brisbane Road	3+	Haven't watched a game from the unique vantage point of someone's flat. Has gotten worse with every development.
Lordswood	Martyn Grove	1	Standard step five setup made better by the occasion.
Luton Town	Kenilworth Road	1	A family trip watching Charlton from the away end, so I went through the entrance between people's gardens before it became cool.
Maldon & Tiptree	Park Drive	2	This includes a match abandoned at half-time, so 1.5 visits.
Manchester City	Etihad Stadium	1	It wasn't empty, so I can't deploy its usual nickname among banter merchants. Mostly remember for Arsenal's banter merchant Nicklas Bendtner showing his 'skills'.

Manchester United	Old Trafford	2	The so-called Theatre of Dreams, if you dream of a tired concrete venue with poor catering. 'Why do they serve Boddingtons when no one outside Manchester drinks that shit,' as one fan sagely observed.
Margate	Hartsdown Park	1	Visit was more about the day out than the ground.
Meridian VP	Meridian Sports and Social Club	1	Don't be fooled by the name, it's a faff to get between the ground and bar.
NAC Breda	Rat Verlegh Stadion	1	Not the biggest drunken party going, but enjoyable, nonetheless, and I've found myself drawn into following their progress from afar.
Norwich City	Carrow Road	1	Garish.
Notts County	Meadow Lane	1	Given how much time I spent in the bar rather than watching the game, I wonder whether it counts at all?
Oxford United	Kassam Stadium	1	Missing an end.
Peterborough Sports	Lincoln Road	1	Lots of random stands added as they've moved up the pyramid. In a slightly sketchy area.
Peterborough United	London Road	1	Walked past Barry Fry on a pre-match tour and he didn't try to sign me. Very strange.
Portsmouth	Fratton Park	1	Saw a Charlton friendly in a sparse crowd and spent all my time trying to listen to how Arsenal were getting on in the Makita Tournament.
Punjab United	Steve Cook Stadium	1	Decent catering.
Ramsgate	Southwood Stadium	1	Another pearl of a Kentish ground near the sea, with a postwar grandstand.

Redbridge	Oakside	1	An underrated gem, easily accessible from the tube.
Saffron Walden Town	Catons Lane	5	Favourite ground in Essex. Worth a visit, or another revisit in my case.
Seraing	Stade du Pairay	1	A traditional English non-league feel in the Belgian second division.
Sheffield FC	At Stocksbridge Park Steels	1	Classic three-sided ground adjoining a cricket pitch, some curved terrace beneath the clubhouse, a covered end and a more charming grandstand than the player it's named after.
Sheffield Wednesday	Hillsborough	1	Didn't rate it when I was younger, especially sat near the drummer. Looked great on a recent drive past.
Silsden	Office Interiors Stadium	1	Lovely setting.
Southend United	Roots Hall	1	Didn't appreciate it in with Orient fans, but never like to see a club in trouble, so hopefully it remains in use.
Sporting Bengal United	Mile End Stadium	1	Big cantilevered stand, which partially overcomes the dreaded running track.
Stansted	Hargrave Park	1	Quaint and quirky.
Stanway Rovers	The Hawthorns	1	Warm and worn.
Staplehurst Monarchs	Jubilee Sports Ground	1	Unremarkable ground made special by the occasion.
St Neots Town	Premier Plus Stadium	1	Struggle to recall much from my visit before I developed a love of non-league; now I often wander into a hedge, watching any action on the adjoining 3G pitch whenever I'm passing.
St Panteleimon	Hertingfordbury Park	1	A reminder that it's better to see the main tenant, although I did get a good look at all the old features.

	LA Construction Stadium	1	Excellent seafood stall.
St Pauli	Millerntor	1	Fun.
Takeley	Station Road	1	Perfectly decent mish-mash.
Tottenham Hotspur	White Hart Lane (old)	2	Complete dump.
	White Hart Lane (new)	1	An improvement, but still miles from a tube station.
Wales	Principality Stadium	4	Steep sides make for a decent atmosphere, which is unusual in a modern international stadium.
Welling United	Park View Road	1	Saw Arsenal reserves play Charlton reserves and got Ray Parlour's autograph. Couldn't tell you anything about the ground though.
West Ham United	Upton Park	2+	Classic East End venue, right down to what appeared to be knock-off Jumbotron screens, with graphics from a bowling alley.
Whitstable	Belmont Ground	1	A very smart setup, retaining a classic grandstand and old covered end, mixed in with some newer bits, making this my favourite ground in Kent.
Wimbledon	Selhurst Park	2	Away fans took over the main stand, which generated a decent atmosphere.
Wingate & Finchley	Maurice Rebak Stadium	1	Nice double-fronted grandstand.
Witham Town	Simarco Stadium	1	Lots of cover. Widely spaced-apart dugouts.
Wivenhoe	Blackstone Stadium	1	One of the better step six facilities.
Woodford Town	Ashton Athletic Track	1	One of the worst running track-obscured views, but atmosphere makes up for it.

| York City | LNER Community Stadium | 1 | Is this a library? Yes, it's also a sport centre, hospital and entertainment complex. |

All of which now has me thinking I ought to visit Juventus, QPR, Unterhaching, VVV-Venlo, Xerez, and Zulte Waregem to have visited a club for each letter of the alphabet.

Appendix II

Current bucket list of grounds I would like to visit as I look towards my next 100:

Club	Ground	Reason
Athletic Bilbao	San Mamés	A unique club who support a Basque version of non-league day, and I quite fancy a trip to Spain.
Avro	Whitebank Stadium	Scran.
Ayr	Somerset Park	Another one *Terrace Edition* made me want to visit.
Bacup Borough	West View	Nearer than Matlock for a ground with a hilly backdrop.
Colne	Holt House	Missed the groundhop game there, and one of their dozen games rescheduled during April.
Crook Town	Millfield Ground	The most visually appealing ground of the classic amateur clubs from the north-east.
Gainsborough Trinity	Northolme	It's not a big detour when travelling south for work and nearly featured in the first 100.
Glentoran	The Oval	An old-school classic.
Go Ahead Eagles	De Adelaarshorst	Fans sounded great in a heavy cup defeat to Ajax that I once caught on TV.
Great Yarmouth Town	Wellesley Recreation Ground	Oldest grandstand in the country.
Greenock Morton	Cappielow	Unfinished business.
Halesowen	The Grove	Ought to explore more grounds in the Midlands, Cadbury Athletic is another standout one, but the Grove promises a good atmosphere if less likely to deliver on the hot chocolate front.

Hastings United	Pilot Field	To see beyond the gates.
Herne Bay	Winch's Field	Along with Deal Town, a likely contender for my next birthday trip to the seaside.
Hitchin Town	Top Field	Recommendation.
Lesmahagow	Craighead Park	Scottish junior grounds seem like a rich seam to mine and I saw some good photos of this one on Twitter.
March Town United	GER Sports Ground	Old grandstand.
Mossley	Seel Park	Vaguely recall a well-designed poster or programme. Possibly a hilly backdrop?
Padiham	Arbories Memorial Sports Ground	Another scenic Groundhop UK venue I missed out on and saw lots of photos to make me feel envious.
Peckham Town	The Menace	To make up for the postponement.
Prescot Cables	Joseph Russell Stadium	Comes highly rated in groundhopping circles.
Queen of the South	Palmerston Park	Ticks off the 'Q', and offers the prospect of a parkrun-match-at-a-characterful-old-ground double. Just need to look up whether there are any pubs with historic interiors or breweries on a trading estate nearby.
Racing Mechelen	Oscar Vankesbeeckstadion	One of the many classic European grounds I've seen pictures of, but one of the few still standing, with a team playing at a reasonable level and that immediately came to mind writing this.
Royale Union Saint-Gilloise	Joseph Marien Stadium	Because I keep missing out and I don't just want to see the art deco main stand from the outside. RCD Jette and RCC Boitsfort are also on my list as backups.
Union Berlin	Stadion An der Alten Försterei	It must be better than wandering around a part of East Berlin that resembled 1970s Moscow, which we did last time.